To Alister,
wishing you a very
happy Christmas, 1974.
Lots of love, Anne.
x x x

Hard Rock

Hard Rock

Great British Rock - Climbs

compiled by Ken Wilson

with editional assistance from
Mike and Lucy Pearson
diagrams by Brian Evans

Hart-Davis, MacGibbon   London

Also by Ken Wilson

The Black Cliff
(with Jack Soper and Peter Crew)

Granada Publishing Limited

First published in Great Britain 1975 by Hart-Davis, MacGibbon Ltd
Frogmore, St Albans, Hertfordshire AL2 2NF and
3 Upper James Street, London W1R 4BP

ISBN 0 246 10565 8

Book designed by Ken Wilson in collaboration with Granada Publishing

Printed in Great Britain by
Fletcher & Son Ltd, Norwich

Contents

North Wales

Pennine and Peak Outcrops

Outcrops and Sea Cliffs in South-West England

List of Illustrations

Preface

British rock-climbing has developed remarkably in scope and quality over the past twenty years. No longer can it be described as the sport of the privileged few, for its present popularity is such that thousands of rock-climbers are to be found on cliffs all over Britain every weekend. The increased number of climbs and climbers has led to an almost insatiable demand for information, for, though some prefer the delights of route-finding by instinct and experience, most climbers take steps to brief themselves carefully both before and during a climb, in order to approach more closely the limits of their ability. Not surprisingly, this demand for information has resulted in a rapid proliferation in guidebook production.

In the present work, we have attempted to go beyond the simple guidebook formula, by studying a number of routes in greater detail. We carefully selected sixty famous rock-climbs from throughout the country and invited a number of experienced climbers to describe these routes in essay form. To enrich the brew further, we collected a selection of crag and action photographs to go with the essays. By these means, we hope to produce an absorbing literary and photographic commentary on the essence of our sport – its climbs and their intrinsic qualities, its climbers and their attitudes and motivations.

Readers will no doubt be interested to know how we chose both climbs and climbers. What constitutes a fine climb? Our contributors have attempted to answer this question in full in the succeeding pages. Certainly there are many qualities that contribute to a climb's reputation: history, singleness of line or, conversely, subtle complexity, good rock, good position, interesting technique, length, consistent difficulty, inescapability, commitment – all are qualities that one looks for, and each of the climbs in this book can lay claim to one or more of these merits.

It was decided from the outset to select climbs in the upper spectrum of difficulty, leaving the many fine but easier climbs to some later volume. The climbs themselves, seventeen from Scotland, eleven from the Lakes, fifteen from Wales and seventeen from various outlying sea-cliffs and outcrops, were chosen by a consensus of opinion among a number of knowledgeable pundits in each area. Thus, while no two people could ever agree on a final selection, the list may fairly claim to be representative, for there was broad agreement on the bulk of the climbs.

Certain routes have been included for some special reason. Historical claims ordained the selection of climbs such as Central Buttress, Cenotaph Corner and Right Unconquerable. One gully was chosen, and two aid climbs. A sea stack made strong representations. There was a risk that the list might be biased towards the harder climbs, for in general the best routes seem to lie around the Hard Very Severe/Extremely Severe level; to redress the balance we added climbs like The Crack, Chee Tor Girdle, Rosa Pinnacle, Great/Bow connection and Engineers' Slabs. We took into account the numbers of climbers using particular areas, and also tried to do justice to the various styles and schools of British climbing.

Nevertheless, it must be stressed that the final list is merely a *selection* of the best routes; there are many more with equal claims to greatness.

The selection of authors involved us in even greater difficulties. The ability to write a few hundred words of golden prose to order is not everyone's forte, although a brief scan of the book will reveal how effectively our contributors have measured up to the task. Our invitation was declined by some, for a variety of reasons. The final cast is nevertheless an impressive one, and expectations have been exceeded. In many cases, original and highly idiosyncratic interpretations were made of a dangerously sterile brief. Some of our contributors, gluttons for work, filled in the gaps by providing more than one essay. In general, we have avoided soliciting first-ascent accounts in the belief that, though interesting in themselves, they usually bear little relationship to the experiences of later parties.

On the photographic side, the response has been tremendous. It was decided at the outset to illustrate each climb with at least one informative crag shot and one pertinent action photograph. To start from scratch with this assignment would have taken years of work, so every known climbing photographer in the country was petitioned; the result was a host of excellent and original photographs. Some keen supporters even took their cameras out specially and devoted valuable climbing time to seeking photographs for this book. Nevertheless, there are weaknesses. In some cases we have been forced to republish well-known shots, and in others we have been unable to obtain any reasonable photograph – poor weather, remoteness and dull north-facing aspects have conspired against us. Despite this, the collection is a good one and should prove of interest to our readers.

Throughout this preface I have referred to 'we' rather than 'I'. This is not a self-indulgent royal 'we' or a platitudinous sop to the contributors. It serves rather to point to the fact that this book is a communal effort by a representative section of the climbing world; an attempt, by those most closely involved, to capture something of the essence of British crags and their climbers. We hope that the layman will find it fascinating, even if occasionally incomprehensible, while the addict, we trust, will be provided with hours of absorbing study.

Acknowledgements

This book could not have been completed without the assistance of a large number of people. A great many climbers have selflessly given their valuable time in order to bring it to completion.

Among the individual helpers, I owe a great debt to my loyal sub-editors from *Mountain*, Mike and Lucy Pearson. Compulsive wordsmiths, their efforts both in this book and in other publications have contributed much to the lucidity of recent mountaineering writing. Certainly my own semi-literate scratchings would be a constant embarrassment were it not for their patient massage. Brian Evans has made a great contribution to the interest of the book with his diagrams, and I am indebted to Paul Nunn, Robin Campbell, Jim Perrin and Ian Roper, not only for their contributions but also for their expert guidance in policy decisions. Among the photographers, I would particularly like to thank Ian Roper, Chris Hall, the late Brian Olver, Greg Strange and Ian Wright for the extra efforts they have made for this book. Thanks are due as well to the photographers' patient 'models' – leaders and seconds – who often went out specially to climb a route in order that photographs might be obtained.

I would also like to record my gratitude to the following for their contributions, photographs, advice and services: Nat Allen, Bob Allen, Neil Allinson, Al Alvarez, Allan Austin, Dave Bathgate, Arthur Birtwhistle, Peter Biven, Chris Bonington, Martin Boysen, Joe Brown, Paddy Buckley, Mick Burke, Dorothy Busby, Frank Cannings, John Cleare, Dave Cook, Jim Crawford, Pete Crew, Leo Dickinson, Harold Drasdo, Ed Drummond, Chris Eilbeck, Nick Estcourt, Al Evans, Brian Fuller, Allen Fyffe, Dennis Gray, Tony Greenbank, Phil Gribbon, Ed Grindley, Peter

Harding, John Hartley, John Harwood, Mike Heller, Les Holliwell, Nigel Horne, Dick Isherwood, Bob Keates, John Kingston, Hamish MacInnes, Jimmy Marshall, Ian McNaught-Davis, Colin Mortlock, Bernard Newman, Dave Nicol, Geoff Oliver, John Porteous, John Porter, Tony Riley, Royal Robbins, Ian Rowe, Klaus Schwartz, Doug Scott, Bill Skidmore, Tony Smythe, Jack Soper, Colin Taylor, Mike Thompson, Gloria Wilson, Brian Wyvill, and anyone else whose name I may have inadvertently omitted.

I would also like to express gratitude to the many writers whose words have either been quoted or used to provide information in the preparation of this book. In particular, I would like to acknowledge those ever-valuable sources of reference, the Journals of the Climbers' Club, the Fell and Rock Climbing Club and the Scottish Mountaineering Club.

Finally, I would like to thank Alan Brooke and his colleagues of Hart-Davis,MacGibbon for their confidence in this project and for their support and enthusiasm in helping to bring it to fruition.

KEN WILSON 1974

The Development of Hard Rock-Climbing in Britain

In the early days of mountaineering the pioneers were content to work their routes up snow-slopes and glaciers in order to gain their summits. Soon they began to realize that in order to pursue their new sport more effectively some skill in climbing rock was needed. So it was that numbers of climbers began to prepare themselves for their seasonal Alpine forays by training on small crags and cliffs away from the big mountains, and slowly the sport of rock-climbing was born.

The detailed pursuit of rock-climbing therefore has its origins from very early in the general history of mountaineering. The main areas adopted for this purpose centred round Austria and Saxony, the Dolomites and the small mountain crags of Great Britain; it is the last with which we are concerned in this book.

The Alpine Club, which consisted of a group of adventurous Victorian gentlemen, was one of the driving forces in the early days of Alpinism, and its members were among the first to start serious exploration of the British homeland crags. After a time, further clubs sprang up, each having local affiliations within the main mountain areas – Wales, the Lakes, the Pennines and Scotland. Such clubs were concerned more with local climbing for its own sake than with Alpinism, although it was a long time before anyone really believed that rock-climbing was anything more than a rather inferior form of practice for the real thing. As the climbs of the day were rarely of exceptional quality this was a not unreasonable belief, but traces of it persist to this day, giving impetus to the tradition that leads many British climbers to the bigger Alpine arena from year to year. So it is that many of today's leading practitioners on rock are equally at home, and indeed very competent, in Alpine surroundings. It is nevertheless true that although rock-climbing still fulfils its original purpose for a large section of the climbing world, almost everyone now concedes that it is an absorbing and worthwhile activity in its own right.

At first, the Victorian pioneers concentrated on the wet, vegetated gullies so typical of British cliffs, but by the turn of the century the number and quality of unclimbed gullies had diminished and climbers turned their attention to more complex routes up the easier faces, buttresses and ridges. Strenuous 'thrutching' was much in vogue. Indeed, many of the chimneys and gullies that were climbed at that time can still be taxing today.

Explorations were made in both the Lake District and Wales. Many crags were discovered and usually one or two gullies were climbed before new areas were sought. The area around Wasdale Head developed into an important centre quite early on, with the result that the cliffs of Pillar, Gable and Scafell received greater attention and were developed more thoroughly than was the case elsewhere.

The leading pioneer of the period was undoubtedly Owen Glynne Jones, an exceptional climber whose attitudes can be recognized as being decidedly modern even today. Jones developed scores of climbs, mostly gullies, throughout the later part of the century, but he also attempted climbs that pointed to new styles which did not emerge until after his death. Belaying techniques were very rudimentary and often dangerous at that time and, although Jones and his friends were skilled at the various rope-tricks then practised, Jones's death on the Dent Blanche in 1899 resulted from a combination of precarious combined tactics and insecure belays, an accident that was echoed in 1903 on Scafell by a similar belaying tragedy when four climbers died.

Following Jones's intense period of exploration there was a lull in Lakeland climbing in the early part of the century. Nevertheless, new styles did emerge, ushered in by the ascent of Botterill's Slab on Scafell. Belaying improved and, by the start of the First World War, developments in technique and climbing skill had combined to allow the ascent of the very difficult Central Buttress, which established Scafell as the leading British cliff of the day.

On the Continent, the years immediately preceding the First World War were particularly fruitful with regard to rock-climbing development. The most advanced European school of the day was centred in Austria, where many difficult climbs were being pioneered in the Wetterstein, the Karwendal and the Kaisergebirge mountains. As the standards of climbing grew harder, it became clear that the momentum of exploration could only be maintained by an attack on the bigger faces, which in turn called for a certain degree of technical innovation. Thus between 1911 and 1913 Hans Dülfer developed a method for making tension pendulums, and Hans Fiechtl was responsible for first employing the piton for aid and protection. Armed with these new techniques Austrian and German climbers put up a number of routes considerably harder and bolder than anything that had gone before.

It is generally supposed that Eastern Alpine climbers accepted the piton with little reluctance. This is a fallacy. Some climbers at that time were deeply critical of artificial aids in climbing, but it was soon clear that the scale and seriousness of the great limestone faces in Austria and the

Dolomites demanded these new techniques if any attempt to climb them was to succeed.

After a brief lull in climbing activity in the years during, and immediately after, the First World War, climbers like Solleder and Wiessner developed longer and harder climbs that relied partially – though never heavily – on the use of pitons, and by the mid-twenties European climbing was clearly set on a course that was to lead to the great developments of the thirties, forming the basis of a style of Alpine rock-climbing that is still accepted today.

How did climbers in Britain react to these revelations? The Alpine Club, with its scholarly traditions and its firm appreciation of the aesthetic aspect of mountaineering, had imbued British climbing circles with a certain aversion towards 'unnatural' techniques. Small wonder, then, that a club that had at one time stoutly condemned the crampon should find the piton objectionable. Before the First World War, rock-climbing in Britain, which had found its highest form of expression on Scafell, was perhaps equal in standard, though certainly not in scope, to contemporary achievements on the Continent: Siegfried Herford's Central Buttress climb, with its complicated rope antics, was technically just as hard in detail as any of Dülfer's efforts. But that was as far as it went, and the situation remained static at this point for several years. Lakeland climbing developed in scope after the war, but standards of difficulty hardly rose at all; Wales remained dormant. Few experienced climbers survived the war years, and protection techniques remained largely undeveloped. It was not until the late twenties that a partial recovery was staged on Clogwyn du'r Arddu by teams led by Fred Pigott and Jack Longland. Here, British rock-climbing had its first serious confrontation with the implications of the piton and, indeed, aid in general. Longland, Pigott and their henchmen were far from being hidebound traditionalists. They were determined to force their climbs and were fully prepared to bend the rules a little in order to do so. On the East Buttress, aid was manufactured with chockstones and slings, while on the West a piton was inserted. But the presence of determined traditionalists within these groups ensured that their climbs were achieved without the use of excessive aid. The debate was pursued in contemporary club journals, whose pages are studded with disapproving comments and sometimes flamboyant rhetoric directed against the piton. Thus while rational pressures for progress might have resulted in a more widespread acceptance of the piton, the propaganda war ensured its almost total rejection and built into the mentality of British climbers an aversion that persists to the present day. However, by rejecting European methods, British climbers also built into their sport a handicap which partially compensated for the lack of scale on the available cliffs. Whereas in Europe many of the small crags got heavily pegged and became merely training grounds for the Alps, in Britain the climbing of such crags developed into an absorbing pursuit in its own right.

One can really date the start of hard free-climbing in Britain from the ascents of Central Buttress and the subsequent Lakes routes, and the first Cloggy routes. Gradually, consolidation took place. In the thirties a whole generation of climbers concentrated almost exclusively on balance-climbing (relying mainly on footwork rather than strong-arm tactics), and a number of elegant routes of this type emerged. Clogwyn du'r Arddu became the centre for the main developments of this period, the most consistent pioneer being Colin Kirkus.

Kirkus and his friends made a number of good balance climbs both in Wales and in the Lakes. Many of these contained long, unprotected leads but as these leads generally took place on rock that was not too steep, the climber just needed to stay in control and work methodically upwards. Routes like Great Slab, Narrow Slab, Rowan Tree Slabs and Mickledore Grooves indicate the tastes of this generation and the style reached its highest expression in 1938 with Arthur Birtwistle's ascent of Diagonal on Dinas Mot.

By the late thirties, however, different styles of climbing were beginning to gain popularity. Kirkus had withdrawn from the front ranks following a serious accident in 1934 (which resulted in the death of Maurice Linnell, another leading climber of the period). His place at the forefront of Welsh climbing was immediately filled by John Menlove Edwards who, though a competent balance-climber, was more at home on steeper and looser cliffs. Edwards's great contribution was the exploration of the steep crags on the north side of the Llanberis Pass – an area which turned out to be ideally suited to the needs of the following generation of climbers. His researches here resulted in the discovery, in 1940, of Brant and Slape, two climbs that introduced a new standard of steepness and technical difficulty to Wales. These climbs were matched by only one other piece of climbing at that time: Arthur Birtwistle's 1938 ascent of the first pitch of Vember, the celebrated Drainpipe Crack, which was perhaps the hardest Welsh lead to be made before the Second World War.

In the Lakes, similarly steep routes were already appearing on the East Buttress of Scafell, notably Linnell's Overhanging Wall (where a piton was used for aid) and Birkett's May Day climb (where three pitons were used for belays). The latter route marked the first improvement in the top standards of Lakeland climbing since the ascent of Central Buttress. There followed a period of development, initiated by Birkett and finally consolidated in the early fifties by Arthur Dolphin.

At this point it is worth considering the attitudes which developed towards the piton during the thirties. Arguments for and against its use had continued to emerge, and it had been employed experimentally by the leading practitioners. Mostly it had come to be regarded as a useful device for aid rather than as a protection method. The two instances of piton use on Scafell have been noted but perhaps the most celebrated piton 'incident' of the thirties occurred when a group of German climbers visited Britain in 1936. Local tempers became frayed when the visitors used pitons on the first ascent of Munich Climb on Tryfan. So outraged were Menlove Edwards and Noyce that they rushed up to Tryfan, repeated the route, and removed the offending ironmongery.

The incident is instructive in so far as the general scorn for piton usage and continental attitudes betrayed an innate complacency that dogged British climbing at that time – protecting our insular world from 'nasty' continental developments. The conviction had arisen that climbers like Kirkus, Linnell and Edwards were vastly superior to their continental counterparts – a feeling that the Munich Climb incident did little to erase. British climbers had remained generally ignorant of the great advances taking place in the Eastern Alps. In retrospect, the achievements of men like Auckenthaler, Vinatzer, Rebitsch, Comici, Cassin and Carlesso, who were doing major climbs of great difficulty throughout the thirties, make the timid British efforts at home seem very unimportant. Unaffected by the outstanding developments abroad, climbing in Britain continued in its sleepy state.

The thirties have traditionally been hailed as the Golden Age of British rock-climbing. With the greater knowledge of hindsight, this description now seems rather exaggerated, particularly when the achievements of the period are set beside those made during the fifties by Brown, Whillans and their contemporaries.

During the Second World War, climbing was adopted by the military authorities as a means of training mountain troops and commandos. Inevitably there was little concern with the niceties of style and ethics, and considerable use was made of pitons, slings and karabiners, and after the war this equipment was more readily available. The end of the war also saw the acceleration of a social development which had begun a decade before and which was to have a significant influence on rock-climbing in Britain. This was the growing involvement of the working classes in mountaineering. The Lake District had remained virtually untouched by this phenomenon during the thirties, although Wales had become popular with ever-increasing groups of working-class walkers and scramblers. But it was in Scotland that the working classes first made their mark in a serious climbing sense.

After a brisk period of exploration around the turn of the century, Scottish rock-climbing had remained comparatively dormant in the years following the First World War. The main preoccupation was with winter climbing (a subject with which we are not concerned in this book), and though a few hardish rock routes were made between the wars there were no serious rock-climbing developments comparable to those taking place south of the border. During the mid-thirties, however, a new breed of climber started to appear. These were the unemployed workers of Clydeside, Dundee and Aberdeen, and by the end of the decade their influence was beginning to be felt. Glasgow climbers from the rumbustious Creag Dhu Club took the lead at the end of the war, and routes of a considerably higher standard started to appear.

Meanwhile a similar revival was taking place in the Lake District under the influence of Birkett, and this reached its zenith in the early fifties with the climbs of Dolphin and Greenwood. Kipling Groove and Deer Bield Buttress are typical products of this period. In Wales, the end of the war was marked by the ascent of the very difficult Suicide Wall by a soldier, Chris Preston. This was an isolated event, however, and well ahead of its time. More fundamental developments were taking place in the Llanberis Pass, most notably in the form of Peter Harding's Spectre and Kaisergebirge Wall.

So it was that the end of the forties saw a greater concentration on hard climbing than had previously been the case. Slightly improved equipment and new social forces formed the background to these advances, and the hitherto mainly middle-class sport now took on a more egalitarian appearance. The advent of the proletarian climber was greeted with some trepidation by the traditional clubs. An S.M.C. writer of the time pointed out that the Scottish mountains had been regarded 'mainly as training for larger mountains and as a practice ground in off seasons for members of the Alpine Club. Such an atmosphere naturally tended to make climbing a sport for the wealthier classes and the new group of climbers thus find themselves not so much heirs to a tradition as discoverers of a secret hitherto kept hidden from their class'. It was rather as if a group of East-Enders had suddenly decided to take up grouse-shooting or polo.

The bastions of British climbing orthodoxy were undoubtedly shaken by the newcomers. But tradition dies hard; although the sport took on a less-privileged image, its latest adherents were subjected to a certain amount of restraint by the world they had entered. Nevertheless harder and better climbs began to appear, the first steps in a revival of British climbing that was to bring it back to a European level of achievement.

In comparison with the traditional middle-class climber the working-class climbers were often fitter, stronger and more able to accept the tough conditions of the British hills. Many of them climbed more regularly, often going out in the foulest conditions to attempt climbs of great difficulty. They trained on rough, tough gritstone cracks, while the middle class continued to tiptoe daintly up their balance climbs. It is all fable and folklore now, but perhaps some of the generalizations contain more truth than many would care to admit.

No one personified this new breed of climber more than Joe Brown. At first a member of the Valkyrie Club which concentrated mainly on gritstone climbing, he was later a founder of the Rock and Ice, which operated on gritstone and in North Wales. Initially his climbs hardly exceeded the standards that were being set in the Lakes and Yorkshire by Dolphin and Greenwood, but the Lakeland impetus was lost with Dolphin's death in the Alps in 1953, and Brown was soon setting the pace. He pioneered scores of excellent routes, most as hard as existing developments and some significantly more difficult. The ascent of Cenotaph Corner in 1952 marked not only a technical advance but also a development of great psychological significance. The Boulder had a similar importance as it showed that Brown was prepared to climb difficult rock for a long way without protection. Some of Brown's other routes of that period, notably The Grooves and Vember, were finer and possibly harder, but it was Cenotaph Corner that captured the imagination of the climbers of the day and became the test-piece for top Welsh climbers over the next decade.

Brown's competence in Wales was matched by similar feats in the Alps. When he and Whillans climbed the West Face of the Petit Dru in 1954, following a spell of Alpine revival by British climbers, they became the first two home climbers to compete on equal terms with the top continental Alpinists since Mummery and Graham Brown.

Much has been written about the prowess of Brown, and no one will deny that his contribution to the quality and standard of British rock-climbing has been outstanding. The reader may gain some idea of his ability by studying those of his climbs featured in this book. He has brought to climbing a rare combination of attributes: keenness, patience, strength, technical ability, eye for a line, competitiveness and, above all, a subtle and mysterious charisma. Few would deny that his place in British rock-climbing remains pre-eminent.

Don Whillans's contributions to rock-climbing certainly matched Brown's. His early involvement with gritstone gave rise to a collection of hard problems. Then came rock-climbing on the mountain crags, first in the company of Brown – perhaps the most powerful twosome ever seen on British rock – but later with others. His Erosion Groove Direct, Grond and Triermain Eliminate set a fierce standard which has stood the test of time. But these were short routes; his bigger climbs like Woubits, Extol, Centurion and Slanting Slab exhibit more of the power with which his achievements came to be associated. No man has been more successful in carving out his personality in terms of rock.

Brown, Whillans and their friends raised Welsh climbing to new heights. Lakeland climbing, on the other hand, despite steady development in standard and scope under the leadership of climbers like Allan Austin, Eric Metcalf and Geoff Oliver, never succeeded in capturing the imagination to the extent that Welsh climbing did during the Brown era. Basically the climbs on offer in each area are much the same. Perhaps Wales, with its cleaner rock, fewer trees and craggier summits, exhibits a more gaunt arena; its climbs, like the castles found in the area, have an air of mediæval power. In contrast, the Lake District displays more sophisticated charms. Its cliffs hide coyly at the ends of long, inaccessible valleys, often disguised by trees or a mottling of lichen. But there is nothing wrong with the climbs themselves: 'They are like little jewels,' remarked one perceptive foreign visitor. 'They have a greater concentration of interesting moves than any climbs I have experienced.' If the climbs of Wales are mediæval in their power, those of the Lakes are surely Tudor in their more subtle attractions. Some of the climbs assembled in this book, like North Crag Eliminate, Gormenghast and Praying Mantis, seem to typify this quality; they do not blazon their merits, but etch them out carefully as one becomes increasingly engrossed. On the other hand, there is nothing subtle about Ichabod and Extol; they are powerful and unyielding climbs, equal in difficulty to the hardest in this book.

In climbing terms, Wales and the Lakes have sufficient in common to bear some comparison: in both areas the cliffs are small and abundant, the climbs hard, the weather mixed and the climbers numerous. But the same cannot be said of Scotland. Here the cliffs are generally far bigger, more remote and more widely spread, the weather usually foul, and the climbers very few in number.

As has been noted, Scottish climbing was initially directed more towards general mountaineering – particularly winter climbing – than towards specialized rock-climbing. In view of the prevalence of bad weather this is hardly surprising. The pattern of development was similar to that shown south of the border – a corps of middle-class climbers being followed by more aggressive working-class groups – but the rock-climbing legacy left by each was less impressive. By the end of the thirties a few hard climbs had been made. During the Second World War, B. P. Kellett made a number of notable solo ascents on Ben Nevis. The post-war period saw further activity, but it was not until the mid-fifties, when Slime Wall, Trilleachan Slabs and Carn Dearg Buttress were developed that Scottish rock-climbing caught up with that of the South. Swastika, Centurion, Carnivore and developments farther north such as Dragon typify this period.

The true flowering of Scottish rock-climbing, however, awaited a further social force – the classless student generation which started to emerge all over Britain in the late fifties. With the end of conscription in 1959 these latest arrivals on the climbing scene rapidly hardened into an identifiable group, less restricted by the pressures of convention or poverty than their predecessors. Longer holidays, a greater degree of financial independence and better transport enabled this new breed of climber to come to the mountains more regularly and to make further steps forward.

It was in Scotland, still relatively underdeveloped despite the advances made by the Creag Dhu, that the potency of the new group was displayed most immediately. Leading the field was Robin Smith. Smith's influence on the course of hard rock-climbing in Scotland was akin to that of Dolphin and Brown in the Lakes and Wales. With a kindred, if older, spirit in the form of Jimmy Marshall he raced across the ice-climbing scene with refreshing panache. His rock climbs were more tangible: Yo-Yo, The Bat, The Needle and Shibboleth were climbs of great power, fully up to the highest contemporary standards being achieved south of the border.

Smith, Marshall and other members of their Edinburgh group – the Currie Lads – brought a new standard of hard climbing to Scotland and alerted other active groups in Glencoe, Glasgow and Aberdeen to the tremendous possibilities that still remained on the great mountain crags. The result was an extensive period of exploration throughout the sixties that has left Scotland with a legacy of many of the longest and best rock-climbs in Britain.

In 1959, while Smith and his colleagues were displaying their powers in Scotland, a number of talented young climbers in Wales were taking advantage of the particularly dry summer to reach the top standards of the day. In doing so, they removed much of the psychological lead that Brown and Whillans had established during their remarkable period of exploration. It was clear after the events of this notable season that a new surge of activity was at hand.

Before moving on to the most recent phase of British rock-climbing it is perhaps important to consider another influence – namely the improvements of equipment and technique. Post-war advances owed much to the greater use of slings and karabiners for protection. It also became accepted practice at this time to allow the odd piton to be used in a climb, usually for direct aid but sometimes just for protection. Such changes may seem slight today, but at the time they gave climbers considerably greater confidence when hard moves were required during long leads. Most important of all, a privileged few were also able to climb on nylon rope which was considerably stronger and lighter than the traditional hemp and manilla ropes.

Another innovation of the period was the vibram-soled boot, which became available as an alternative to the old-style nailed boot. The idea met with some resistance at first but it was later widely accepted. The vibram-soled boot, and its subsequent adaptation into a lighter technical climbing shoe (the *kletterschuhe*, an imported German invention which replaced the gym-shoe) greatly assisted improvements in climbing standards in the decade after the war.

Throughout the post-war period, the equipment itself underwent steady improvement, as did the techniques involved in its use. At first, the great strength of nylon led climbers to believe that very thin line was adequate both for slings and ropes, but it was soon realized that this was not the case. The thinner ropes were found to cut easily in the event of abrasion and to melt quickly under heat friction; karabiners without screw gates could open one another if used together; vibram soles were likely to slip on greasy rock, and certain designs of piton pulled out very easily under strain. In many cases it took a tragedy for these lessons to be learned.

The adoption of new techniques was also a process that was subject to traditional pressures. Pitons, for example, were still used sparingly, as is indicated by Brown's first-ascent dictum of no more than one or two pitons per climb. Restricted piton use, however, may also have owed something to the poor quality of the soft iron pitons of the day and the difficulty of placing them in hard mountain rock. As spikes and cracks for chockstones are easier and quicker to use, natural protection became the order of the day in areas where these are numerous. The granite cliffs of Cornwall and the Cairngorms, however, are less susceptible to natural protection, and here pitons were used more readily on the harder climbs.

Many of the steeper climbs of the early fifties kept to well-defined crack lines, which succumbed to the hand-jamming techniques used by gritstone-trained climbers and also permitted the use of chockstone protection. The chockstone idea, which had started with Pigott's climb in the twenties, had been gradually improved with ever-increasing skill until by the end of the fifties it had reached the height of sophistication. Climbers were inserting minute pebbles into very thin cracks and then carefully threading line slings behind them with makeshift wire-threading hooks. It was not long before someone thought of threading small nuts on to line slings, the nuts acting as portable chockstones.

This idea rapidly caught on, and at once the protection possibilities multiplied. The reamed hexagonal nut used at first was soon replaced by specially designed soft metal wedges with a variety of tapers, sizes and sections, providing yet another ingredient for further climbing developments.

Other equipment improvements also played a part in the surge of development. The *kletterschuhe*, which remained in vogue until the early sixties, was itself superseded by another form of rock-climbing footgear. By the mid-fifties expert climbers had already started using a specialized French rock shoe known as the *P.A.* (after the French climber, Pierre Allain), which allowed very delicate climbing on small holds. The same period saw the introduction of strong webbing tapes, which multiplied still further the running belay possibilities. There was also an improvement in the quality of piton design, following important American influences, and the stronger and more versatile perlon rope took the place of laid nylon.

In conjunction with these improvements, there was activity in all areas of British climbing. In the Lakes, 1960 was an exceptional year, marked by the appearance of Ichabod, Extol, Gormenghast and Astra. Subsequent years saw further important discoveries, with Austin playing a leading part. In Wales, the emergent young climbers had as their most gifted members Martin Boysen, Peter Crew and Barry Ingle, and much hard climbing took place under their leadership, with Great Wall, The Skull and The Pinnacle Girdle marking important achievements. Brown also played his part, making extensive explorations on the cliffs of Snowdon South and West. Scotland was the scene of sustained activity when the weather permitted. Smith was killed in the Pamirs in 1962 but exploration continued, spearheaded mainly by the Edinburgh group but bolstered also by Creag Dhu climbers led by Cunningham and McLean. Later in the decade the Edinburgh dominance became less marked, as a new breed of climbers without any obvious affiliations began to move freely about the mountains. This did much to blur the old partisan divisions that had hitherto typified Scottish climbing. Nowadays there is a far broader base of experience and many accomplished climbers are at work developing new routes and repeating the great climbs already established.

By the end of the decade the improvements in equipment and the various social and economic changes that have been mentioned enabled large numbers of climbers to experience the satisfaction of hard rock-climbing. The rank and file were now able to embark on routes of considerable difficulty; in 1960 quite modest grades had been the norm, but by 1970 thousands were performing regularly at Very Severe standard and hundreds operated above that grade. With the increased effectiveness of the various forms of protection, this trend has continued and some climbers (usually very able ones) are now beginning to feel that the traditional balance between commitment and safety has swung too far towards safety. Certainly, climbers now have to extend themselves more if they are to find the same emotional and spiritual rewards which their predecessors of the thirties and forties enjoyed in the course of their infrequent 'big leads'. It may be that the trend towards hard solo climbing, which became marked during the sixties, is related to the feeling that conventional climbing has become 'too safe'.

The growing popularity of climbing has led not only to increases in the numbers of climbs and climbers, but also to an improvement in the quality of climbs and in the speed with which great climbs become accepted as such. For, though there are exceptions, it is generally true to say that the finest climbs in Britain are among the harder grades, and the stage has now been reached where most serious climbers, given adequate fitness, experience and determination, can hope to do the majority of routes described in this book at some point in their climbing careers. Ten years ago such a statement would have been laughable.

So far this commentary has been limited to the mountain areas of Great Britain. No survey of British climbing would be complete, however, without generous reference to the part that outcrops have played in the development of the sport. Traditionally, Pennine and Peak gritstone has been of the greatest importance in this respect; its development has largely paralleled developments in the mountains, and often the same pioneers operated in both areas. Usually, climbing on gritstone has been technically rather harder than the corresponding mountain climbs. Although a number of good climbs were made on gritstone before the Second World War, the heyday of this type of climbing undoubtedly came in the fifteen years after the war. The reasons are not hard to find. Flanking the Pennines are the great industrial centres of Leeds, Bradford, Sheffield, Manchester, Derby and Nottingham, and the outcrops formed an ideal training ground for the poorer, working-class climber who was unable to pay regular visits to more distant mountain areas. A tremendous amount of effort and enthusiasm was therefore channelled into gritstone climbing.

Immediately after the war the leading figures were Dolphin (in Yorkshire) and Harding (in the Peak); their efforts were later consolidated by Brown, Whillans and Austin. By the end of the fifties, the gritstone edges were studded with testing routes. The predominant skill needed here was jamming, and those who fully mastered this technique were capable of extraordinary feats.

Recently the emphasis has swung from gritstone exploration to limestone. For many years this rock was considered inferior for climbing purposes. The early pioneers had sampled it and been unimpressed and its development languished. In the fifties it was dragooned back into service to give emergent Alpinists a crash course in artificial climbing. Ironically, climbing development thereby went full circle. By adopting limestone crags as training grounds for the Alps, climbers were echoing the very start of rock-climbing in Britain. In the early days it had been the mixed climbing of the Western Alps that had demanded

rock practice, but now it was the great aid routes of the Dolomites that demanded specialized techniques and soon a collection of accepted artificial test-pieces emerged to satisfy this need. Kilnsey Main Overhang is generally considered to be the best such climb.

It was not long, however, before the historical cycle repeated itself yet again: climbers found that armed with their improved equipment, limestone climbing was neither as dangerous nor as unpleasant as they had thought, and it began to be developed as a free-climbing form. Many routes which had originally been pegged were climbed free, and numerous discoveries were made. New guidebooks brought increasing numbers of climbers to limestone and by the end of the sixties the rock had disgorged hundreds of routes, many of them very impressive and testing despite their limited length. Carnage, Sirplum, Debauchery and Alcasan represent some of the finest products of this era.

Divorced from the mainstream of climbing in the mountains and the Pennines, the limestone climbing in the Avon and Cheddar Gorges has traced a rather different path. Avon has always been a centre of free-climbing. Its development began in the early fifties and proceeded steadily until the mid-sixties, when a sustained period of energetic exploration made it one of the best limestone cliffs in the country. Longer routes (up to 400ft.) admittedly can be found in near-by Cheddar, but so far Cheddar has failed to become a popular area, partly because of its dank, overgrown aspect and partly because of the danger to tourists from rock-falls. Nevertheless, its finest climb, Coronation Street, has rapidly acquired an outstanding reputation.

In considering the development of British outcrop climbing, the part played by sandstone should not be ignored. The two main areas, one centred on Frodsham and Helsby and the other in the vicinity of Tunbridge Wells in Kent, have always had their talented devotees. Their proximity to large centres of population has ensured that the sandstone outcrops have been microscopically developed, and the standard of the climbing is now extremely high. Many outstanding climbers have derived great benefits from sandstone training.

Finally, consideration must be given to yet another extremely important offshoot of mainstream climbing – the increasingly popular pursuit of sea-cliff climbing. The first serious sea-cliff exploration took place in Cornwall, for years a haunt of the Climbers' Club. The Second World War brought groups of marine commandos to train on the Cornish sea-cliffs. The association persisted after the war, and development reached a peak in the mid-fifties when the marines and the C.C. men made a concerted effort of exploration. Bishop's Rib, Suicide Wall and String of Pearls were the finest products of the period; even Joe Brown put in an appearance to add the awe-inspiring Bow Wall. But despite these developments sea-cliff climbing was not taken seriously for at least another decade. In Wales the Alpha Club, having virtually picked Cloggy clean, turned its energies to the search for new rock. The prime discovery was an impressive belt of sea-cliffs dropping into Gogarth Bay from Holyhead Mountain. Developments here started in 1964 and continued feverishly for several years. The result was a new major climbing area that added yet another dimension to the already varied qualities of Welsh climbing.

The significance of the Holyhead discovery was considerable. New rock was becoming scarce in the mountains; furthermore, the mountain areas had always suffered a prolonged off-season, during which winter weather tended to make hard rock-climbing unattractive. Winter had traditionally become a time for climbing on outcrops, practising pegging, or searching for ice (a relatively rare commodity in England and Wales). With the emergence of the Tremadoc area in the late fifties Wales had been able to offer good rock-climbing conditions throughout the year, but the new-route interest at Tremadoc was soon exhausted (the highpoint being Brown's ascent of Vector in 1960). Craig Gogarth therefore came as a timely development, providing a really comprehensive all-the-year-round centre, and offering climbs of great length (by Welsh standards), difficulty and seriousness.

These discoveries triggered off a renewed interest in sea-cliff climbing throughout the country, and climbers everywhere scoured their coastlines to see whether they too had a dormant 'Gogarth' waiting to disgorge a flood of impressive routes. Much attention was paid to the traditional sea-cliff areas in Cornwall, Lundy, Gower, Swanage and Aberdeen, and completely new areas such as Tintagel, Carn Gowla, Pentire Head, Blackchurch, Berry Head, Baggy Point, Lydstep, St David's, Cilan Head and St Bee's emerged. Sea stacks, particularly those off the northern coast of Scotland, were also climbed – a craze in which the late Tom Patey played a pivotal role. The Old Man of Hoy was undoubtedly the finest discovery in this respect.

Another interesting by-product of sea-cliff climbing was the tremendously exciting and not unserious pastime of sea-level traversing. This had been practised sporadically for many years, but the general move towards sea-cliff climbing led to the discovery of a number of very long and entertaining sea-level traverse expeditions.

In 1960 the climbing world was primarily linked to the mountains and mountaineering skills, but the time may come when a large proportion of the country's rock-climbs will be situated away from the mountains on extensively developed sea-cliffs. This will undoubtedly add to the interest of the sport, but whether it leads to any significant divergence between a large section of rock-climbers and those generally skilled at mountaineering – a prediction that has been made for years – is doubtful. Sea-cliff climbing will probably remain a useful and exacting section of the sport, enabling the climber to improve his skills ready for the real object of his ambitions – the great routes of the mountains. The possibility of remaining at peak fitness throughout the year can only result in a further improvement in standards on the high mountain crags in the summer.

And what of the future? The signs are that the current preoccupation with hard technical test-pieces on outcrops will spread to the mountain crags of Wales and the Lakes, bringing in its wake a greater concentration on physical fitness, training and technique. Sea-cliff climbing will probably become even more popular, with many more routes being developed, and finally there should be a steady exploitation of the remote mountain crags of Scotland.

Rock-climbing is becoming an increasingly international sport, and there is already a growing tendency towards taking holidays in rock-climbing areas such as Romsdal and Yosemite instead of in the traditional Alpine regions. A similar trend occurred during the fifties and early sixties, when the Dolomites enjoyed great popularity for a period. Climbers at that time became keen to brush up their artificial climbing, and it may be that interest in Yosemite will lead to a greater concentration on the advanced technical aspects of the sport. In this context, the happenings on St John's Head and Strone Ulladale may not be just isolated events, but pointers to future trends.

Britain will never be one of the world's major climbing areas, but historical coincidence and isolation have given us an inheritance of small but rewarding climbs. It is a valuable inheritance from which thousands will gain years of exciting and absorbing recreation – some have made it the centre of their lives.

SCOTLAND 1 Dragon and Gob

by Paddy Buckley

'Carnmore is the most wonderful place in all Britain; remote, vast and beautiful in a fashion not found elsewhere in the Highlands.' This challenging statement was made by Mike O'Hara in 1958. He went on to say that two of the routes compared 'favourably with the best climbs elsewhere'. Dragon was 'steeper and more exposed than Mur y Niwl, with a finer outlook. The difficulties are rather greater . . .' Fionn Buttress, 'the best climb in the region', was judged to be 'slightly harder, slightly more exposed, and . . . more enjoyable than Sheaf'. Eleven years later, Ian Rowe gave it the distinction of being 'one of the finest climbs in Scotland'. As a sustained mountaineering expedition at VS standard, Fionn Buttress has few equals. Its twelve enjoyable pitches offer continuous interest and sensational exposure on perfect rock. But the line is somewhat artificial and most of the difficulties are, regrettably, avoidable.

Carnmore is also one of the remotest crags on the mainland of Britain, and it is certainly the most inaccessible of all those featured in this book. It lies seven weary miles from the nearest road; the nearest pub is even farther. The six-inch map gives the name in Gaelic, Càrnmór; the English spelling, hallowed now by use, derives from the building at the foot of the crag, a shooting lodge owned by the Whitbread family. From any distance, the size and scale of the cliff are lost in the sprawling mass of Beinn a' Chaisgein Mór (2811ft.). Even from the barn, its appearance can still prove deceptive. It is 800ft. high and faces south-west; the rock, Lewisian gneiss, is superb: rough, tough, clean and reliable. There is little vegetation except in the Central Bay, an oasis of very steep grass and heather, which is grazed by wild goats. In contrast to the forbidding aspect of Cloggy or Càrn Dearg, Carnmore has a pleasant, friendly appearance, basking in sunshine: a crag for shirt-sleeves. Its steepness, however, is very impressive and most of the routes have considerable exposure.

Although the Fisherfield area has been visited sporadically since 1909 by S.M.C. members, the development of climbing at Carnmore is relatively modern. The first climb, Diagonal, was put up in 1952 by Ted Wrangham and Arthur Clegg. Twelve more climbs were added in 1956 and 1957, mostly by Mike O'Hara and other members of the Cambridge University M.C., but over the next ten years only a dozen or so new routes were written up, although several parties climbed here without leaving any record of their explorations.

The most prominent feature of the cliff is the great red corner, first climbed by Carrington and Jackson during a heatwave in June 1968. Left of the corner, the almost vertical Upper Wall is bisected by a slanting line of overhangs. This is the line followed boldly by Gob, while Dragon finds its way, unbelievably, through the roof at its highest and most intimidating end. The Upper Wall is no place for compromise. So far it has produced six magnificent routes at HVS, three by English parties – Dragon, St George and Sword – and three by Scots – Gob, Abomination and Carnmore Corner. The earliest, climbed in 1957, was Dragon, now a classic, the touchstone of a leader's mettle. Gob came next, put up in 1960 by Dougal Haston and Robin Smith: so far it has not had its due share of glory, being overshadowed by the reputation of its neighbours. Dragon is awesome, rather introspective; Gob is a mind-blower, packed with gusto and excitement: a star of the future. All the climbs on the Upper Wall suffer a little from the disadvantage of starting from the Central Bay, already two-thirds of the way up the crag. An entry by one of the routes on the Lower Wall should therefore give the right perspective and sense of achievement.

The pedestal on Dragon, like the dentist's waiting-room, is a place for anxious thoughts . . . It was comfortable enough and quite secure, but the knowledge of what was to come made me sharply aware of the immediate surroundings. Below, the crag had quietly unreeled over 700ft. of exposure; above, in every direction, loomed enormous overhangs; to my left, the plummeting groove of Abomination appeared extremely hostile; to my right, St George tiptoed delicately past, as though to avoid this fierce Dragon; the breaks in the roof taken by Gob and Sword were

Routes Dragon, Hard Very Severe, 340ft.; Gob, Hard Very Severe, 420ft. Best approached via the Red Scar Entry, Very Severe, 510ft.
Cliff Carnmore Crag, Beinn a' Chaisgein Mor, Wester Ross.
First Ascents Dragon – G. J. Fraser and M. J. O'Hara, April 1957; Gob – D. Haston and R. Smith, April 1960.
Map Reference O.S. Sheets 19 or 20, 1–50,000 Sheet 19 (ref. 984773).
Guidebooks S.M.C. *Northern Highlands Area* by I. G. Rowe; *Selected Scottish Climbs*, Vol. 2, by H. MacInnes.
Nearest Road The end of a private road at Kernsary (ref. 893793). Prior permission should be sought before using this – parking fee £1·10. It is possible to park at various points along this road or at Poolewe which adds a further 3½ miles to the walk.
Distance and time from cliff 7 miles/1000ft. Allow 3–5 hours.
Good Conditions The crag dries quickly and the climbs are not unduly affected by damp conditions. Avoid midsummer (midges) and the stalking season (12 August–20 October).
Campsites and Bunkhouses Good campsites and an out-house of Carnmore Lodge immediately below the cliff.
Bibliography C.C. Journal 1958: *Highland Dragon* by M. J. O'Hara (a first ascent account). Mountain 22: *The Last Great Wilderness* by P. Buckley (an overall appraisal of climbing in this area).

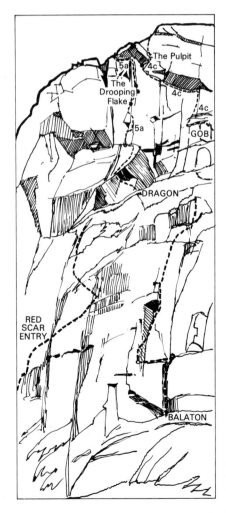

Left: Moving up past the drooping flake of Dragon to the start of the traverse. *Climber: Mick Goad*

Below: The exposed traverse of Dragon. The route continues across to the sunlit rib on the left and follows this to the top. *Climber: Martin Harris*

emergency exits only – for desperate emergencies. That pale slab of the first pitch, weirdly decorated with long strands of grey-green lichen, its 100ft. run-out casually protected by one hopeful runner, that pale slab which seemed so steep for an overture, now appeared quite flat as I waited for the finale. A boulder from the top would fall free for 200ft., hit it once, and never touch rock again until it reached the bottom.

I was loth to leave my pedestal. I felt quite chuffed with the groove and wall pitch I had just led. Technically, this is the most difficult pitch: steep, thin, fierce and delicate, with enough alternative possibilities to keep a leader on his toes. On its merits I tried to convince myself of my chances for the next pitch. No sale. I knew, how well I knew, that all the technical skill in the world, all the balance, would be useless, should I run out of steam on that crucial traverse. The technique was to relax, I told myself, not to get gripped when unable to stand in balance. But it was a technique I had failed to master in almost thirty years of climbing. The knowledge that I'd done the route before should have helped, but it didn't. Like a visit to the dentist.

I couldn't even remember the most economical route to the drooping flake. A dead vertical crack led to the smooth yellow peapod. Was this the way, or was it better on the right wall, or on the left, or perhaps *via* the groove in the corner? Droopy is overhanging and is ascended by jamming arms, knees, feet and anything else into the deep crack on its right. It is not a problem which allows an elegant solution. Having jammed yourself into a position of comparative security, you can crouch down for a rest, clutching Droopy to your stomach, backside in the air, feet a-dangle, contemplating the Dragon's innards. Or, if this is *infra dig.*, you can ride Droopy *à cheval*, but possibly not for as long.

Stand up, bridge and move left to the rib and the tiny ledge below the pegs. It was here, during the first ascent, that O'Hara made his sensational cat's cradle stance, suspended in slings from two leafpegs (the originals were still being used in

1973!). Modern dragon-slayers, armed with Moacs and Clogs, prefer to take their belay on a sloping ledge in the corner just beyond the finger traverse, where they can give advice and comfort to their seconds. The situation is undoubtedly impressive. The traverse is short, a mere ten feet, but it lies across a rigorously vertical wall that is undercut and overhung; anyone coming unstuck here and unable to help himself would present serious problems. Technically the crux is not hard; as a boulder problem at ground level it would give no difficulty. *In situ*, however, the build-up of pressure caused by exposure, seriousness and the demands made on tiring fingers, gives it a very high grip rating. It is also quite inescapable. You will remember it all the days of your life.

Gob, on the other hand, has a lower grip factor. It is just as exposed, just as serious and more evenly sustained (though less difficult), but there is one important difference: the climbing is all in balance. Since much of it is beneath an overhanging roof above a steep wall, Gob has consequently become one of the most exhilarating climbs at Carnmore. The line, though seemingly circuitous, has a classic simplicity: the line of least resistance. The laconic description in the guidebook is a gem of brevity, Scottish style. It only fails to mention the fact that you will need 150ft. of rope. Protection throughout is excellent; indeed, one has to miss out possible runners now and then to reduce the drag on the rope.

The first pitch, after negotiating the initial overhangs by a side-step, leads to a superb wall, with cracks and a corner groove giving sheer delight. Then a fantastic traverse is made along the fault under the vast roof, with the crux at a sort of giant swallow's nest half-way along the eaves. A jammed wire sling was installed there during Easter 1973, and it has removed much of the anxiety previously encountered. The route continues along the fault all the way to a very reassuring pulpit stance where the exit through the overhang becomes obvious at last. Pete Rowat's direct finish is a better variation than the original; it goes straight up from the break-out to an overhanging crack in a corner, and finishes magnificently at the very top of the cliff.

Left: The traverse through the overhangs on Gob to the pulpit. The lower section of the route reaches this point by a long traverse under the lower overhang. *Climber: Pete Gray*

SCOTLAND **2** **King Rat and Goliath**

by Greg Strange

Winter and the wet weep have gone. It is June on Creag an Dubh Loch. Already the sun is filtering through the walls of the doss, yet it is only four in the morning. Will the good weather hold? The distant rushing of water is borne on a cool breeze that creeps around the slabs and walls and sends crazy ripply shadows across the loch. Yes – the dark loch, the silver sands, and that immense crag. Central Gully Wall basks in the early morning sun, its pink and grey slabs resembling the scales of a monstrous reptile. The granite looks desperately smooth, seamed only by vertical cracks and grooves. What a magnificent cliff! What great lines!

King Rat and Goliath, just two of those lines, offer between them perhaps the greatest introduction to climbing on Creag an Dubh Loch. As individual climbs they are superb; but their significance goes beyond their physical qualities, for they were the product of almost twenty years of spasmodic exploration. Few crags of comparable size and excellence have developed so slowly. The reasons may be obvious, remoteness and dampness being the major handicaps. Weatherwise, the Dubh Loch is no more fickle than other Scottish mountain crags, but it is certainly remote. Not only is there a six-mile walk-in, but the crag is also far removed from the popular climbing scenes of the south. The Dubh Loch remains part of a climbing backwater where modern trends and techniques have been slow to influence a staunch mountaineering tradition. The advent of P.A.s, chrome-moly steel pegs and jam nuts certainly made it safer to venture on to the open faces; nevertheless, few of the modern classics were climbed before the late sixties.

The Central Gully Wall has two major facets, the great frontal face and a more beetling though shorter wall higher up the gully. The continuity of this steeper section is broken by three prominent corners, Vertigo Wall, Goliath and The Giant. It was here that early exploration was concentrated. After his remarkable 'nails' ascent of Vertigo Wall in 1954, Tom Patey turned his attention to The Giant. Thinking that the overhanging lower corner was impracticable, he discovered that it was

possible to reach the corner *via* an exposed traverse from below Vertigo. Several epic attempts were made on this line, the most notable being that by Dick Barclay and Alec Thom, in 1956. Having omitted to leave a companion to safeguard an irreversible tension traverse, the pair found themselves trapped over halfway up The Giant. Anxious friends on the plateau tied two ropes together and hauled them to safety. Ten years passed before The Giant fell to Bathgate, Ewing and Brumfitt.

But there was still another: Goliath was first tried by Jim McArtney in 1967. Accompanied by Brian Lawrie, McArtney managed to climb the steep corner above the tension traverse; but, just as in his attempt on King Rat, his luck ran out. He was forced to retreat, having overcome the major difficulties, and the climb was completed two years later.

Goliath is the gentle giant of Central Gully Wall. It follows a fine natural line through impressive rock scenery and gives a great variety of interesting climbing and situations. Above all, it has atmosphere. The approach up Central Gully is, to say the least, thought provoking. Huge boulders, precariously balanced on unstable scree, are a constant reminder of the forces of nature. That massive, wedged block used by the direct start appears to be supporting the entire crag. Some day gravity will triumph and Goliath will be no more.

The first pitch is a long rising traverse, Etive style. It looks easy, but after 8oft. you become aware of the increasing drop. Above the second overlap a good peg runner inspires confidence and you actually find holds on the old tension traverse. A fine pitch. Now comes the crux which is the very antithesis of the delicate friction climbing gone before. The corner is very steep for 3oft. An awkward move from the belay brings a pull-up on to a small ledge; an out-of-balance move right then enables you to gain sufficient height to reach a good jug. It is now possible to go right, but the true line continues straight up the fault, easing gently before going over a bulge with good holds to a large depression.

Once again the character of the climb changes. The large diagonal corner with its

Routes Goliath, Hard Very Severe, 500ft.; King Rat, Hard Very Severe, 950ft.
Crag Central Gully Wall, Creag an Dubh Loch in the Cairngorms.
First Ascents Goliath – B. Findlay and M. Rennie, June 1969; King Rat – J. Bower and A. Fyffe, June 1968.
Map Reference O.S. Sheet 41, 1–50,000 Sheet 44 (ref. 235824).
Guidebooks S.M.C. *Cairngorms Area*, Vol. 5, by A. F. Fyffe; *Selected Scottish Climbs*, Vol. 2, by H. MacInnes.
Nearest Road Car Park at the head of the Loch Muick road (ref. 313853). Follow the private road along the west side of Loch Muick and continue up a good path from Glas Alt Shiel to the crag.
Distance and time from cliff 6 miles/1000ft. Allow 2–3 hours.
Good Conditions Between May and October. The crag dries slowly. Allow at least one week after heavy. rain though it can dry more quickly in warm and windy weather.
Campsites and Bunkhouses There are several good bivouac boulders below the cliff and a good campsite at the head of Dubh Loch.
Bibliography S.M.C. Journal 1970: *Creag an Dubh Loch A'la Carte* by John Grieve.

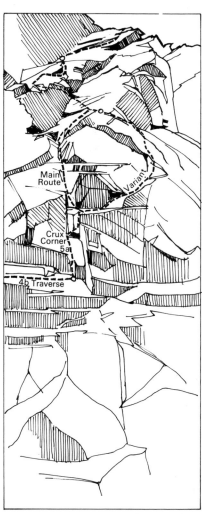

Left: Looking up the line of Goliath. The leader is taking the right-hand variant, having climbed the crux corner. *Climbers: Dougie Dinwoodie and Cynthia Heap*

Top left: The traverse across the initial slabs of Goliath.
Climber: Dave Stuart

Bottom left: The final pitch of Goliath. *Climber:* Bob Harris

Below: The aid moves through the big overlap of King Rat.
Climber: Dave Stuart

vertical left wall dominates the remaining pitches. You wonder where to go next. Away to the right the final corner of Giant cuts a perpendicular course through blank walls; but the rock directly above seems to lie back. A short slab corner starts the third pitch and soon you emerge below a smooth slab. Delightful climbing follows up a good nut crack, then a traverse to the right edge and so by a blocky crest to a stance halfway up the big corner. The last pitch is superbly situated. Although technically straightforward it provides a fitting climax to this great route. A line of holds leads out across the slabs to a series of cracks. Good jams, great holds, a satisfying sense of exposure, and suddenly you are at the top.

King Rat is the most prominent crack system on the great frontal face. There can be few more aesthetically pleasing routes. It traces a perfect line to the plateau, almost 950ft. of excellent and very continuous climbing. At 200ft. the crack system leads over a large roof. Due to considerable foreshortening this fearsome object dominates the climb. It certainly dominates your mind. For 50ft. the climbing is quite steep with small flaky holds, uncharacteristic of the face. You feel uneasy on this unfamiliar rock, but soon a left traverse leads out from the dark recess on to the sunlit face. The roof looms above. An airy slab with ample holds lands you in a small cave. After great contortions you reluctantly swing away left on the first shaky peg. It holds. Clip into the next. God this is steep! Only two pegs for aid! Reach high. Fantastic jugs and you are on a good ledge. Apprehensions are dispelled and you really begin to enjoy the climbing. What's next? Two long run-outs of sheer delight. Continuous climbing up cracks, corners, short walls and slabs, never easy, never hard, but always interesting.

At the top of a corner you reach Waterkelpie Wall. Slabs and a peculiar mantelshelf lead to a belay. The next pitch is the crux. It starts with the leaning corner of Waterkelpie, which is often wet; but there are a few helpful tufts of grass on the ledge above. Soon you are below the jutting block overhang. You don't like the look of that rusty old leeper. Find a better runner. A

John Mothersele

9

Left: Looking up the line of King Rat. The route is grossly foreshortened.

strenuous pull and a long reach to grasp a flake hold; a quick step right above the block. Not quite up yet. A side-pull, then good holds lead up left and back right to a spacious ledge. The angle eases off now, but there are still two good pitches before the maze of vegetated blocks below the plateau.

Thus a dream momentarily becomes reality and lives for ever as a memory. A memory of two magnificent routes on a huge lonely crag. Of boundless views across sweeps of granite. Of steep walls, smooth slabs, grooves, cracks and long serious pitches. Few climbers visit Creag an Dubh Loch. Are you prepared to make the effort to be one of the few?

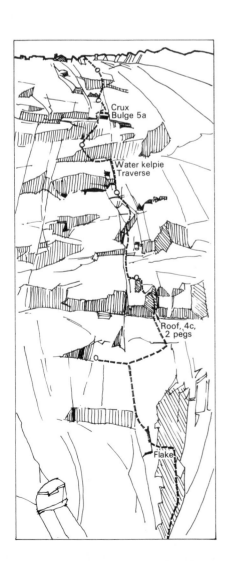

Hamish MacInnes

11

SCOTLAND 3 The Needle

by Ian Rowe

Sit by the rough shores of Loch Avon and sense the malevolence of those ancient glaciers; like gargantuan navvies they have just left for a tea break and will soon return. The great cliffs wait in limbo; they know of forces far greater than those exerted by the puny humans burrowing in their sides; they sleep on, closed brethren of the moving ice and the inexorable fingers of winter frosts.

The Cairngorms have long been the province of the Aberdonian. Approaches are long and climbs were always hard won in terms of work and accumulation of knowledge. It is natural that the Cairngorm devotee should be defensive and should climb there to the exclusion of other areas. It is a long and inconvenient drive to Glencoe from Aberdeen. Natural, then, that Malcolm Smith should reflect this insularity and ignorance of contemporary standards in his classic guide of 1961. Seldom can a guidebook editor have committed himself as fatally as Smith did in his description of Shelter Stone Crag.

'There are few chinks in its grim armour. The Central Slabs . . . are manifestly impossible. This is also the case with much of the rock forming the great vertical bastion to the right of Central Slabs, unless mechanized techniques are employed to excess.'

The refutation of this will be brief. There are now three routes on the Slabs and four on the 'bastion'. This does not include the late R. H. Sellar's Citadel (put up in 1958) which takes an indifferent line between the two features and suffers by comparison with Needle, the first of the iconoclastic *tours de force* by 'outsiders'. Cairngorm climbers are no longer complacent and now fill a role which their energy has long deserved. Shelter Stone Crag today provides the best modern routes of the group.

Needle goes up the middle of the 'great vertical bastion'. What could be more natural to Robin Smith? How could such intellect and ability refuse the Editor's naïve and unwitting challenge? How could a rope like Smith and Agnew fail to climb anything they set their minds to? Davy Agnew, the epitome of the Creag Dhu hardman, not such a puny human that the cliffs could afford to rest easy. The rope must

have shot up the first two pitches towards that tempting skylight which is the eye of the Needle.

On the final section of the lower slabs there is an overlap larger than the ones below, and the traverse across its wall is sparse of the holds for the hefty pull you feel you deserve. Balance and guile are needed to gain the slab above.

At the end of the pitch the character of the climb is changing and you are no longer a neat and balanced technician choosing holds like a connoisseur at an auction. The crag has steepened and you gratefully take what you can get and use it to the full.

A steep flake leads delightfully to a ledge from which a delicate traverse left is made. At the end there is a nasty little wall. The holds are all wrong. Having attacked it, you again feel that a jug is deserved, but the recess above is sadistically sparse. You will be grateful to get to the belay, a fine eyrie with no view but the greater panorama of the sky and the valley walls opposite: a fine place to imagine the struggles of your second.

The lead-hogger will make sure that his second leads the next pitch, a short rising traverse right to a large ledge on the open face. This will leave him with the 'Crack for Thin Fingers', a one-move problem for the shorter man and no real trouble to the taller specimen with the correct digital dimensions. Smith's description is no doubt a reference to Agnew's discomfiture. The latter's fingers are better suited to medium-sized bong cracks. The move is in a blank corner, a contorted layback on the left fingers while the right hand rises to a good hold.

Some indifferent scrambling follows, and a short traverse left across a small slab leads to a belay below the final deep chimney. At last you begin to thread the Needle. Not far left is the imposing corner of 'Steeple', which was created by Kenny Spence, John Porteous and Mike Watson, in August 1969, and which is acquiring a growing reputation. Bridging is recommended for the first pitch of the chimney, not only because it is less strenuous, but because you are then elegantly suspended above the

Route The Needle, Extremely Severe, 870ft.
Cliff Shelter Stone Crag, Loch Avon Horseshoe, Cairngorms.
First Ascent R. Smith and D. Agnew, summer 1962.
Map Reference O.S. Tourist Map of the Cairngorms, 1–50,000 Sheet 36 (ref. 003015).
Guidebook *Selected Scottish Climbs*, Vol. 2, by H. MacInnes.
Nearest Road The Cairngorm Car Park below the chair-lift (ref. 996053). Take the chair-lift to Cairngorm, cross the summit and drop down to Loch Avon.
Distance and time from cliff 3 miles/500ft. ascent–800ft. descent. Allow 1 hour.
Good Conditions Dries quickly on sunny days except after prolonged bad weather or if there is still snow on the ledges. The route should be completely dry.
Campsites and Bunkhouses The Shelter Stone (a famous bivouac site) is just below the crag and there are campsites close by. There is also a campsite near Glenmore Lodge and the car park.
Bibliography S.M.C. Journal 1969: *Shelter Stone Crag* by J. Renny (a general history of the crag). S.M.C. Journal 1971: *Tall Story*, c. 1834.

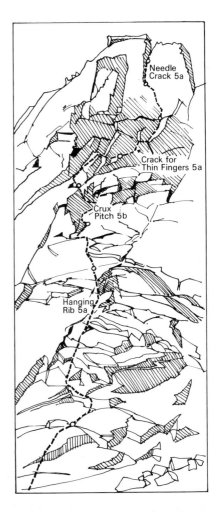

Greg Strange

lower slopes. It is a good moment, for the difficulties are over.

The last pitch worms through some chokestones (traditional spelling). It is a refreshingly old-fashioned and surprising finish to a unique modern climb, a watershed of Cairngorm history.

Above: The difficult moves on pitch four of The Needle. *Climbers: John Ingram and Greg Strange*

Left: The Crack for Thin Fingers. The climber has to move up into a strenuous layback position and reach up for the holds on the right. *Climber: John Ingram*

Right: The start of the Needle Crack. *Climber: Lynn Jones*

14

SCOTLAND **4** **Centurion**

by Robin Campbell

Few British crags are as intimidating as Càrn Dearg Buttress. Take the old Nevis path on a crisp winter night. As you follow the long drooping curve towards the hut, the buttress looms above you black with menace, blotting out the moon. Even when seen on a warm summer morning, bathed in sunlight, its sheer size impresses. Whatever your feelings on leaving the hut, when you stand below the 1000ft. plunge of the crag's high right edge, listening to the slow drip of the bottom overhangs, only if you are exceptionally brave or insensitive will you not feel a twinge of anxiety.

Objectively, however, the buttress is not unaccommodating. Its major difficulties are confined to the first 400ft., and the rock is the familiar old volcanic andesite, similar to that of Glencoe, the Lake District and North Wales. The crag abounds in good natural up-and-down lines, and holds are plentiful and sound except in a few areas, notably the middle pitches of Sassenach. O'Hara and Downes, who made the second ascent of that route, were appalled by the looseness of the flakes in the great chimney pitches, but these have long disappeared.

Exploration of the crag is of fairly recent date. Before 1954, the only routes were Routes I and II on the left of the buttress (the former was climbed by Hargreaves, MacPhee and Hughes in 1931, the latter by Kellett and W. A. Russell in 1943) and Evening Wall on the extreme right (climbed by Rolland and Ogilvy in 1940). Kellett was an extraordinary man. A conscientious objector in the last war, he was put to work in the Forestry at Torlundy at the base of the mountain and, perhaps as a demonstration of the sincerity of his objection, he spent the war years making a series of extremely courageous climbs on Ben Nevis, many of them solo. He must have been attracted by the splendid lines of Càrn Dearg Buttress, and there is evidence that he climbed what is now the first pitch of Centurion with the idea of traversing across into Sassenach chimney. He died in 1944 while engaged (most probably) on an ascent of the simple Cousins' Buttress. Ironically, he had a climbing partner on this occasion.

In 1954, Joe Brown and Don Whillans (acting on information received) investigated the great right-hand nose of the buttress and found a most unnatural and improbable way through the lower overhangs to the foot of the big dark chimney splitting the front of the nose. After that all went relatively smoothly. This route, Sassenach, should have served as a warning to local climbers (emphasized by the name) that the magnificent line of corners to the left would not long remain inviolate. The warning did not go unheeded. Indeed, it was unnecessary, since Noon and Cunningham from Glasgow, Marshall from Edinburgh and Patey and Brooker from Aberdeen had already tried the line of Sassenach before the 1954 ascent.

The next route to fall, Centurion, is undoubtedly the finest natural line on the cliff and is one of the most challenging climbs in Britain. It follows a great 500ft. corner which slashes down through the lower overhangs from the sweep of slab high on the buttress. Above the slab the fault continues through the upper overhangs to finish on a terrace some way below the buttress's highest point. The Scots had tried the line: indeed, Marshall had climbed most of the crucial second pitch but was defeated by circumstances beyond his control. However, local response to the stimulus of Sassenach was too slow and the route fell in August 1956 to Bob Downes and Don Whillans. Downes had already that same summer produced a route on the Minus Face, Minus One Direct, which, though not as hard as Centurion, is, in my view, superior in quality.

In the crag's subsequent history, Scottish climbers played an appropriate role, the last two real natural lines, The Bat (a line of corners between Centurion and Sassenach) and The Shield Direct (the lower part of a fault-line on the extreme right of the nose), falling to Robin Smith and Marshall respectively.

Centurion is not now considered a hard climb. Even in 1962, when I first climbed it, it was generally recommended as a fine bracing excursion, a nice safe route for budding VS leaders to cut their teeth on, an evaluation likely to be reinforced by its frequent ascents and by Norrie Muir's solo

Route Centurion, Hard Very Severe, 650ft.
Cliff Càrn Dearg Buttress, Ben Nevis.
First Ascent D. Whillans and R. O. Downes, August 1956.
Map Reference O.S. Tourist Map to Ben Nevis and Glencoe, 1–50,000 Sheet 41 (ref. 163723).
Guidebooks S.M.C. *Ben Nevis* by J. R. Marshall; *Selected Scottish Climbs*, Vol. 1, by H. MacInnes.
Nearest Road A lay-by (ref. 137763) on the Fort William/Spean Bridge road, one mile east of the Distillery. A path leads from here directly into the valley below the cliff.
Distance and time from cliff 3½ miles/2800ft. Allow 3 hours.
Good Conditions Allow two or three dry days after prolonged bad weather, but the route can dry quickly after a superficial wetting.
Campsites and Bunkhouses S.M.C.'s Charles Inglis Clark Hut below the cliff. Campsites by the hut or in Glen Nevis.
Bibliography S.M.C. Journal 1958: *Shirt Sleeves on Ben Nevis* by B. E. H. Maden (an account of an early ascent).

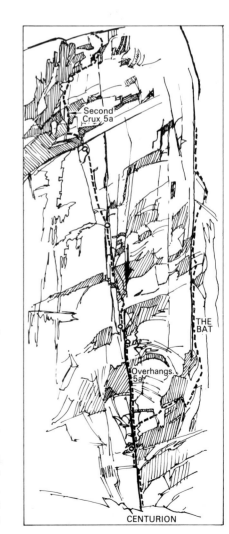

CENTURION

ascent in September 1971. However, it is perhaps rather more serious than that. During a recent encounter, I was much impressed by the demands on muscle stamina posed by the second pitch: one would be ill-advised to venture on to it after a long lay-off. As a route its structure is simple and satisfying. There is a stiff little pipe-opener of a pitch, deceptively steep, which leads to the bottom of the 120ft. open corner which forms the great second pitch. This is an exercise in the logistics of muscle as much as anything else. There is no move that is particularly daunting, but none are easy and few can be made without considerable assistance from the arms. Natural protection is plentiful and nuts can be inserted at will in the main crack, but the climber who over-indulges himself in this way faces a lot of hanging about in awkward positions and may require extensive aided 'rests' before he wins through. On the other hand, a fresh, fit climber making a bold approach may wonder what all the fuss is about!

After this pitch, there are two further interesting pitches of comparatively moderate difficulty in the corner, before the crack runs out in a long straightforward section to meet the upper overhangs. Here,

there are comfortable ledges where a residue of tins, etc., testifies to their popularity as a lunching place. The indolent may now continue by the traverse of Route II, to reach the easier rocks on the right, but the final pitches should really not be missed. The first one is very awkward technically but is only a two-mover. An initial weird thrutch crosses the lowest overhang and then one embarks on a fantastic leftward excursion through groves of tottering spikes and flakes to teeter under the next band of overhangs on a diminishing ledge. Here, careful footwork allows subtle handholds to come into play; once one is correctly positioned the roof is easily passed to move back rightwards by a simple slab. The last few feet of the pitch cause difficulties on account of the rope drag produced by the zigzag line, but this can be avoided by using only one rope for protection and finishing the pitch on the other. The final pitch requires a little careful route-finding through the last overhang but is not really troublesome.

That, then, is Centurion – undoubtedly *the* classic modern rock-climb on Ben Nevis, when difficulty, quality, historical interest and amount of traffic are taken into account.

Left: The second pitch of Centurion. This long and difficult pitch, generally considered the crux of the climb, works strenuously through the overlaps above the climber. *Climber: John Kingston*

Above: A view from the start of Centurion's second pitch. The overlapping slabs followed by The Bat are beyond the climber. *Climber: Sam Crymble*

SCOTLAND **5** **The Bat**

by Paul Nunn

Route The Bat, Extremely Severe, 1000ft.
Cliff Càrn Dearg Buttress, Ben Nevis.
First Ascent R. Smith and D. Haston, September 1959.
Map Reference O.S. Tourist Map to Ben Nevis and Glencoe, 1–50,000 Sheet 41 (ref. 163723).
Guidebooks S.M.C. *Ben Nevis* by J. R. Marshall; *Selected Scottish Climbs*, Vol. 1, by H. MacInnes.
Nearest Road At a layby (ref. 137763) on the A82 Fort William/Spean Bridge road, one mile east of the Distillery. A path leads from here directly into the valley below the cliff.
Distance and time from cliff 3½ miles/2800ft. Allow 3 hours.
Good Conditions The climb needs several days of dry summer weather to come into condition after bad weather.
Campsites and Bunkhouses S.M.C.'s Charles Inglis Clark Hut below the cliff. Campsites by the hut or in Glen Nevis.
Bibliography S.M.C. Journal 1960: *The Bat and the Wicked* by Robin Smith (a now classic account of the first ascent).

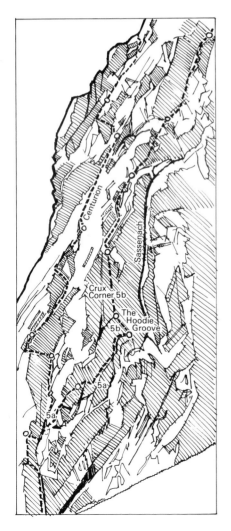

The swelling bulges and roof-grey slabs between the giant groove of Centurion and the black slit of Sassenach's upper chimney are the epitome of modern rock climbing challenge. No obvious route attracts the eye. Instead, every positive feature militates against vertical progress. Slabs are attenuated above and below by smooth bellied bulges; vertical cracks are faint and discontinuous, except for a high corner descending into space quite close to Sassenach.

A rock feature devoid of suggestion provides a challenge not only to strength and skill, but also to cunning – an essential in the act of creation. There is an originality quite specific to the conversion of rock impossibilities into climbs. Mere craftsmanship is not enough – it is artistry beyond the average which is essential to free climbing in an over-vertical world fraught with potential blind alleys.

Robin Smith, author both of the climb and of an unsurpassable account of the first ascent with Dougal Haston in September 1959, had just this combination of talents. Taking advantage of the brief cessation of the late summer monsoon which concentrated upon Scotland, while England and Wales basked, Smith launched on to the buttress from Centurion with R. K. Holt, and made a linking traverse to Sassenach, below the challenge of the corners carving through the upper bulging wall. In a series of epic outings, Smith completed the climb with Dougal Haston. It required more aid than he liked, but the competitive screws were on and the chips were down as darkness threatened to end the last possibility of success . . .

'So I was very sly and said we had to get the gear and climbed past the roof to the sling at the pebbles. . . . There I was so exhausted that I put in a piton, only it was very low, and I thought, so am I, peccavi, peccabo, and I put in another and rose indiscriminately until to my surprise I was past Dougal's ledge and still on the rock in a place to rest.'

After three falls, some dramatic retreats, and much adrenalin, the climb was securely done: one of the greatest, and at that time one of the hardest routes on Càrn Dearg,

despite Smith's characteristically whimsical misgivings and an escape up Sassenach which left the final grooves to the editing of Haston and Marshall.

The nose of Càrn Dearg is utterly unyielding below two slabby tilted breaks cutting through overhangs at a hundred feet, and Sassenach only just creeps through the right extremity of this barrier by its most ferocious pitch. Entry to the buttress must be indirect to be free-climbed, and is achieved by taking Centurion's initial wall. The wall is climbed to an ample, notchy ledge below the massive, sliced-out, corner groove. After a few feet in this magnificent corner, an upper and broader slab, suspended over the lower bulges, provides the link with the centre of the buttress. The compact, pinky-grey rock forces an uncertain and delicate traverse, without much protection, to the haven of a gloomy perched block under the overhanging prow of the buttress. Beyond this belay the slab is sliced away and, after a slight ascent, a step right leads to a groove which veers inwards at a dramatic angle a few feet below the traverse line, while bulging out above. This blind, bottomless, black-streaked corner, lost amid the overhangs, is the one and only unattractive option, taken by insecure steep bridging moves up right, if it is possible to avoid a slide into the impressive void between your knees. There is a belay a long way to the right on a comfortably insulated slab near Sassenach's chimney.

The 'hoodie groove' is a queer Triermain-like problem, mossy, very steep and with too few holds. It was once done with a sling, but one wonders if it wasn't more difficult once you were in it to launch off again. The second, out of sight, relaxes his mind in oblivion. Or should do!

The belay lies on a little slab hanging off the base of the towering walls of the culminating corner, the climb's *raison d'être*. In the midst of this, a crack rears to a gritstone-like roof and then narrows in the perspective of upward sweeping rock.

Forever steep, encumbered with chockstones, the crack calls for muscle-power to attain the roof and a piton runner. Remarkably good jams then materialize, and a combined layaway and jamming tactic provides the solution to the roof and the crack above. But there is a piton in place and it is hard to reach, though no doubt less so than it was to put in. Then the crack is less difficult but very steep, with jams and leg jams and chockstones, like some Alpine granite horror. A sweat up the fierce but now not too difficult crack leads to a terrace and the easing, rambling walls and occasional bits of looseness. As progress accelerates, the sense of scale is lost on the extensive reaches of the great buttress, and concentration is deflected on to the terrace descent, the possibility of a little snow-shooting in P.A.s in Number 5 gully and brews in the citadel of S.M.C. restrictive practice.

The Bat is perhaps a great non-line: a connoisseur's delight, with its devious complexity and its unwillingness to reach the point. It does not look very logical, and maybe it isn't, but it feels right in ascent. After all, its wanderings are not fortuitous – they are forced by the sheer unco-operativeness of the rock. There is an objective to be attained in this magnificent ramble, the reward which is the near-alpine smooth walled corner, the grand finale to one of Smith's finest legacies to British climbing.

SCOTLAND 6 Trapeze

by Allen Fyffe

Aonach Dubh, the last and most westerly of the Three Sisters of Glencoe, is a squat, cliff-encircled ridge jutting out from the elegant triangle of Stob Coire nan Lochan. On the east side the cliffs are open and pleasant, while the north face is predictably steep, gloomy and dark. The west face, on the other hand, is a complex sprawl of ledges, gullies and buttresses. From the road it appears as a great three-layered cake cut up into so many vertical segments.

The Middle Ledge, a narrow horizontal fault at one-third height, scores across the top of the Lower Tier, an unpleasant area of poor rock, vegetation and seeps. Above is the Middle Tier, a line of variously shaped buttresses up to about 250ft. high; this area, undercut in places but clean and distinctive, is in turn capped by the Rake, the second horizontal fault. The broad grass terrace of the Rake runs the length of the cliff below the Upper Tier, an area of small buttresses, ridges, slots and slabs – clean, solid rock in fields of turf.

Vertically the west face is divided by a series of deep wet gullies, numbered from one to six, which split the cliff into a series of buttresses (lettered A to G). The largest gully, Number 4, appears as a great dark funnel in the centre of the cliff, opening out in the Upper Tier to form the Amphitheatre, a miniature hanging corrie. In the Middle Tier, the gully runs between the narrow, tapered E Buttress on the left and the smaller, squatter F Buttress on the right; below, it descends the Lower Tier as a nightmare of loose rock, vegetation and water.

From the front, E Buttress appears as a pleasant pillar of rock, but things look different when a traverse is made along the Middle Ledge into Number 4. The south face of the buttress, overlooking Number 4, rears up for 500ft. as a great leaning mass of andesite. Going up the gully below this face, one passes a smooth tilted wall, a large corner, a region of steep walls and perched ledges and, finally, a broad cracked overhanging rib. The big corner is the obvious line. First the corner, broken then vertical; then a long slab ramp sweeping up to abut against the overhanging top half of the buttress; and finally an area of over-

hanging grooves and cracks and over-lapping tile-like slab: this is the line of Trapeze.

The cliff's development began in 1898, and over the next fifty years most of the gullies and buttresses were climbed. But it was not until 1958 that exploration of the big corner was started. In the summer of that year, Jimmy Marshall and Derek Leaver climbed the corner and slab, a piece of bold climbing and fine route-finding. Because of some of the antics involved, they named the route Trapeze.

The climb starts as an easy vegetated ramp which leads to the corner proper, the 70ft. crux. Twin cracks snake up the corner: not nice cracks, but ones which open and close, giving sharp edges and sloping pea-pods. Right from the start the climbing is energetic; awkward laybacks and jams, bridging moves and side pulls for 20ft. until the ledge is reached. Here, one can sit and recover, and rig up some protection. The climbing continues in the same style to below the bulge near the top, at which point a nut can be placed from a vague resting position in a crouched bridge. Above, the cracks widen and vee out. A right hand-jam, pull up then push down, feet in the crack, then a hold in the left crack and up, gratefully, on to the ledge and into a secure cave. Belay and hide, surrounded by rock, with no need to hang on.

The slab ramp follows: easy climbing for 140ft. on small square holds, a complete contrast to the fight below; then into a belay niche amid the junipers where the ramp loses itself in the walls above. A few moves up and right round the corner complete the next short pitch to a spacious ledge perched high on the face. Exposure returns with a rush. The wall above this undercut perch rears up with frightening smoothness. The way is not clear and the angle not easy, the rock is compact and the holds slope out. Near the left end of the ledge is a line of poor holds. Careful balance climbing on the almost perpendicular wall leads, after about 20ft., to holds you can get your hands round. These, in turn, lead to the top of the wall where a diagonal line of slab and corners goes up and right to the second half of pitch four. The groove, gently impending

Route Trapeze, Extremely Severe, 450ft.
Cliff East Buttress, West Face of Aonach Dubh, Glencoe.
First Ascent J. R. Marshall and D. Leaver, Summer 1958.
Map Reference O.S. Sheet 47, 1–50,000 Sheet 41 (ref. 144557).
Guidebooks S.M.C. *Glencoe and Ardgour*, Vol 2, by L. Lovat; *Selected Scottish Climbs*, Vol. 1, by H. MacInnes.
Nearest Road A82 at road junction (ref. 138567).
Distance and time from cliff ¾ mile/1200ft. Allow 1 hour.
Good Conditions Allow two to three dry summer days.
Campsites and Bunkhouses Bunkhouse and Youth Hostel in Glencoe Village; S.M.C. Hut Lagangarbh (6 miles); Campsites along the valley.

Tony Riley

but equipped with holds, hangs in space, looking forward to the slabs above. 130ft. from the ledge they arrive, with a small belay niche. The way is now obvious, up the slab rightwards to a crack – steep but easy – then the route is no more. The top of the buttress, almost 500ft. above the start – Trapeze ending up on top.

Above: The easier slab section after the difficult, initial corner of Trapeze. *Climber: Ken Jones*

Above and right: Two photos of the lower section of Yo-Yo (*see following chapter*). The smaller picture shows the initial damp bulges; the leader is tackling the layback near the end of the first pitch. The larger photo shows him just completing the first pitch. The climb continues up the corner to the dark chimney, which is climbed with difficulty to a second ledge. The third pitch (grossly foreshortened) moves up the ramp on the left and then returns to the steep groove on the right which is followed to the top. *Climber: Bill Lounds*

Aonach Dubh, Glencoe

SCOTLAND 7 Yo-Yo

by John Porteous

Aonach Dubh harbours two famous rock faces, both developed in the late fifties. On the west face, the sunny disposition of E Buttress attracts many an aspirant who might otherwise have turned his talents to the brooding north face. The latter is dominated by Yo-Yo – a great *dièdre* cutting vertically through the main wall, clearly visible from the Glencoe road 1500ft. below. The sun hardly penetrates the gully bed, where snow often lies until midsummer, and the dripping overhangs demand patience from those who wish to ascend them.

The main feature of the cliff is Ossian's Cave, a gaping 200ft. high abscess which, until the visitors' book vanished from its box, was the only reason for anyone going near the place. Most of the climbing is to the west of the cave on a short (300-400ft.) but lengthy buttress (the girdle extends for 1000ft.). The majority of the climbs terminate on the ill-named Pleasant Terrace, the normal descent route, above which the cliffs continue at an easier angle for another 200-300ft. In general the rock is solid Glencoe granite, providing sharp, fingery, incut holds and thin, parallel cracks and corners, which improve the further one traverses away from the Cave.

In Wales, Brown's routes inevitably mature into classics; in Scotland, Smith's routes fall into the same inevitable category. Bold and direct, they personify the climber. The effort expended in early attempts on Yo-Yo is well reflected in the name, each repulse providing the spring of enthusiasm for the next attempt. Today's route, damp though it may be, bears little resemblance to the vegetated ledges and cracks experienced by the original ascensionists.

Rob Campbell, writing in the Scottish Mountaineering Club Journal, adequately summed up the problems encountered during early attempts on the route: 'Whillans had a stab at it in 1958, but, unaccountably, turned back after passing the first overhang. Then in 1959 Smith and Hughes climbed it

in two days. Smith spent something like four hours hanging on the bottom overhang, wiping the rock dry with a towel, before he eventually won through. To date the climb has only had three ascents. This route must rank with the best in the country.'

Yo-Yo is generally regarded as tougher than any of the E Buttress trilogy (Trapeze, Big Top and Hee-Haw) and is a good preamble to Shibboleth, being shorter and better protected than the latter, but more strenuous and sustained. The first fifty feet are generally regarded as the crux: they constitute a rising traverse left to breach the initial overhang, followed by a short, steep crack leading into the classic layback, which gradually eases off to a large sloping ledge and the first belay. (This section is similar to the first pitch of White Slab on Clogwyn du'r Arddu.)

The second pitch is one of the most spectacular in Glencoe. From the ledge, the corner is climbed with difficulty for forty feet. At this point the crack widens into an overhanging chimney, jammed with rattling chockstones round which the climber entwines his arms as he lunges out and up over the prow, with nothing but thin air between his feet and the screes below. Although the main difficulties are now over, the final pitch maintains the tempo, being deceptively steep and strenuous, particularly to a leader weakened by the overhangs below. Again the crack is followed, either direct to Pleasant Terrace, or via a short excursion on the left wall, twenty feet from the top.

At this point, most parties descend by the terrace, but it is possible to continue the route for another 200ft. on the upper tier. This section was completed by Smith, with Moriarty, in May 1960, but it does not compare in any respect with the lower section, and is generally ignored.

Yo-Yo is today accepted as one of the best climbs in Scotland and by any standards deserves to become a classic.

Route Yo-Yo, Extremely Severe, 300 ft.
Cliff North Face of Aonach Dubh, Glencoe.
First Ascent R. Smith and D. Hughes, May 1959; Extra Finish – Smith and J. Moriarty, May 1960.
Map Reference O.S. Sheet 47, 1–50,000 Sheet 41 (ref. 157563).
Guidebooks S.M.C. *Glencoe and Ardgour*, Vol 2, by L. Lovat; *Selected Scottish Climbs*, Vol. 1, by H. MacInnes.
Nearest Road A82 at Achtriochtan Farm (ref. 156572).
Distance and time from cliff ½ mile/1500 ft. Allow 1 hour.
Good Conditions Allow three dry summer days.
Campsites and Bunkhouses Bunkhouse and Youth Hostel in Glencoe Village (3 miles); S.M.C Hut Lagangarbh (5 miles); Campsites along the valley.
Bibliography S.M.C. Journal 1964: *The Ugly Sister* by Robin Campbell.

27

SCOTLAND **8** **Carnivore**

by Jimmy Marshall

Creag a' Bhancair is located just west of the entrance to Coire na Tullaich, the great North Western corrie of Buachaille Etive Mor. The best approach is from Laganggarbh, the S.M.C. hut, with the crag about half-a-mile distant to the south-west and of unusually easy access for Scotland.

Close acquaintance soon dispels the outcrop image as the crag looms large, vertical and bulging in great porphyritic walls of apparent impregnability. Early visitors climbing routes on the easier flanks compared the central configuration to the side of a railway tunnel!

The only serious attempts on the face were made by the Creag Dhu M.C., who with traditional indifference made repeated sorties from a point deemed appropriately honourable and central to the crag. There, a deceptive groove, probably still marked below by a deep hole in the moss, burned up their effort and enthusiasm, until Don Whillans came upon the scene to resolve the problem by an entry pitch, starting away on the left. At a later visit he teamed up with John Cunningham in an attempt which got very high on the face but terminated in the big crack above the pitch 5 traverse. Now in possession of the key to the route, Cunningham quickly returned with Mick Noon to complete it by means of a traverse pitch of splendid exposure and difficulty. They named the route Carnivore.

Not to be outdone, Whillans returned to the scene to complete his line up the big crack, providing a more direct and harder finish of some 8oft., naming it Villain's Finish.

Years ago, winter went early, leaving no recourse but to climb rock, so a few good weekends were spent burning the winter fat off. Then we ran into Noon, the babbling enthusiast.

According to him (he probably wanted to keep us away from some other place) there was only one climb in the Glen; Carnivore, 'the greatest thing since sliced bread'. No repeat had been made, so after a few beers and an epic Noonie session of gesticulations, grunts, wee pinches here, strong fingers there, ropy traverses, slings in spikes, fantastic thin air traverses, turning us all dizzy

before the small beers did, we deemed the route worth looking at and retired worrying about weak wrists, winter flab or an alternative escape to a warm pleasant day on Etive's slabs.

Late next day, big Elly and I drifted off towards Creag a' Bhancair in leisurely fashion, stopping for tea at Lagangarbh. After all, with such an easy access it's only natural to savour to the full the absence of toil.

Cursory exploration soon disclosed the start away to the left and the line of the lower traverse, all in splendid confirmation of Noon's eloquence; so off I went, up the groove. Holy cow! it's steep. At the top panic takes over and I rattle down as fast as not falling off allows. O.K. the leisure's over; now in serious vein the hard exit is tackled, heaving the fat carcass up and gasping at the grimness of it all. It's a good start for tuning up so, moving better, it's up and easy to arrange a kind of runner, move right, find a peg, then, feeling great, negotiate the traverse. Sure enough, there's a wee spike for a sling (good old Noon), so the whole thing goes as smooth as silk. Some climb! I bring on Elly. His part is

Route Carnivore, Extremely Severe, 650ft.
Cliff Creag a' Bhancair in Coire na Tulaich, Glencoe.
First Ascent J. Cunningham and M. Noon, August 1958; Direct Finish — D. Whillans and D. Walker.
Map Reference O.S. Sheet 47, 1–50,000 Sheet 41 (ref. 217552).
Guidebook S.M.C. *Glencoe and Ardgour*, Vol. 1, by L. S. Lovat.
Nearest Road A82 at layby (ref. 216560).
Distance and time from cliff ¾ mile/500ft. Allow ½ hour.
Good Conditions Dries quickly in summer.
Campsites and Bunkhouses S.M.C. Hut Lagangarbh (½ mile); Campsites near Kingshouse (3 miles) or in Glencoe (3 miles).
Bibliography Interviews with Cunningham and Whillans in Mountain's 14 and 20 respectively; Cambridge Mountaineering, 1969; *A Visit to Scotland* by Richard Isherwood.

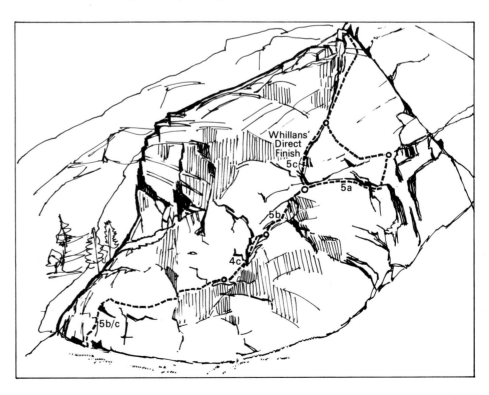

infinitely worse than mine; if he peels he'll plough a great hole in the moss! We try to arrange a fancy running rail belay; our rope mechanics aren't up to it, but he soldiers on and we're together again on the big ledge. Higher up, Elly takes a belay in a grassy nook, where I find him warming in the afternoon sun. Things are going well; we're happy and raring to go.

Collecting the gear, I follow the crack above. The climbing gets delicate again and the exposure impressive as I arrive at a sloping shelf. Above, an overhung crack

recess slants away out of sight. (That's where Whillans stopped. No wonder, it looks deadly! But doubtless he'd return to settle the score.) To the right a horizontal crack runs under a roof. This is the way; it looks hard, so I place a peg runner and proceed hand-jamming under the roof, fitting chockstone slings galore! Eventually I reach a lovely thread and arrange a sling stance, puffingly, pantingly, to rest. What a situation: nothing but clear air and plummet. Noon was right, this is some climb! But where the hell does the route go

effort! In the struggle a peg is lost, along with a lot of strength: I'd better get on with it! This time it's easier, a sleeve over the hand for the wet undercut. I place a mini peg and tap it into place. The arms are giving out, so I sling the hammer on the peg, fumble for a krab, then – Whee! off into space, gripped with fright, that rope's running a long way, Whang! It'll never hold . . . but it does and I'm dangling in the middle of a bland slab wall. Shattered shouts elicit no response from Elly, so I pull up a few feet to a thin grass edge, to ease the gut. The grass rolls out of the crack. To hell with this. Arm over arm I go up the rope like a scalded cat to the comforting haven of the thread. Absolutely knackered I clip on and hang there, a jabbering wreck. Sense eventually returns, though little from the other end of the rope. Having had enough, the traverse is reversed in full retreat to the piton, communication re-established with Elly and a rappel made to reunion. All becomes clear; he was sound asleep in his wee nook during my downfall.

Howling with hilarity and relief, by aerial rappels and swings to regain the rock we effected an enjoyable retreat to tea and toast.

Shortly after (but not before being presented with my hammer by a grinning Walsh from the second ascent), John Maclean and I were back on the trail, he taking the lower section, I reserving the upper traverse for the return bout. This time it went beautifully, with John at the peg belay, level with the traverse. Across the roof to the thread, no vertical variations this time, but up and across by the continuing overhang fault, negotiated with a couple of pegs. It was so obvious – the previous antics seemed insane.

The situation was still exciting and the difficulties continued to the small cave, passed by in favour of a belay on the large grass ledge at the far end of the traverse.

The next two pitches, over rough brown slabs, went leftwards then up, with seeming ease, by balance-climbing to the top.

As Noon said, a great route, the best in the country . . . till tomorrow's edition, that is!

now? There's a break in the overhang here, the traverse fault continues over to the right. Only two pegs and karabiners left, so I recover some slings from the traverse, deciding that Cunningham would go up and launch off up the wall.

The rock rears out, pushing savagely. Christ, what a grappler! I'd better get a peg in, but both hands are fully occupied hunting friction on a wet undercut. No! No! this won't do, down before you fall down, a desperate scrabbling retreat to joy at the thread stance. Phew, what a bloody

by Martin Boysen

Route Shibboleth, Extremely Severe, 550ft.
Cliff Slime Wall on the North Face of Buachaille Etive Mòr.
First Ascent R. Smith and A. Frazer, June 1958.
Map Reference O.S. Sheet 47, 1–50,000 Sheet 41 (ref. 225545).
Guidebooks S.M.C. *Glencoe and Ardgour*, Vol. 1, by L. Lovat; *Selected Scottish Climbs*, Vol. 1, by H. MacInnes.
Nearest Road A82 at Altnafeadh (ref. 221563).
Distance and time from cliff 1 mile/1300ft. Allow 45 minutes.
Good Conditions Several days of dry summer weather.
Campsites and Bunkhouses S.M.C. Hut Lagangarbh (1 mile); Campsites near the Kingshouse and in Glen Etive.

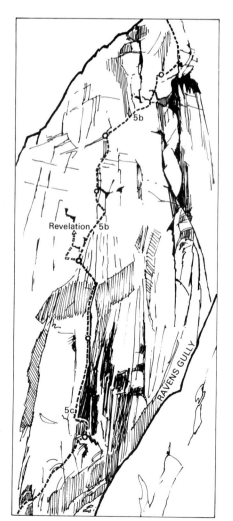

Although most climbs provide intense enjoyment at the time, the pleasure is often short-lived and the memory soon becomes indistinct. But, thankfully, this is not always the case and some climbs have a special significance which makes them stand out sharply. Why this should be so is difficult to fathom. The climb must be good, well situated and, I suppose, hard, for greater satisfaction comes if one is stretched to one's limits. It helps if one has looked forward to a climb with a keen anticipation nursed over the years. Ideally, too, the climb should have a certain rarity value, making devaluation in time unlikely. If, after all this, the climb lives up to or even exceeds one's expectations, it becomes a great climb. For me, Shibboleth was such a climb.

I first heard of Shibboleth in Chamonix, after a chance meeting with Robin Smith who first climbed it with A. Frazer in 1958. Smith had by this time gathered a reputation as a strong climber, a reputation which I knew to be justified for I had once climbed alongside him at Harrison's Rocks. He moved slowly, with great certainty, and was strong and very good. The alpine season had by this time come to a premature end, and I returned to England in a minibus, half-crushed by the mighty presence of James Moriarty – otherwise known as Big Elly. He, too, had spent time on Shibboleth, and he hinted with a knowing smile of its delights. He seemed, if anything, overkeen that I should try it, and this all served to whet my appetite.

However, I had to wait many years before I could try the climb, and it was not until Whitsun 1967 that an opportunity presented itself.

The weather cleared miraculously as we reached Glencoe and, after a few days of lazing in the sun and padding over the open slabs of Etive, I felt ready for sterner stuff on the high north crags of the Buachaille.

Shibboleth lies on the aptly-named Slime Wall, the large left retaining wall of Great Gully, which is itself one of the most forbidding recesses to be found in our mountains – an awesome cleft. As Mike Yates and I approached the foot of the climb, great patches of winter snow melted slowly

in the gully bed and, encouraged by the perpetual shade, green slime oozed from the first rocks. Only the upper wall, shining white and smooth, offered escape from the oppressive gloom.

The first pitch follows easily – as for Guerdon Grooves – but the second breaks out left to gain a steep, weeping crack. I am a slow starter and need time to warm up, so it was with a sense of shock that I found myself, after only a couple of moves, committed, unprotected and hanging uneasily from greasy and sloping holds. I swung up awkwardly, out of balance, and reached a wet mossy crack. After a few insecure jams and a layback, I gained the comparative safety of an old and twisted peg. Was I fit enough? I felt the nagging fear. The crack continued, still hard but drier, until at last a small stance appeared.

The third pitch gives a foretaste of the delectable climbing ahead. The rock is rough and bubbly, the holds numerous but small and not easy to spot. After the brutish climbing below, it is a delight to move delicately, savouring the subtlety of each friction hold. The pitch traverses slightly left then up to reach a small stance, which is unreassuringly close to Revelation Flake.

The next pitch constitutes the crux. A huge wall rears up steeply, unrelieved by cracks or other features. The description is vague, ominously singling out a halfway jug as the only feature worth mentioning. I have seldom felt so nervous before setting off on a pitch. The process of climbing is mercifully totally absorbing, but I felt fearful; lost on the wall, with nothing to go for. No runners relieved the tension of the climbing. Each move is hard, although no move is harder than the next, but as the rope runs out in a single sweep the sense of exposure increases terrifyingly. The hands begin to tire, and I felt an urgent need to hurry to obtain rest; but the climbing is precarious and steep and allows no rushed, unconsidered moves. A traverse right, then left and up, until at last holds appear. A ledge, and the pitch is done. Relief follows, then admiration; such a pitch will never, thank God, be made easy by nuts or wires; it will always remain a test of nerve.

With tension released, the remaining

climbing follows easily. The details are now vague; the difficulty was over and the top was reached.

Released from the confining concentration of immediate rock, we could at last enjoy the glorious day. I felt inspired by the climb; it was the culmination of the holiday. Later that night, still exultant, I ran over the moonlit peaks until, exhausted, I lay on a cool rock – content.

Right: The impressive Slime Wall of the Bauchaille with the black streaks indicating seepages that rarely dry. Raven's Gully is the diagonal line on the lower right corner of the photograph

Ken Wilson

Raven's Gully

by Hamish MacInnes

There is something traditionally Scottish about gully climbing, and indeed it seems to have created a certain class of climber: one fond of loose, greasy rock, revelling in the masochistic pastime of thrutching up waterfalls. Most mountaineers associate gully climbing with the era terminating at the end of the Second World War. From the pioneering point of view, this was the case, for it was in the 1950s that the last of the great gullies was climbed. Today, however, some of these climbs are done frequently, and even in the light of modern techniques many are still formidable. Considering that some were ascended as far back as 1885, a few were outstanding climbing achievements.

Waterpipe Gully, in the Cuillins, is one of the classics. Over 1000ft. long, it makes an entertaining day and the loose rock provides an insight into the psychology of Victorian climbers – they were perhaps not as prudent as we are led to believe!

Gardyloo Gully on Ben Nevis has only been climbed two or three times in summer. As well as being an exacting day's outing, it allows one to study the trash of a bygone age, when conservation meant pitching litter into the most readily available receptacle – in the case of the old observatory, Gardyloo Gully.

On the other side of the mountain, Graveyard Gully, later to be renamed Surgeon's Gully, has still not been climbed in its entirety. Only a short distance from the Glen Nevis road, it provides mountain scenery on a grand scale and a liberal amount of pure Ben Nevis water.

Farther south again, on the Isle of Arran, is Ben Nuis Gully 3. The first ascent in 1901 was an amazing exploit. Not only is this still a route of considerable difficulty; it is probably one of the best climbs on the island.

The Cairngorms do not have the same wealth of gullies as the Western Highlands, while Glencoe offers a greater number of difficult gullies per square mile than any other region in Scotland.

For many, The Chasm of Buachaille Etive Mòr typifies the best in Scottish gully-climbing, and indeed it is hard to find a more enjoyable route. The first ascent was

done in 1920 by Mr and Mrs Odell and M. Stobart.

Clachaig Gully has, of course, been immortalized in Bill Murray's book *Mountaineering in Scotland*, while Tom Patey immobilized that 'fateful day' in song, when he wrote:

> On the Wall of Jericho,
> They shouted 'Will it go?'
> As he hung on a hair-trigger hold.
> He answered not a word
> And he rose like a bird,
> Through the mud and the slime and
>   the cold.

The mud, etc., may be true of Clachaig Gully, though it still remains the most popular climb of its type in Scotland.

In adjoining Glen Etive, splitting the hillside of Stob na Broige in three gashes, each rising from a central common gully, is Dalness Chasm, whose branches provide serious climbs by any standards.

However, I feel that one Glencoe gully stands out above all others – Raven's Gully. Even today, this route repulses good climbers and, considering it was done in 1937 by a party led by Jock Nimlin, it is assured of its place in climbing history.

The gully separates North and Cuneiform Buttresses and, though a mere 450ft., it has packed into it a concentration of climbing problems which few climbers of today would overcome in worn nailed boots!

As in the case of many outstanding climbs, the first ascent was done more or less by accident. The party of five – Jock Nimlin, with Barclay Braithwaite, N. Millar, J. MacFarlane and A. N. Other – set off across the bogs from Coupal Bridge. It was a damp June day and the friends were intending to try a route on the Rannoch Wall.

They looked up at the wall and Jock said: 'It doesn't look much use, does it?'

The wall was running with water. 'Nae it disn'ae,' replied one of his Glaswegian colleagues.

'Let's go round and have a wee look at Raven's Gully. I believe a party has got up to about pitch three.'

'D'ae ye mean it hasn'a been climbed?' said A. N. Other, looking at Jock.

Route Raven's Gully, Very Severe, 450ft.
Cliff North Face, Buachaille Etive Mòr, Argyll.
First Ascent J. Nimlin, B. Braithwaite, N. Millar, J. McFarlane and A. N. Other, June 1937; Direct Finish – J. Cunningham, W. Smith and T. Paul, May 1948.
Map Reference O.S. Sheet 47, Glencoe, 1–50,000 Sheet 41 (ref. 225545).
Guidebooks S.M.C. *Glencoe and Ardgour*, Vol. 1, by L. Lovat; *Selected Scottish Climbs*, Vol. 1, by H. MacInnes.
Nearest Road A82 at Altnafeadh (ref. 221563).
Distance and time from cliff 1 mile/1300ft. Allow 45 minutes.
Campsites and Bunkhouses S.M.C. Hut Lagangarbh (1 mile); Campsites near Kingshouse or in upper Glen Etive.
Bibliography *I Chose to Climb* by Chris Bonington, Gollancz, London, 1966, (account of first winter ascent).

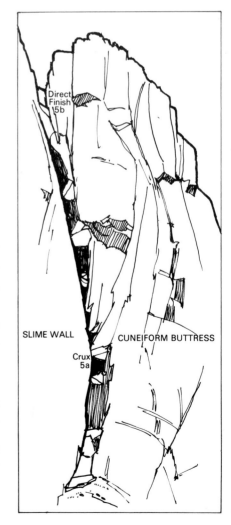

SLIME WALL   CUNEIFORM BUTTRESS

Direct Finish 5b

Crux 5a

Ken Wilson

Above: Pitch four of Raven's Gully, the crux of the climb, where a huge chockstone has to be turned by some very steep moves on the Slime Wall. The grooves to the left of the climber are taken by Guerdon Grooves and the big corner of Shibboleth can be seen in the top left of the photograph. Cuneiform Buttress is on the right. *Climber: Bill Skidmore*

will discover some day that gully-climbing is the most strenuous form of mountain exercise. By the time Jock had led them all on one long rope to the foot of pitch 6, he was exhausted.

I don't intend to pun when I say that these working lads climbed on a shoestring. They were certainly very hard up. Their boot nails were badly worn and they were waiting until the Glasgow 'Fair' before forking out on new ones. Barclay was the exception, as he sported a new set of ship-yard-made nails. These were the days of combined tactics, and Jock's shoulders, and later his head, retained for some time to come the impressions of the Glasgow tricounis. His head was Barclay's last 'stepping stone' before a determined launch on this, the 'Bicycle pitch'. His subsequent leg-flailing attempts ended with him sliding back down on Jock, whose injuries were endured in typical Glaswegian fashion – loud and expressive.

Eventually the pitch did fall to the home-made nails, and beyond this point, Jock, feeling perhaps that there was less danger in the van, took over.

At the top of pitch 8, near a point where a natural rock arch spans the gully, the stalwarts took a line up to the left. Straight ahead is the Direct Finish, which was later to be climbed by John Cunningham, Bill Smith and Tommy Paul of the Creagh Dhu Mountaineering Club, in 1948.

Here, in two run-outs, the last problem was reached – the Corkscrew Pitch. It was dark now, and the party still had to drive back to Glasgow for work the following morning. However, they reached the top, tired but elated.

After the first ascent an aura of impregnability once again shrouded the gully. Many attempts failed – usually with leaders falling off at pitch 4.

Jock Nimlin told me that when the rock climbing guide was published Raven's was rated as 'Very Severe in rubbers'.

'This,' he said, 'confirmed our original impression that pitch 4 was moderately impossible in aged nailed boots.'

'Aye, that's right, laddie, we can have a look at it.'

'Having a look' is a ubiquitous expression, used much in Scotland, meaning either that a serious attempt may be intended or just literally a look if it seems too hard, or if one is off form.

It turned out to be a serious look. Before Jock knew what was happening he had climbed up to pitch 4, which is the crux of the climb. It was about here that the previous attempts had failed.

Jock didn't use runners on this section as is done now. He led up round the awkward overhang with the 'Thank God hold' in the crack above.

No doubt some thesis-minded climber

SCOTLAND **11** **Swastika**

by Robin Campbell

Beinn Trilleachan, mountain of oyster-catchers, dips its smooth eastern flank in the headwaters of Loch Etive, the long sea-loch which cuts deeply into Nether Lorn in North Argyll. This is the setting celebrated in one of the most beautiful Gaelic sagas, the land where the ill-fated Deirdre and her lover Naoise lived secretly in their *grianan* (an idyllic residence where deer could be slain from the windows and salmon caught at the front door), before Deirdre returned to Ulster to die at the hands of the treacherous King Conchobar. Tir Dearduil is a region of great natural charm: 'A pen for the sun is Glen Etive,' sang Deirdre as she sailed reluctantly for Ireland. Few climbing grounds enjoy such a splendid combination of sun, sea and graceful snow-tipped peaks (for the high season there is the late spring). The peaks are well spread, giving a sense of spaciousness which contrasts sharply with Glencoe's cosy clutter to the north. The valley-bottom, too, is markedly different, with its wild rhododendrons and the wooded river which surges and glides through rock-pools and tunnelled waterfalls.

Beinn Trilleachan's side has lost a patch of skin. Halfway up the flank a sweep of granite slabs lies like an enormous pink scab on the hillside. On these slabs is to be found a kind of climbing which, eighteen years ago when the first routes were made, was quite unknown in Scotland. For the granite has been exposed on the bedding plane, providing in the centre of the cliff a single, six-acre slab, flawed only by two horizontal overlaps. The slab lies at a mere 40°, but, being granite, positive holds are rare almost to the point of irrelevance; progress can only be made by seeking natural lines of weakness, usually cracks or shallow scoops where the climber can proceed by means of friction holds. These special circumstances give the Trilleachan Slabs an ambience unique in Scottish climbing. The warm pink slabs, the pleasant prospects north to the Buachailles of Etive and south to Beinn Cruachan, and the majestic sweep of Ben Starav across the loch, all combine to build an atmosphere of tranquil security; and yet, for the climber embattled on the central slab, with the last

protection point far below and no comforting ledge or hold available, fear can tighten its grip, causing the hands to sweat, the feet to slide and scrabble, the stomach to lurch in anticipation of a fall. No one has died there yet, but many have felt the rough granite grind and tear their flesh. It's not only the sides of Beinn Trilleachan that are scabbed.

Swastika was the first route to tackle the great central slab directly. Exploration of the face began in June 1954, when a Cambridge University party, consisting of Eric Langmuir, Mike O'Hara, J. A. Mallinson and Miss Joyce Tester, found a way up the leftmost of the four huge overlapping corners which bound the left-hand side of the crag. The route, Sickle, was heavily vegetated and not of much account. The

Route Swastika, Hard Very Severe, 685ft.
Cliff The Etive Slabs of Beinn Trilleachan, Glen Etive, Argyll.
First Ascent M. Noon and E. Taylor, June 1957; Direct Start – B. Robertson, R. Holt, F. Harper and A. McKeith, October 1964.
Map Reference O.S. Sheet 54, 1–50,000 Sheet 50
Guidebooks S.M.C. *Glencoe and Ardgour*, Vol. 2, by L. Lovat; *Selected Scottish Climbs*, Vol. 1, by H. MacInnes.
Nearest Road At the Loch Etive pier at the end of the minor road down Glen Etive (ref 108449).
Distance and time from cliff 1 mile/1000ft. Allow 45 minutes.
Good Conditions Dries quickly but avoid very hot days as the rock temperature can become unpleasantly high.
Campsites and Bunkhouses Grampian Club Hut, Inbhirfhaolain (ref. 158508); Campsites by the lochside or in upper Glen Etive.
Bibliography Mountain 8: *Nutless Guts for Gutless Nuts* by Robin Campbell.

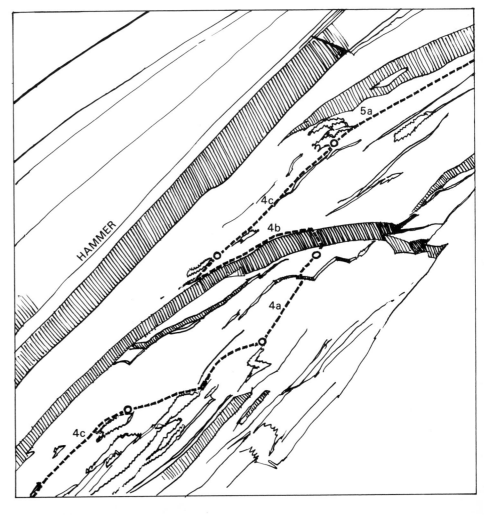

next day, however, Langmuir, O'Hara and Mallinson followed the right-bounding edge of the slab by a series of cracks: Spartan Slab was a fine route then, but it is even finer now that years of use have widened the cracks and removed all necessity for direct aid.

The next developments came three years later, from the Creag Dhu, during a period when the club's ascendancy in Scottish climbing was almost complete. Mick Noon, John Cunningham and various others lined the slabs with a series of magnificent routes: in the spring, the three remaining corners, Claw, Hammer and Agony, fell; then, in June, Noon and Taylor found Swastika.

The climb begins quietly enough. Some way left of the Coffinstone (a flat, funereal slab where layabouts and wives sunbathe, stirring occasionally to jeer or criticize) a crack slants rightward up the slab. It yields easily enough to determined climbing, but can cause trouble to the climber who dallies at its crux trying to place the two unnecessary pegs mentioned in the original description. A second, easier pitch leads to a belay below the first great overlap. Noon and Taylor used pegs to cross this, but again these are now unnecessary, and those who employ them will merit the jeers of the sharp-eyed critics below. A strenuous heave and mantelshelf and you are on the upper slab. Above, the rock is flawless, but at your feet there is a turfy crack, the Moustache, which forms a straggling wisp of possibility leading horizontally leftwards above the lip. A long way left you reach a comfortable ledge, construct a belay with angle pegs placed upwards, and enjoy the view while your partner struggles outwardly with the overlap and inwardly with the prospect of a desperate pendulum across the lower slab. Now comes the heart of the route, the great quartz band, a six-inch ladder of tiny flat holds which leads in two pitches to the second overlap, 200ft. above. Neither pitch is easy and neither can be protected. Perhaps the second is the most taxing: it keeps its hardest moves right to the end, and moisture often weeps down the slab from the grass ledge above. In such conditions one is strongly tempted to forget technique

and rush blindly up the slab to grab the grass, but the appalling consequences of a slip make this eminently resistible! To my mind these pitches, like many of the Trilleachan cruxes, excel because only courage will get you out of the danger you have invited – and surely that is the essence of mountaineering. No one ever reverses an Etive crux: once started there is

nothing for it but to grit the teeth and make the moves.

Now there is a choice: the purist, going well, can join the Long Wait by a short rightwards traverse and finish by that route, climbing free throughout. But the old finish, with its noisy banging and rattling, rounds off the climb nicely. To the left, a crack takes you through the overlap with the help of a peg and a sling on a spike. Above, a short slab brings you to the 40ft. overhanging wall which tops off the great slab. The final aid pitch, traditionally climbed without etriers, boasts perfect peg cracks and provides the mechanically unsophisticated with a pleasant half-hour of manic bashing and thrashing to purge the tensions of the delicate adventures down below.

Above: The central section of the Etive Slabs. The four climbers in the centre of the photograph are on Swastika and The Pause. Swastika breaks through the overhang directly above the moving climber and then traverses left along the Moustache (clearly seen on the lip of the overhang). The climber on the extreme right is belayed in the crevasse stance of The Pause. *Climbers: unknown*

Island of Hoy, Orkneys

The Old Man of Hoy

by Chris Bonington

Route East Face Route, Hard Very Severe, 460ft.
Crag Old Man of Hoy, Isle of Hoy in the Orkney Islands.
First Ascent R. Baillie, T. W. Patey and C. J. S. Bonington, 1966.
Map Reference O.S. Sheet 7, Pentland Firth, 1–50,000 Sheet 7 (ref. 175009).
Guidebook *Selected Scottish Climbs*, Vol. 2, by H. MacInnes.
Nearest Road Take the Ferry from Scrabster to Stromness and Stromness to Hoy. Take a taxi to Rackwick Bay. Path from here diagonally left up hillside to the cliffs above the Old Man.
Distance and time from cliff 1½ miles/900ft. Allow 30 minutes.
Good Conditions Dries quickly in summer.
Campsites and Bunkhouses Campsites and a Youth Hostel at Rackwick Bay.
Bibliography *One Man's Mountains* by Tom Patey, Gollancz, London, 1972; *The Next Horizon* by Chris Bonington, Gollancz, London, 1973 (both books contain accounts of the first ascent and references to the subsequent TV extravaganza).

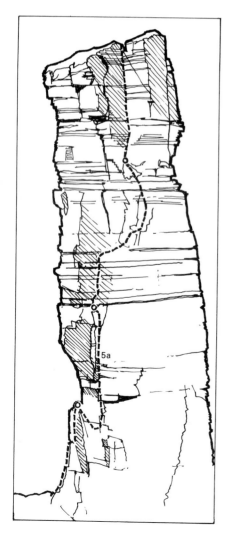

The Old Man of Hoy, immortalized by the BBC's most successful climbing extravaganza, has perhaps had its reputation threatened by the very nature of its exposure. In the summer of 1967 the BBC turned the Old Man into a magnificent climbing circus, with an all-star cast – Joe Brown, Ian McNaught-Davis, Peter Crew, Dougal Haston, Tom Patey and myself – backed up by climbing camera teams comprising Hamish MacInnes, Ian Clough, John Cleare and Rusty Baillie, plus around a dozen climbing Sherpas, fifty or so camera technicians and a platoon of Scots Guards! We gave the Old Man the lot – a completely new route up the South Face by Joe Brown and Ian McNaught-Davis, artificial climbing and bolting on the South East Route by Dougal Haston and Peter Crew, high trapeze acrobatics by Tom Patey and myself, plus a bivouac half-way up the Old Man. And yet, despite all the fanfares (which, incidentally, provided the actors with several exciting and extraordinarily enjoyable days), the millions who watched were given quite a good insight into the very best – even if a little theatrical – sea stack climbing.

The Old Man of Hoy is undoubtedly Britain's finest sea stack; it can probably also claim to be Britain's most rewarding summit, in that it is 450ft. high, juts out from the sea above Pentland Firth with only a narrow rocky peninsular to join it to the mainland, and even dominates the cliffs which flank it. The easiest route to the summit is HVS, the others which have been placed on it being more difficult. It also has the attraction of remoteness. Lying off the western coast of Hoy, it faces out to the Atlantic with only the tiny islands of Sula Sgeir, North Rona, Sule and Stack Sterry between it and the Americas, so that it takes the full blast of the Atlantic storms.

The Old Man itself is formed from comparatively soft Orcadian Sandstone, but perhaps an explanation of its survival is the fact that it stands on a plinth of granite. The waves have, no doubt, curled their way round the softer rock which flanks the plinth, to erode it away. At one stage there was an archway linking the Old Man to the island, but this must have collapsed at some

time and the Old Man is now linked to the mainland by a clutter of huge boulders. It stands square-cut, in places slightly pendulous, overhanging its base on three sides, its summit approximately the same diameter as its base – around about 100ft.

Although there are legends of an intrepid, elderly islander having climbed the Old Man as the result of a wager, it is unlikely that anyone made a serious attempt before the early summer of 1966, when Tom Patey, that indefatigable pioneer of unlikely crags and sea stacks, focused his attention on the problem. Patey recruited Rusty Baillie and myself for the attempt and in June that year we had our first sight of the Old Man from the 'St Ola' steamer, which makes the run from Thurso, on the mainland, to Stromness, in the Orkneys. From Stromness there are no regular ferries and it is necessary to charter a fishing boat to take you across into Scapa Flow to the north side of Hoy. The island itself is split by a valley which leads to Rackwick Bay, which lies on the south side of the island. At Rackwick there are a few cottages and a small unattended Youth Hostel. From here, a walk of a couple of miles over open, pathless moorland leads to the cliff head opposite the Old Man of Hoy.

The outer defences of the Old Man are provided by skuas which have an uncomfortable habit of dive-bombing the unwary climber. For the first ascent we selected a route up the east face: easy climbing for about 80ft. leads to a commodious platform on the south-west corner of the pillar. At this stage the only problem is presented by nesting fulmers and their chicks, whose defensive mechanism is to spew a gob of particularly malodorous puke, with unerring accuracy, straight into your eyes. The next pitch was the crux of the climb. On the first ascent we used artificial techniques freely, but on subsequent ascents, both in the TV spectacular and since, the pitch has yielded to free climbing. An airy downwards traverse leads into a small niche roofed by a square-cut overhang; an awkward hand-jam enables the climber to pull over this on to another small ledge, where he is once again in balance.

The next section of the climb is splendidly

Right: The difficult section on the second pitch of the
Original Route on The Old Man of Hoy. *Climber: Rusty
Baillie*

impressive, although it is easier than it
looks from below. A broad impending
crack, too wide for a comfortable hand-jam,
but too narrow to get your body right into
it, sweeps up in a great rounded bulge. It is
in a corner, however, so that the climber
can get some help from either wall, and
there are the characteristic horizontal,
though rounded, ledge-like holds you so
often get on sandstone. One of the principal
problems is the softness of the rock, which
gives it a ball-bearing-like texture, tending
to make feet and fingers slide with off-
putting ease. This pitch is about 70ft. long,
and must rank as one of the outstanding
rock pitches in Scotland. There are some
good chockstones for runners near the
bottom of the crack and the rest of it should
go without the need of any further artificial
protection.

In a way, it's a pity that the most outstanding pitch of the climb is so near the
bottom, but even so, this pitch has an
extraordinary feeling of exposure, which is
accentuated by the constant movement of
the sea below, crashing against the little
peninsular which joins the Old Man to the
mainland. Above, the climb deteriorates for
about 130ft. – the angle drops off, the rock
assumes an almost mud-like texture, and the
climbing is little more than mild VS. You
can pick your way almost anywhere up the
right-hand side of the pillar until you reach
the foot of a clean-cut vertical corner which
leads to the top. The standard of this final
pitch is barely severe, for the rock has
become sound once again and fingers curl
reassuringly around big jugs; it is possible
to bridge airily across the corner. In spite
of the ease of climbing, however, it is a
wonderfully elating pitch – sheer to the very
summit move, as you pull up on to the little
square-cut, grass-clad summit.

Then come the exhilaration and sheer
sensual comfort of lying on the soft turf on
Britain's most inaccessible summit, with the
prospect of an Alpine-style descent by abseil
as the only means of retreat. In this respect
it is advisable to leave a rope on the steep
second pitch, since its top overhangs the
base and also involves a traverse. A direct
abseil from the top of the second pitch
would require a doubled, 400ft. rope, and is

Chris Bonington

free all the way to the deck.

There are, of course, other routes on the Old Man of Hoy, but I suspect that none of them have quite the satisfaction that the original route gives; it has the charm of being the most obvious natural line up the Old Man, and that second pitch is sufficiently difficult to give anyone some food for thought.

Chris Bonington collection

Chris Bonington

Left: Finishing the second pitch. *Climbers: Rusty Baillie and Tom Patey*

Top right: The first-ascent team established half-way up the Old Man, trying to work a line up to the final corner. *Climbers: Rusty Baillie, Tom Patey and Chris Bonington*

Bottom right: The final corner/crack. *Climber: Tom Patey.*

Blaven, Isle of Skye

13 The Great Prow

by Phil Gribbon

Route The Great Prow, Very Severe, 380ft.
Cliff East Face of Blaven.
First Ascent W. Tauber, N. Ross, W. T. Band and P. Gribbon, June 1968.
Map Reference O.S. Sheet 25, Portree, 1–50,000 Sheet 32 (ref. 532216).
Guidebooks S.M.C. *Cuillin of Skye*, Vol. 2, by J. W. Simpson; *Selected Scottish Climbs*, Vol. 2, by H. MacInnes.
Nearest Road At the head of Loch Slapin (ref. 561216). Follow the north bank of the All't na Dunaiche to Coire Uaigneich, then climb directly up towards the Blaven/Clach Glas col. Alternatively climb the East Ridge towards the north summit of Blaven and descend the gully on the west side of the Great Prow.
Distance and time from crag 1½ miles/2200ft. Allow 2 hours.
Good Conditions Dries quickly in summer.
Campsites and Bunkhouses Camp west of the Strath Mor river estuary, or on the raised beach at Fasilean.

The great Prow was hidden in the shadows of the blue mountain. The western isles shimmered in the sheen of the calm sea. The sharp sgùrrs of the Black Cuillins cut the horizon in an evanescent row of teeth.

The heat of a summer's day reflected from the ridge. Above the Blaven-Clach Glas col, sitting in the heather and shading his eyes from the glare, he looked at the north walls of the mountain.

Blaven had been untouched for years. Its potential had been discovered and developed in the end. It was the familiar story . . .

The old guidebook had tried to preserve its anonymity: uninspiring, low-grade routes; names like East Face, Central Buttress and Northern Ridge, linked with the pioneers, Abraham, Pilkington and Naismith. It was a lost land, full of doubtful Diffs and impossible Mods. The mysterious aura remained intact, surviving the cryptic journal entries inserted by the inveterate new-route exploiters who snatched out the minor lines. The well-worn trade routes of the Glenbrittle resort controlled the Skye scene. Blà Bheinn was forgotten . . .

The Great Prow sits astride the East Ridge of Blaven. It is a big, angular pinnacle, a dark dolomitic tower of weathered gabbro that juts out from a banded curtain like the battered bow of a monstrous longship. A symbol of affirmation raised to the heavens in a gesture of sublime indifference, it derides and challenges in the same breath.

The Great Prow breaks into the broad, tilted avenue of boulders below the bealach. Its blunt profile rises for over 300ft. in a series of overlapping and overhanging creases interspersed with brief slanting ledges. On one side there is a huge slab, on the other a splintered sliver of rock, both suspended on an overhanging pedestal. A faultless line runs beside the cloven splinter to a final headwall, the direct line to a twisted figurehead framed against the sky.

Red deer wandered undisturbed on the mountain. The Great Prow was unique and inviolate.

One day, four climbers stood at the base of the splinter, laughing hysterically. They had been bitten by midges and burnt by the sun; their energy had been sapped in the pulsating furnace of distant Sron na Ciche, their amusement at the imaginary belays lurking in the shade had palled in Coire Lagan. They knew that cool asceticism could be practised afresh on the walls of Blaven.

They made admirable excuses. Some years before, the Professor had conceived the route in the dank flank of the lonely hill. He felt that he had justified himself, and now he wished to use his camera. Teeser had remembered his gloves, Mitey M'oose was lethargic. Superspan owned P.A.s, and besides he was long, leggy and levitatious. He was the automatic fore-runner.

The problems were noticeable. The first pitch was an overhanging crack. Soon Superspan was 30ft. over the scree. The spectators grinned, but the leader groaned from his perch while he runnered a rotatable chockstone rattling within the crack. He was being forced outwards, away from the blank left wall and the ragged right edge of the crack. He tugged at the second stone, swinging and bridging until he could stand on it. Lodged below an awkward bulge, he extended his illusory inches to reach far up the crack, his toes flexed on the sloping holds, and pushed out by the bulge. He made a sequence of quick moves; a runner was close at hand. A side clasp on the left edge, a real handhold on the rock above, and he was creeping up the steep slab.

'Mild VS,' he murmured, but the Professor, gripped in anticipation, raised his eyebrows in disbelief.

'Stand away!' It was an imperious command, announcing the stones that arced parabolically down towards their sulphurous impact on the scree. 'C'mon, next.'

The crack continued up the second pitch. 'This is no bother,' he called, confidently. 'Sure, sure, we know,' replied the Professor, but without conviction because he had been treated to similar gross understatements on other occasions.

They watched his expanded swing out on to an exposed edge, and then the layback into the crack. They were glad that he gave a cursory acquiescence to tradition by

Right: The Great Prow. The first-ascent party can be seen strung out up the route. *Climbers: Wilf Tauber, N. Ross, W. T. Band and Phil Gribbon*

placing a runner, before backing into the steep, severe scoop that funnelled up to the notch where the splinter abutted against the headwall. The 240ft. crack was complete.

Three-quarters of the party were soon draped on the Great Prow. 'Wha' a sight!' thought the Professor, who couldn't see a thing. Untying, he stumbled out on to the scree with his head down and quickly snapped some frantic photos of the dwindling figures. He could see that Superspan was having trouble with his second, who was remonstrating disgustedly at the choice of belay. The loop flicked off in a shower of tiny spikes, and the Professor ran for cover again.

The crucial third pitch ran over a vertical wall. It was a spectacular traverse rising in a rampant catenary to the skyline. Twin grooves strung along the wall marked out a fragile line of weakness as the route freed itself from the splinter's clasp and touched tremulously on the web of space.

The traverse held animated time. With outstretched limbs, Superspan began a slow, sidling shuffle, his toes seeking out minute holds pitted in the groove. Pale, peeled fragments trickled down the cliff. Teeser, who was paying out the rope, watched carefully, while Mitey M'oose dozed unconcernedly at the first belay, and the Professor shook his jammed camera in abject fury.

The traverse led on to the stepped slabs that ended below the final nose. Superspan paused to savour his situation, before pulling unhesitatingly on the jammed block perched on the edge of space and moving up into the sunshine.

Well he remembered that day on the Great Prow. The tremendous holding power of the coarse gabbro had helped the feeling of tension to disappear and be replaced by an air of relaxation. How satisfying had been the traverse away from the splinter!

A car rumbled across the bridge by Loch Slapin. A burn winding through Glen Sligachan looked coolly inviting. A white cumulus cloud towered up beyond the stained screes of the Red Hills of Skye. The Great Prow stood mute in the silence of the centuries.

The Scoop

by Doug Scott

The Strone is remote. To reach it, the climber has to motor through Skye, take a two hour ferry across the Minch, and then travel another seventeen miles by road and track to the lonely Glen Ulladale. Now the Strone is revealed, a sphinx standing sentinel over its broken blocks, the puddle of Loch Ulladale, and the desolate moorland stretching away into the mist. The cliff emerges gradually from the hillside, a long low wall growing higher and ending abruptly in the black, overhanging north-west face.

This face dominates the Strone as the Strone dominates the Glen. Its omnipresence is felt from the start, but the difficulties are not appreciated until one is standing at the foot of the crag; from there the face is seen to be a monstrous scoop, overhanging its base by 150ft. This enormous depression, 500ft. high, was gouged out by the ice sheets which, not so long ago, slithered smoothly over the top of the Strone and cascaded down, plucking blocks of rock away.

The Strone's metamorphic rock is mainly fine-grained Lewisian gneiss, but mica schists and brittle quartz bands are common. In the scoop itself, blank leaning walls, crackless dihedrals, and shallow cracks, together with furrows of earthy schist and frail, brittle flakes, minimize the scope for free climbing and render aid-climbing problematical.

The obvious line, to which the eye is naturally drawn, winds up the centre through open hanging corners capped with square-cut overhangs. It is the line where all the branch lines meet from left and right – the aesthetic line. The pleasures of the route are more evident on reflection; at the time, it is the concentration and the exhilarating situations that the climber will relish. Continual exposure and the strenuous nature of the climbing preclude the enjoyment of pure balanced movement and fast rhythmic aid work, for overhanging walls of this nature consume hours of concentrated aid placement. One pitch can take a full day, whereas a vertical wall on similar rock may only take an hour or two.

In fact, the first ascent took 30 hours' climbing time, spread over several days. Our initial optimism turned out to be essential, as the first pitch was hard (though not the hardest). An attempt to free-climb up on to tempting ledges was soon thwarted by crumbling mica: pegs were found more applicable. One was already in place – a bent and twisted relic of an abortive attempt by a Sheffield team.

The wall above this peg appeared encouragingly strata-seamed, but closer inspection revealed only wrinkle-scarred rock. It took none of the gadgets we had. We turned to taping fickle flakes for direct aid, and cautious silent progress was made for some 20ft. A vertical crack accepted blades which, laced together, gave confidence for a move right; a crack tack enabled a further move right, a tension traverse under the leaning wall, with back arched and the meat of the body held in to seduce the rock and maintain that precarious balance over the growing void. The shattered cracks of the main line led to a hidden sit-down ledge; here an open corner bristled brittle flakes, loosely slotted behind one another to accept chocks and tapes better than peg wedges. For 20ft. on, only the tips of our knife blades and rurps bit into the rock of the corner; but growing anxiety dissolved on the discovery of an unexpected lie-down ledge, 200ft. up. Climbing on up reiterated the Strone's bulging reality. Pegs were thumped up into the earthy mica of a square-cut roof; the band of soft loose muck continued above, and pegs plopped out as we stepped off them. Jamming a wet dingy hollow led to a pink quartz dihedral where the pegs at last rang true. Then another change in perspective as another black roof hung over us: no hardship, for there were good pegs to hold a clean fall into harness and space.

From a peg fixed high under the third roof, we slithered down a slimy wall and made a pendulum round the corner to a second lie-down ledge. This roof was in fact the base of a detached block; chocks were used nervously to minimize outward pressure. Now the scoop reared out in a final flourish, with upside-down cracks that diminished in width. A hairline crack finally petered out into blank overhanging rock.

After three hours' deliberation and effort, a bolt was placed (perhaps subse-

Route The Scoop, A4, Extremely Severe, 560ft.
Cliff Strone Ulladale, Harris, Long Island, Outer Hebrides.
First Ascent D. Scott, J. Upton, M. Terry and G. Lee, June 1969.
Map Reference O.S. Sheet 12. Isle of Lewis and North Harris, 1–50,000 Sheet 13 (ref. 079137).
Guidebook Selected Scottish Climbs, Vol. 2, by H. MacInnes.
Nearest Road At the dam at Loch Chliostair (ref. 069101). Car Ferry from Uig (Skye) to Tarbert (Harris). Take the A859 and the B887 to Amhuinnsuidhe. From here a private road leads to the dam. Follow a good footpath over a col into Glen Ulladale.
Distance and time from cliff 2 miles/400ft. Allow 1 hour.
Good Conditions The crag overhangs and stays almost permanently dry except in driving rain.
Campsites and Bunkhouses Good campsites and bivouac boulders below the crag.
Bibliography Mountain 7: The Big Scoop by Doug Scott (an account of the first ascent with route description). Other references to the cliff in S.M.C. Journals, Vols. 151, 153, 157, 159 and 161.

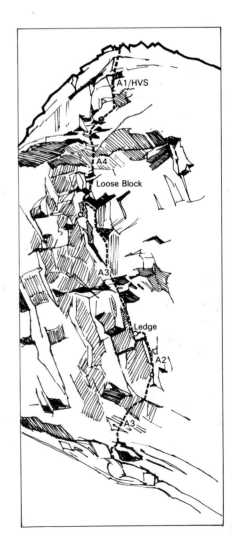

Ken Wilson

Ken Wilson

Left: The first pitch of The
Scoop during the first ascent.
The leader's trail rope is being
blown by a strong updraught.
Climber: Doug Scott

quent parties can chop it by using copper-heads). It was our only escape now, for the lower pitches had been de-pegged. From its comfort we used a bong in a hammer-sculpted pocket and then snug baby angles smashed up into the roof one after another to go over the lip. 150ft. of A1, HVS up a

wet brown streak and over balancing blocks, and we were scrambling to the top.

It may not be everybody's cup of tea, but as an exercise in imagination and ingenuity, as on swings high above the moor and the lake, it is a unique experience in fear and fascination.

Above: Moving up past the detached block to the smooth overhanging section on pitch four.
Climber: Doug Scott

Rosa Pinnacle, Isle of Arran

South Ridge Direct

by Ian Rowe

Route South Ridge Direct, Very Severe, 1100ft.
Crag Rosa Pinnacle, Cir Mhor, Isle of Arran.
First Ascent J. F. Hamilton and D. Paterson, September 1941.
Map Reference O.S. Sheet 66, 1–50,000 Sheet 69 (ref. 965429).
Guidebooks S.M.C. *Arran* by W. M. M. Wallace; *Selected Scottish Climbs*, Vol. 1, by H. MacInnes.
Nearest Road Steamer from either Fairlie or Ardrossan to Broderick. Cars unnecessary on Arran. Cycles can be hired (75p) and taken some way up Glen Rosa.
Distance and time from cliff From Broderick – 7 miles/2000ft. Allow 3–4 hours.
Good Conditions Dries quickly. Any sunny day will do.
Campsites and Bunkhouses Good campsites in Glen Rosa.
Bibliography *Undiscovered Scotland* by W. H. Murray, Dents, London, 1951 (account of early ascent). Other references in S.M.C. Journals, Vols. 122 and 127.

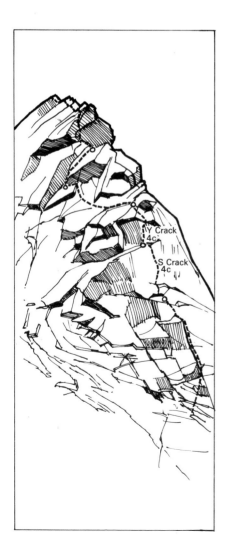

Arran moves like a vast steamer up the Clyde. Or rather the waves and troughs of granite model the surface of the Clyde far below, and you are the captain of the ship. On the corrie walls schools of fault lines sweep past, carrying the eye easily from one place to the next.

Movement can be your theme for the day. Nothing has to be tedious, not even the approach. The finest access is from Beinn Tarsuinn by the A'Chir Ridge; by the time you see the Pinnacle across Coire Bhuidhe, you will know the granite and will be moving with heightened awareness of an effort more than that of mere ascent.

The Pinnacle is defined less by its summit than by its South Ridge and West Flank. The summit, of course, should be that of Cir Mhor, but they are a hundred yards apart. There should also be some final difficulty or characteristic shape to lend definition; the Rosetta Stone would do, but it is off to one side. No, the Rosa Pinnacle is a ridge first and foremost, and the climb on the crest is the supremely logical line.

In sequence, the three principal pitches are the S-Crack, the Y-Cracks and the Layback. The guidebook gives the credit for the first ascent to J. F. Hamilton and D. Paterson in September 1941. In September 1940, however, Hamilton and G. S. Roger climbed the route, avoiding the Y-Cracks on the right, and Hamilton was able to examine their feasibility from the top. Furthermore, Hamilton must have done the route twice in September 1941, with Paterson and R. Grieve respectively. Grieve's account suggests that Hamilton wished to straighten out the route with him and, while the article is not specific, the implication is that they climbed the Y-Cracks. Yet, eight years later, Hamilton advised W. H. Murray that the climb would be 'Severe' in rubbers and that there would be two hard pitches, an S-shaped crack and a layback. Could he have forgotten about the Y-Cracks? Does the fact that Hamilton climbed the route twice in one month imply something more intriguing than comprehensive exploration?

Grieve's day in 1941 is noteworthy. He started from Pirnmill on the west coast at 7 a.m., climbed over Beinn Bharrain to

Loch Tanna, descended to Glen Iorsa and went up Garbh Coire Dubh to meet Hamilton at the head of Glen Rosa. Later he returned to Loch Tanna and reached the road by Glen Catacol – after a 'Great Day' of seventeen hours.

In eagerness to get to the bottom of the S-Crack I have not noticed difficulties in the first hundred feet or so; the climbing is pleasant and reassuring.

The S-Crack curves, sly and snake-like, to a large ledge. The rock is as rough and hard as anywhere on Arran and, while vice-like hand-jams are there if needed, a subtler and less mortifying approach can be adopted. Try to keep the skin of your knuckles intact – it may be needed later. It is possible to stay in balance without great expenditure of energy, and there is much joy in that. Up right, then left and right again up to the final slot, where the left hand drifts up and sinks into a memorable hold – not so much a jug as a very large porridge bowl, which should rhyme with the howl you will be delighted to let rip.

The ledge is broad and comfortable, a fine resting place between attempts at the Y-Cracks which bulge overhead. Only philistines will climb the cracks at the first launch. Far better to savour more than once the exposure and the safe if strenuous holds in the parallel faults. It is also necessary to memorize the sequence of hand movements at the top, for this is the crux. And when you go over, don't forget to take your feet with you. A friend was once embarrassed to find his foot firmly wedged in the crack below.

The Layback lies on the left flank of the ridge. There need not be much layback work in the pitch, for it can be completed on the slab by a line of small but adequate holds. However, the purist or layback-freak can go all the way; this, with impressive understatement, is known as L. S. Lovat's Variation.

What follows is not difficult, but well sustained. A confident party could dispense with the rope and enjoy solo scrambling. It is here, perhaps, that the theme of movement is better exemplified. The rock is perfect and the difficulties are behind. Your

command of the situation has a fascination
which adds its own momentum. The chimney at the junction with Sou'wester Slabs is
marginally strenuous but very positive.
Near the top, the Terrace may be taken to
flank the summit of the Pinnacle on the left,
but keep to the crest.

And don't forget the Rosetta Stone.
Climb it *on* your backside, facing out, if you
cannot manage it more conventionally, i.e.
with your backside *et cetera* . . .

Robin Campbell

Scafell

Central Buttress

by Geoff Oliver

Seen from Hollowstones, the majestic sweep of walls, buttresses and clefts that is Scafell Crag presents a picture of omnipotence; a surging mass of igneous rock, frozen into immobility by the passage of time. Centrepiece of the primeval display, flanked on either side by deep fissures, the Central Buttress stands stark, uncompromising and inescapable. This was how the early pioneers of the nineteenth century saw Scafell and they accordingly confined their activities to modest exploration of the easier paths and gullies, gradually familiarizing themselves with the savage surroundings. The process continued progressively for a hundred years and the resultant host of criss-crossing routes has inevitably robbed Scafell of its aura of impregnability. Given a fine day, the crag now suffers the indignity of scores of parties disporting themselves on its most exposed bastions. Nevertheless, when the sky darkens, and mist swirls in the gullies, dampening the rock and chilling the body, the importunate intruders are cut down to size and the cliff regains its mastery.

Before the outbreak of the First World War, British rock-climbing was still in its infancy. In the Lake District, the few mountaineers who gathered at Wasdale Head sought climbing problems of the kind encountered in the Alps, and no attempt was made to seek out difficulty. Apart from the audacious leads made by O. G. Jones on the Pinnacle and F. Botterill on the slab that bears his name, the main defences of Scafell remained unprobed until Siegfried Herford, a young undergraduate from Manchester University, and his friend George Sansom first came to Wasdale. Unlike the other visitors, they had no Alpine experience, having learned their climbing on the short but difficult courses on Derbyshire gritstone; like many others since, they soon proved that gritstone skills could be applied with equal success to major crags. In 1912 they completed the Direct Route to Hopkinson's Cairn on the Pinnacle Face, a line formerly considered unjustifiably dangerous after the fatal accident of 1903. Further exploration led to the ascent of Hopkinson's Gully, another unsolved problem of long standing, and a girdle traverse of the whole crag, from Deep Ghyll to Central Buttress.

On this expedition, while traversing the Oval, the pair were struck by the possibilities of the Flake Crack, which later proved the key pitch of Central Buttress. Finally, in April 1914, with snow patches lingering at the foot of the face, they laid siege to C.B. Three days were taken in all, the first being more of a skirmish to sound out the Great Flake's defences. When conventional methods of ascent failed here, the climbers devised a rope cradle by threading a spare length of rope behind a chockstone; when Sansom was safely installed, Herford (who, being a gentleman, had removed his boots) swarmed over his body and reached the top of the flake. Some idea of how difficult their contemporaries considered the pitch can be gained from the words of C. F. Holland, the last man on the rope: 'Suffice it to say that I had two ropes on and climbed up a third, finishing in a state of utter exhaustion after a wild haul at a knotted loop that Herford had thoughtfully placed in just the right position.'

Their climb ranked as the most serious in the country, and was certainly a major step towards raising the role of British rock-climbing from mere Alpine training to a sport in its own right. Herford, in fact, was fated never to see the Alps, as the war now intervened. Ironically, the War Office considered him unworthy of the commission he requested, and this natural leader of men died in France two years later as a private soldier.

For almost two decades C.B. remained the most serious expedition in Lakeland, and not until the exploration of the East Buttress was its supremacy questioned. With the general raising of standards it was inevitable that the Flake Crack would eventually be led without the use of combined tactics. In 1931, Menlove Edwards, a climber more associated with Wales than the Lakes, made the important breakthrough, raising the reputation of the climb to its former level. The driving spirit of the thirties also produced a direct finish and variation start, climbed by F. G. Balcombe and A. Mullan respectively, and the com-

Route Central Buttress, Hard Very Severe, 470ft
Cliff Scafell Crag on the north side of Scafell.
First Ascent S. Herford, G. Sansom, H. Gibson and C. Holland, April 1914; First unaided ascent – J. M. Edwards, W. Stallybrass and M. Pallis, August 1931; Direct Finish – F. Balcombe, J. Wright and J. Files, June 1934; Variation Start – A. Mullan and H. Thompson, July 1939.
Map Reference O.S. Lake District Tourist Map, 1–50,000 Sheet 89 (ref. 208068).
Guidebook F.R.C.C. *Scafell Group* by G. Oliver and J. Griffin.
Nearest Road Minor road along Wasdale at Wasdale campsite (ref. 181076).
Distance and time from cliff 2 miles/2200ft. Allow 1½ hours.
Good Conditions At least four dry summer days.
Campsites and Bunkhouses F.R.C.C. Hut, Brackenclose; Barn at Wasdale Head Hotel; Wasdale campsite.
Bibliography F.R.C.C. Journal 1921 (account of first ascent). Numerous references in books and magazines since then.

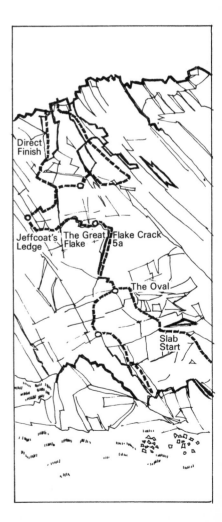

Ian Wright

bination of these and the Flake (climbed free) imparted a thoroughly modern flavour to the route.

The role of C.B. at the present has changed considerably. No longer the ultimate test for the tiger, it is now a trade route within the capabilities of numerous climbers, a fact that often leads to a queue at the Oval. Many an unfortunate wretch has struggled on the Flake Crack to the accompaniment of derisory banter from the impatient watchers below.

Scafell is usually at its most benevolent in June, so this is the ideal time for an attempt on C.B. As a number of other parties will doubtless have the same intention, an early start is advisable. The approach from Wasdale is steep and gruelling, making the arrival at Hollowstones and the last water supply a welcome excuse for a rest. From this point, the line of the climb can be traced; if one is new to the crag, it is hard to believe that the small rock splinter in the middle of the face is the legendary Flake Pitch. However, the vastness of the crag soon falls into place during the long scramble up scree to the Rake's Progress and the foot of the buttress. The pioneers reached the Oval from the left, over grass-covered rocks. The accepted route now takes a series of narrow slabs and walls, providing a foretaste of the sterner stuff ahead. At the Oval, a pleasant grass-covered ledge, the crux of the climb obtrudes forcibly on the senses.

A huge flake, partly detached from the face, forms a 65ft. crack on its right side, the upper part of which is gently impending. For 30ft. this is straightforward, as a diagonal crack leads across the wall to join the main fissure. Above this, the crack attains that awkward width, too narrow for the body, but too wide for satisfactory hand-jams. Overhead can be seen the base of the most famous chockstone in Lakeland, threaded with a depressing array of aged

Left: The crux pitch of Central Buttress. The leader is starting to climb up the side of the Great Flake. The final section of this pitch involves a series of difficult layback moves. *Climber: unknown*

Leo Dickinson

and ageing slings. Under its protection, a precarious wedged resting position can be achieved while one surveys the final 12ft. of the crack.

The obvious mode of attack is a layback up the slightly impending edge of the flake: a most committing step, for the edge is disconcertingly smooth and the right wall devoid of encouraging rugosities. The top of the chockstone seems to offer a foothold, but once embarked on the layback it is found that the feet must be kept well to the right to maintain equilibrium. Any attempt to stand on the chock would result in a swing out, and ultimately off.

Laybacking to the top of the Flake is very tiring on the arms, so it is advisable to make the first attempt tell. (The second man should note that if the rope is run behind the Flake to give an added feeling of security it invariably snags on an undercut projection, leaving him to perform a one-armed layback while he clears it. It is better to place a sling on the extreme end of the Flake and pass the rope down the outside.)

After the drama of the Flake Crack, the traverse to Jeffcoat's Ledge becomes a veritable walk. However, the climb shows its teeth again in the shape of a series of delicate traverses to the right with a wide sweep of nothingness as a back-cloth, before it peters out into easier slabs leading to the summit plateau of Scafell.

Looking at C.B. strictly as a piece of rock to be climbed, it makes a very satisfying ascent; but there is much more to it than that. It has a sense of both past and present, spanning, as it does, almost sixty years of climbing endeavour. In climbing it, one can identify in a small way with names of the past: Herford, Edwards, Balcombe, Linnell, Kirkus. If the next sixty years should see the climb relegated from the ranks of the Very Severes, the effects could only be good in that a greater number of climbers could enjoy it.

Right: A view from the top of the Great Flake showing the easy but sensational pitch that follows. *Climber: Steve Suthorn*

Ichabod

by Allan Austin

The East Buttress of Scafell – a name to conjure with. The finest crag in the Lakes. High on Scafell, just below the summit, staring out over upper Eskdale and facing north and east, it is an impressive place. A great lonely crag. Its walls overhang. Water drips out from the crag instead of down. Greenery is virtually non-existent. The sheer bulk of its sweeping grey rock and barrel shape induces in a climber a feeling of insignificance. Massively constructed in iron-hard rock, it possesses a string of the finest lines in the district.

I was suitably impressed.

We stood there, reading the description and sorting out the gear, with that huge corner hanging high above. It appeared to be totally inaccessible. A thin stream of water descended from it, losing itself in spray long before reaching us.

'You'll be O.K. – the water's clear of your route.' It was Ian Roper ('Sherpa' to the climbing world), reading my thoughts. I looked round. I had already lost out. Chris (Chris Mitchell, who was killed in Norway in 1968) had picked up a rope and was soloing up the long easy gangway that starts the climb, leaving the other rope – and all the gear – for me.

There are essentially two pitches: one with the reputation of being a chopper, and the following one, which is said to be harder but safe. There was only one pitch for me. I mean, I have responsibilities . . . a man with my craft and skill . . . and my family to think of. I was a natural for the hard, safe pitch. Chris was a bold young man, a natural for the chopper. He was also an astonishingly mature 18-year-old, a thoughtful youth, and he was occupying the stance with great determination. Indeed, he insisted that it was a pitch for an old and steady hand – like myself. I felt unable to agree, but Sherpa and Ken Wood, halting their preparations for Phoenix, urged Chris to stand, or rather sit, firm. There was a perfect barrage of light-hearted chatter: Sherpa reminisced about his gripping ascent, a tale liberally embellished and embroidered since its last telling; pseudo-encouragement from the belayed Mitchell was interspersed with pointed comments

from Wood about my climbing skill, age, and so forth. They enjoyed themselves hugely. What a party! I was understandably less keen.

A great undercut ridge separates the corner of Ichabod from the crack of Phoenix and, nestling under the ridge is a bottomless niche. The old entry for Phoenix went left here, but today only teams bound for Ichabod come this way.

I remembered that Eric ('Matey') Metcalf, one of the great Lakeland climbers of the late fifties, had once spent several hours in this niche with Ron Moseley (Ron's second day) attempting the traverse I was about to make. A fanatical purist, Matey believed that climbing rocks meant just that. No aid was to be used. And he had failed. On the following day, as a direct result of this failure, Moseley took the other way out of the niche to make the first ascent of Phoenix.

Well, we would see. . . .

Out across the smooth wall on the right was a steep little groove, with a peg halfway for encouragement and aid. I left the comfort of my niche and headed for the peg. It wasn't far, a few feet perhaps, but I was already feeling the strain when I reached it. It was the prototype 'ancient peg', a pathetic piece of crumbling rust. Occasionally, when there is no other way, I can put cowardice behind. This was such an occasion: I decided to try it without a peg. It was only a few moves anyway; I was almost there.

Matey's words echoed back from the past: 'We were almost there, only inches to go, but the wall was too steep; we never made it.'

He was right. As I hadn't the guts to use the old peg, I'd have to use my own. At the first blow, the flake I was hammering creaked ominously outwards and threatened to come off. I was appalled: a few millimetres of rust – or a peg I dared not drive.

Sweat was trickling along the top of my eyebrows by the time I reached the corner. Bonington's old channel was still there, a relic of the second ascent. Without a moment's hesitation I clipped in, took a breather, collected myself and unsteamed

Route   Ichabod, Extremely Severe, 240ft.
Cliff   The East Buttress of Scafell.
First Ascent   G. Oliver, G. Arkless and L. Willis, May 1960.
Map Reference   O.S. Lake District Tourist Map, 1–50,000 Sheet 89 (ref. 210067).
Guidebook   F.R.C.C. *Scafell Group* by G. Oliver and J. Griffin.
Nearest Road   Minor road down Wasdale at Wasdale campsite (ref. 181076).
Distance and time from cliff   2 miles/2600ft. Allow 2 hours.
Good Conditions   Three dry summer days.
Campsites and Bunkhouses   F.R.C.C. Hut, Brackenclose; Barn at Wasdale Head Hotel; Wasdale campsite. Campsites below North Face.

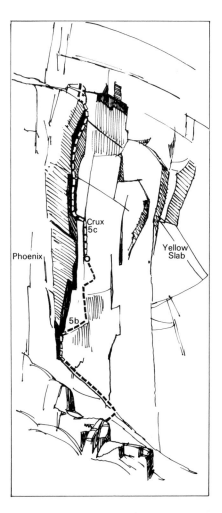

Below: The difficult traverse on the first hard pitch of Ichabod. *Climber: Ed Grindley*

Ian Roper

my specs. Then on again, up the corner until it petered out a few feet below the stance.

On the first ascent, in 1960, Geoff Oliver made a long and harrassing traverse out to the right, followed by desperate climbing to get back to the ledge. I did not need Sherpa's account of the irreversible moves and appalling out-of-balance climbing to make me try elsewhere. To say I was reluctant to traverse is an understatement.

But things weren't as desperate as all that. I intended to go straight up. I had done my homework, and I had Daniel Boone's word for it: 'It's steep up there, but there's a jug. Take your time and work it out.'

So I took my time and when I reached the ledge the problem shrank to measurable proportions. A foot, in fact. I had to reach a lot further, or grow. As attempt succeeded attempt, my arm grew and eventually dropped into a jug. I was up.

So there I was, 'belayed round the mountain', standing on the stance (which is not really a stance at all), trying to avoid the stream which Sherpa had assured us would be somewhere else.

Still, I wasn't grumbling. It was almost comfortable. It's wonderful how relaxed one can become when it is someone else's turn for the sharp end.

There was only one way to go from here – straight on up. Chris was wedged across the corner about 20ft. above my head. He was wearing socks over his P.A.s in an attempt to make them grip. But sticking feet didn't help his sliding fingers. I cursed for the fiftieth time – no water indeed! Chris seemed to have been there for hours. My feet were continually pushed into the pointed toes of my P.A.s, with painful results! I marvelled at Chris's self control. There was no pulling on, or standing in, slings. If the climb was going to go, it was going to go legitimately. Eventually it did, and Chris disappeared over a bulge, moving continuously and with so little fuss that I hardly realized he'd cracked it. The rope ran out until there was none left, and it was my turn.

It was a delightful little corner: lots of cunning little moves and delicate bridging. True, it was wet and greasy – but that didn't detract from the enjoyment. Then came the

Below: Having completed the traverse the leader has to climb a short corner and get on to a slight ledge on the right. From here, more difficult moves allow the main groove line to be regained. The climbers on the left are on Phoenix. *Climbers: unknown (on Ichabod); John Yates and Dave Morris (on Phoenix).*

crunch. I couldn't for the life of me find anything to pull. Something would have to be done quickly. I couldn't let the young whippersnappers above think that I was in difficulties. It wouldn't do at all. I was the one who was supposed to be showing them the way. I finished up trying to mantelshelf out on to the left-hand rib.

It was a round, sloping boss and threatened to precipitate me into the truly awesome depths. An extra coil or two dropped around my knees – slack to enable me to appreciate the situation! By dint of getting a knee on, wedging a shoulder against the wall, and pushing my finger into the moss on the bulge above, I managed to achieve a position of verticality above that evil little glacis.

Panic died and I waited a minute or two for my heavy breathing to subside before continuing. The rope was taken in, grudgingly and reluctantly it seemed, but the crisis was past. I could now enjoy the long, relatively easy crack which ran straight up to join the last two or three feet of Yellow Slab. My would-be nonchalant exit on to the top was spoilt by my usual ham-fisted attempts on the last moves of that climb and I graunched my way out, puffing and panting, to be surrounded by three grinning faces.

There was a pause, then: 'Hard?' said Chris.

I started to say how pleasant and attractive it had all been. And then I stopped.

It had been a great lead on his part. I would have been proud to have made it myself.

'Hard,' I admitted. 'I nearly didn't make it.'

His grin broadened. 'We were hoping you'd fall off.'

I started to smile.

'I'd have stood in a sling if you hadn't been there,' he confessed.

It was my turn to laugh. What a team! And what a climb!

Ken Wilson

59

THE LAKE DISTRICT 18 Central Pillar

by Paul Nunn

At the core of the Lake District's finest mountains lies the roadless expanse of upper Eskdale. Unattainable without walking, it is one of England's most beautiful valleys. Esk Buttress complements the wilderness caught between Scafell and Bowfell, for while the valley is wide, open and treeless, the crag is towering, stark and steep, an archetypal precipice, unbroken by major gullies or obvious ledges.

This grandiose setting is not belied by its climbs, the finest of which is undoubtedly Central Pillar. Early explorations groped up its lower reaches towards the formidable upper brow of rock which caps the crag, blocking direct exit from it. Explorers like George Bower, Alf Bridge and R. J. Birkett were forceful assailants, but all were deflected by the upper bastions. A great hiatus appeared in the development of the cliff in the 1950s. It was too steep and smooth for all but a few pioneers before 1959 and they did not come. All existing climbs avoided the upper wall at the crag's centre.

After this lull and a few exploratory peerings from all angles, Esk Buttress was subjected to the indecency of a mass assault on a fine June Sunday in 1962, the day of an appalling accident on nearby Scafell's East Buttress. Allen Austin, spidery Jack Soper and Eric ('Matey') Metcalf were beaten to the crag by Peter Crew and Mike Owen, and were forced to compensate by producing Red Edge and Black Sunday. The 'first team' off from Langdale picked the plum while, less than a mile away, two other climbers of the '59 generation died below the East Buttress.

The climb has some great characteristics. Following Bridge's Route, it gains height easily at first, climbing pleasant slabs and little walls of solid grey rock between ledges for over 200ft. Then the rock steepens, the pillar proves intractable at pre-1945 standards and the old route is forced off into the protective recesses of Square Chimney.

Above the upper ledge of Bridge's Route, a slabby expanse eases a little where it abuts on to the deep V-cleft of Trespasser Groove, to the right of the main face of the Pillar. No obvious line suggests itself, but a few moves upon squarish holds reveal a traverse out on to small holds in compact rock. Careful balance climbing leads out diagonally to a small stance in a V-groove. Though it has been used as a belay, this seems ill advised; piton scars mark the back of the groove. The grey-green rock above offers a few small holds leading to a bulge. The rock gives away little and after a series of difficult moves a long reach out right is probably irreversible. Beyond, a mossy slab is perched below another barrier of beetling walls, and a piton provides a belay at its upper edge.

The second man, belayed in this position, is excellently placed to apprehend his leader's fate. A slight traverse on to the wall, which tilts out above the groove below, leads to a piton. Despite the situation's unsuitability for such antics, a series of boulder problems ensues. A pull out on to a block is both insecure in itself and leaves doubts as to the block's stability. After standing on the block a long grope upward to holds in a quartzite band is the only escape. The band is seized, pulled on to and traversed to a cool haven in Bower's Route.

Beyond there lies only a classic polished crack and the rocky dome of Esk Buttress's summit, with magnificent views down towards the lower valley.

The climb is certainly great, though it appears deflected, for one never climbs the upper wall direct; instead there are cunning side-steps, which almost push one off the Pillar. Yet this attenuation is not an overwhelming price to pay, and the validity of the route rests assured, despite or even because of the deviousness of the particular solution.

Route Central Pillar, Extremely Severe, 495ft.
Cliff Esk Buttress, Eskdale.
First Ascent P. Crew and M. Owen, June 1962.
Map Reference O.S. Lake District Tourist Map, 1–50,000 Sheet 89 (ref. 224065).
Guidebook F.R.C.C. *Scafell Group* by G. Oliver and J. Griffin.
Nearest Road The Hard Knott Pass. Park at approx 236015 off the road and walk directly to the crag via Birker Fell. Alternatively approach from Eskdale and Taw House (ref. 220106).
Distance and time from cliff 3 miles/700ft. Allow 1½ hours. Slightly longer and higher from Taw House.
Good Conditions Allow at least two dry summer days after prolonged bad weather.
Campsites and Bunkhouses F.R.C.C. Huts, Brackenclose (Wasdale) and Rawhead (Langdale). Youth Hostels in Eskdale and Duddon Valley. Camping in Duddon Valley and Taw House.
Bibliography Climber and Rambler, October 1966: *Esk Buttress* by C. Bonington (with detailed account of the events leading up to the first ascent).

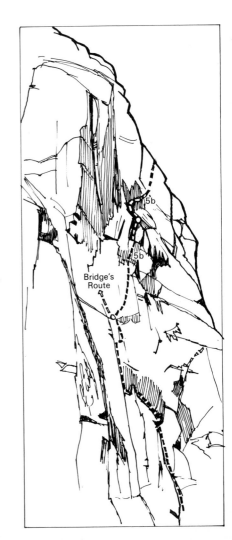

Bridge's Route

Chris Hall

Left: The first hard pitch of
Central Pillar, with a party on
Bridge's Route in the
background. *Climber: Gordon
Higginson*

Right: The strenuous 'boulder
problems' on the crux wall of
Central Pillar. *Climber: Ed Grindley*

THE LAKE DISTRICT 19 Gormenghast

by Colin Taylor

Heron Crag is by far the most popular of the few valley crags on the western side of the Lake District. It boasts over a dozen high quality routes which are often dry when the high cliffs are out of condition. The crag can be reached by a twenty minute walk up Eskdale from the foot of Hardknott Pass, but the best approach is along the track past Taw House which leaves the road about a mile before the pass. As you walk along the path from the end of the track, the crag gradually emerges from the hillside. It presents a very steep profile formed by a pillar about 300ft. high. This pillar is in fact the central section of the crag and is bounded on both sides by deep crack and corner lines. On the left the crag is more broken, with several corners, but to the right there is a steep mossy wall which overhangs by several feet at the bottom.

The first routes were only climbed in 1955. Heron Corner (V Diff) and Babylon (S) follow crack lines left of the main pillar. Bellerophon (VS), climbed in 1958, takes the corner right of the pillar. The best, however, was yet to come. In March 1960 Les Brown, then working down the road at Windscale, climbed his modern classic right up the central pillar to put the crag properly on the map. Gormenghast immediately became popular and has remained so ever since. In the next year Austin and Metcalf added a Direct Start and Whillans a Direct Finish. Half-a-dozen or more routes have been climbed since, the most important being perhaps Flanker and Spec Crack on the mossy right-hand wall and Iago up the centre of the pillar right of Gormenghast. But these routes have only recently started to receive repeats, and the most popular line on the crag is still undoubtedly Gormenghast.

The line of the route is easy to find. About 40ft. from the base of the central pillar a ledge forms a niche below an obvious crack. The original start, no longer described in the guidebook, involved a semi-hand-traverse directly on to this ledge from a few feet up Babylon, round the corner to the left. Almost everyone now does the direct start. The steep wall gives good climbing with little difficulty apart from a fingery pull-up at half-height; this, however, can be well

protected by a tape round a nearby spike. The ledge above is rather constricted and there is usually a belay peg in place.

A long and imposing pitch now lies ahead. The first 20ft. up the wall well left of the crack are the hardest and not really protectable. The rock is compact and slightly overhanging. An initial jug is followed by three mantelshelf moves on flat holds each a little more precarious and committing than the one before. At the last, if you arrange your feet carefully, you can rest a little. Just above and to the left is a fairly good although rather old peg to allow full recovery. This section seems to take either a very short or a very long time to lead. It is all a matter of confidence, although a long reach gives a considerable advantage. The angle now relents slightly and easier moves up right lead to the safety of the crack. After a few bridging moves, a swing out right from the crack marks the end of the difficulties and the groove above leads to three belays in about thirty feet.

The main pitch over, there is a choice to be made between the direct and original finishes. The former, a single pitch, is the more impressive, but the latter offers two pitches, both of some interest. Right of the belay, an awkward pull up past a block leads to a jammed flake below the final wall. The direct finish now continues straight up, trending right at the top. The initial bridging moves up the smooth shallow groove are quite difficult, but thereafter, above a small overhang, the holds improve. The original route traverses right from the same jammed flake; in a fine position, it leads round the arête to above a niche which is gained by an awkward ten foot reverse layback down a thin crack protectable by spike runners. The belay is further up right on the edge of Bellerophon. The last pitch is often used as an escape from the top crack of that route. It follows the edge above the belay to a curious ledge on the left which leads further left to the top of the crag.

Route Gormenghast, Hard Very Severe, 300ft.
Cliff Heron Crag, Eskdale.
First Ascent L. Brown and A. Atkinson, March 1960; Direct Start – A. Austin and E. Metcalfe, 1961; Direct Finish – Don Whillans and A. Ashworth, 1961.
Map Reference O.S. Lake District Tourist Map, 1–50,000 Sheet 89 (ref. 222030).
Guidebook F.R.C.C. *Great Gable* by P. Fearnehough.
Nearest Road From Eskdale follow farm track to Taw House (ref. 200106).
Distance and time from cliff 1 mile/200ft. Allow 20 minutes.
Good Conditions Dries quickly in winter or summer. Adjoining routes stay damp for some time however.
Campsites and Bunkhouses Camping at Taw House or in Wasdale; F.R.C.C. Hut, Brackenclose (Wasdale).

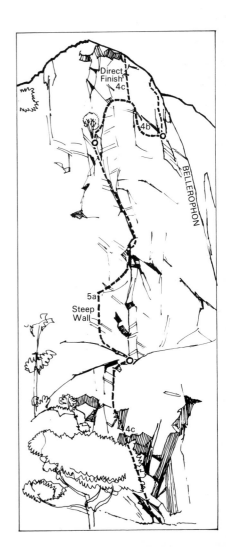

Ken Wilson

Right: The crucial second pitch of Gormenghast. Having surmounted the steep wall, the second man is moving rightwards to the groove/crack that leads out to the easier-angled rock above. The pitch continues to the tree stance occupied by the leader. *Climbers: unknown*

Below: The original third pitch traversed up and round from the tree and descended this exposed crack to link up with Bellerophon. *Climber: Mike Kosterlitz*

Left: A distant shot showing the climber in a position identical to that of the previous photograph. The Direct Finish goes straight up the edge of the buttress. *Climber: unknown*

Ken Wilson

THE LAKE DISTRICT **20** **Engineers' Slabs**

by Paul Nunn

At the head of afforested Ennerdale, a few hundred yards from the point where an ancient track linking Langdale and West Cumberland leaves Aaron Slack, Great Gable plunges into a steep, craggy north face. Though large and of good rock, it is broken by numerous ledges and vegetated gullies, a disappointment after drinking in its forbidding aspect, characteristically gloomy, cold and often wet.

Yet, set in this chaos of detached buttresses and wandering gullies, there is a steep, compact, rectangular wall, a grey block of Lakeland granite almost two hundred feet high and quite unspoiled by ledges or vegetation. This wall is a 'slab' only in name, for it is slightly convex, providing steep sustained climbing in a remote and unfrequented mountain environment. At mid-height it is split by overhangs; these, in turn, are vertically bisected by a steep chimney and crack line which suffers only one minor discontinuity. This fine line, from base to summit of the cliff, was ascended in a remarkable manner by F. G. Balcombe and his companions in 1934.

It was a feat of considerable boldness, lost in the obscurity of the twenty years which elapsed before a repetition. It compared favourably with the notable achievements of others on Scafell and in Wales. The climb, Engineers' Slabs, must have been sparsely protected, given the techniques of the time and the few stances, whatever the nature of the engineering involved. Yet it was neglected, left to its geographical isolation and persistent dankness, the challenge of its considerable technical difficulty ignored. Only in the fifties was the climb regenerated, to become a Very Severe classic worthy of the fine dry day which is ideally required for its ascent.

Above a vegetated gully the 'slab' rears abruptly, with the lower cracks of the climb oozing a little slime in all but the finest conditions. Awkward moves lead up to a small stance below uncompromising-looking cracks which prove shallow, with a peculiar distribution of holds. A small stance is reached at about 80ft. Even with nuts a piton belay is probably advisable on this and the subsequent stance.

The long stride right to reach a continuing steep crack reveals the mounting exposure. The cracks above are steep and eventually demand a layback before a good ledge can be reached below the final groove. Traditionally, these moves must have been almost totally unprotected while the second remained virtually belay-less below.

There remains a steep V-groove, climbed by back and foot, and only dry in the best summer weather. During dry spells in early Spring this groove can retain winter verglas, even when the rest of the climb is dry; at such times an escape up a steep arête on the left is necessary to complete the climb. Both escapes are quite difficult, even under modern conditions; on a hemp line, without protection, the lead of the groove was remarkable.

Instead of retracing one's steps to the foot of the cliff, the finest way to complete the climb is to continue over the summit of Gable and descend by one of the ordinary paths (boots can be carried up in the second man's sack for this purpose).

Somehow this climb goes beyond normal rock climbing and is almost a mountaineering route, feeling much greater than its small size justifies. It is this special quality and particular atmosphere, together with an inescapable character, which creates the unique appeal of a remote, isolated and infrequently ascended climb.

Route Engineers Slabs, Very Severe, 180ft.
Cliff Gable Crag, Great Gable.
First Ascent F. Balcombe, J. Shepherd and C. Cooper, June 1934.
Map Reference O.S. Lake District Tourist Map, 1–50,000 Sheet 89 (ref. 213105).
Guidebook F.R.C.C. *Great Gable* by P. Fearnehough.
Nearest Road B5289 at Honister Hause.
Distance and time from cliff 2½ miles/1000ft. Allow 1 hour.
Good Conditions One of the slowest-drying crags in the Lake District. Allow at least four dry summer days.
Campsites and Bunkhouses Youth Hostels at Honister Hause and Black Sail (Ennerdale); Campsite at Seatoller, or in Wasdale.

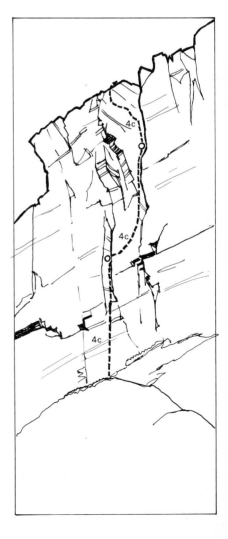

Left: Looking down the final groove of Engineers' Slabs. *Climber: unknown*

Right: The difficult first pitch of Praying Mantis (*see following chapter*), with the leader climbing the difficult corner/crack. *Climber: Martin Barnicott*

Chris Hall

by Ian Roper

Route Praying Mantis, Hard Very Severe, 260ft.
Cliff Goat Crag, Borrowdale.
First Ascent L. Brown and S. Bradshaw, May 1965.
Map Reference O.S. Lake District Tourist Map, 1–50,000 Sheet 89 (ref. 245175).
Guidebooks F.R.C.C. *Borrowdale* by P. Nunn and O. Woolcock; *Borrowdale A Climber's Guide* by P. Ross and M. Thompson.
Nearest Road At the end of a rough track from Grange to Hollows Farm campsite (ref. 250167).
Distance and time from cliff ¼ mile/300ft. Approx. 10 minutes.
Campsites and Bunkhouses Youth Hostel at Keswick; F.R.C.C. Hut, Salving House in Rosthwaite; C.H.A. Hostel at Seatoller. Campsite below the cliff.
Bibliography F.R.C.C. Journal, No. 59: *New Wine from Old Bottles* by P. Nunn.

It is scarcely surprising that the exploration of Goat Crag took place only sporadically. The obvious exposures of rock on its eastern flank are too broken to offer good climbing, while its gloomy northern wall was, until 1964, so vegetated that the would-be climber could scarcely see the rock for the trees! Nevertheless, the history of the crag is a long one. The Abraham brothers climbed nearby Mouse Ghyll in 1899, and an alpine guide, Angelo Dibona, visited the crag in 1924. Development continued fitfully until 1964. The present appearance of the northern flank bears little resemblance to the Goat Crag of those earlier years. True, several large trees remain which must have been there in 1924, but the grass has gone, great carpets of it, the cracks have all been cleaned to make way for the nut and the hand-jam, and a score of modern climbs now decorate its walls.

The event which catalysed this change occurred in the spring of 1965, when Les Brown made the first ascent of Praying Mantis, having spent a whole winter gardening the climb in great secrecy (leaving the first 70ft. to the last!). It must have been an epic ascent, for those who made early repetitions of the climb compared it in difficulty with Dovedale Groove. Now that the holds have been thoroughly cleaned, the difficulty has diminished somewhat, but the climb still remains a serious undertaking. Thus was Goat Crag rescued from obscurity. The climb sparked off a spate of activity which brought the crag to maturity inside two years, a record scarcely equalled by any cliff of comparable extent anywhere.

Even today, looking across from Grange, it seems impossible to the casual observer that the gloomy and vertiginous northern wall of Goat Crag could yield climbs of quality, certainly not of the quality of Praying Mantis. Closer acquaintance, however, reveals that the crag is bigger and steeper than first appearances suggest; in particular, the eye is caught by the yellow overhangs and the blank featureless aspect of a bulbous buttress, which is less verdant than the rest of the crag.

The buttress plunges vertically into the ground, and is split by two large corners.

That on the left contains large overhangs and is eschewed for the easier-looking one on the right. A tree some 70ft. above the ground provides a haven, but is only won with difficulty. The corner crack is smooth and strenuous and leads to an *impasse* in a niche. Out leftwards the climber must go, on large holds at first. These diminish with the angle, and it is with relief that the leader reaches the tree. Here he can hear, but not see, the struggles of his companions on the horrors below. The party is reunited on the stance, then split again as the leader plunges on up a staircase of collapsing turves, besmirching all beneath with eroded earth. Above are bulges, to the right more bulges, so left again is the only way. The wall is steep and the holds small, but a smooth, water-worn groove at an easier angle is soon attained, and yields with surprising ease. A delightful little stance is reached by an elegant move to the right and the climber attaches himself to the wide variety of hardware normally in position.

The situation is impressive. Above and below are overhangs. To the left is a belt of damp overlapping slabs, and to the right a delicate patchwork where the moss has been removed from the holds. All around is the verdant scenery of mid-Borrowdale, with Derwentwater and Skiddaw forming a fitting backdrop. Even the predations of the tourists in nearby Grange seem to belong to another world. Falcons and rooks squabble in their eyries, while the second advances stealthily to the tiny sanctuary.

The line now leads delicately back to the right, to a pair of footholds and a rusty peg where the first few parties belayed. The overhangs above have now relented and a steep wall, climbed surprisingly awkwardly with subtle undercuts and historical jams, leads to a slab of superb rock and a final heather cornice.

It has been said that a climb can still be great, without excelling in all the factors which contribute to greatness. This is perfectly true of Praying Mantis. The line is not simple, nor is it inescapable, though escape would not be easy to effect. Much of its charm lies in its variety of techniques and situations; for my money the stance at the end of pitch two is one of the finest

The third pitch of Praying Mantis, where the route traverses delicately to the right between the bulges.
Climber: Terry Parker

anywhere. The climb lays no claim to extreme difficulty, although a few moves on the first pitch could be trying to those not proficient at hand-jamming; yet the route as a whole is rarely easy, but yields to sound and varied technique with no tricks or frills. Also, the crag is scarcely inspiring, and perhaps it is the pleasant surprise of doing a route of such quality on such a cliff that is one of the climb's finest attributes.

Gimmer Crag, Great Langdale

THE LAKE DISTRICT 22 The Crack

by Ken Wilson

High above Langdale stands Gimmer Crag, a 300ft. shoulder of rock, proudly outlined on the edge of the Langdale Pikes. The rock is hard and good and the sunny south face is criss-crossed with routes steeped in the atmosphere of the twenties. One can imagine nail-booted Fell and Rockers lurching their way up Bracket and Slab and heaving painfully up the grotesquely desperate Amen Corner, watched by groups picnicking on the slopes below. Out of sight of Langdale and the picnickers is the north-west face, steeper and more serious than the sporting south side. Most of its climbs echo this mood. The best line on the face is The Crack. While the nearby Kipling Groove contains a greater concentration of appetizing moves set in finer positions, The Crack is longer, easier and better sculptured – a classic climb hemmed in by more difficult but lesser companions. A developing VS leader or an unfit expert will find it testing enough. A succession of tricky moves and well situated pitches builds up gradually, though never unpleasantly, to the final crux section. True to tradition, The Crack reserves its climax to the end: sated, the climber pulls over the top to relax on Gimmer's accommodating summit ledges.

The climb is reached by toiling arduously up the gully below the face. Here, the crag assumes its full height above, with soaring grooves and ribs accentuating the perspective. A prominent, curving groove with a crack in its bed appears to lead directly up to these difficulties. In fact, the initial pitch unfolds fairly easily, until an interesting leftward traverse brings greater technicalities and a sharper standard. The second pitch starts with a precarious mantelshelf move followed by slightly easier climbing up an open slab. Gradually one moves back right to regain the crack, which is now hemmed in by a steep corner, leading in one impressive sweep to the top of the crag. One long pitch, packed with exhilarating climbing, brings one to the top. The hard section is half-way up, where the crack becomes blocked by an overhanging wedge of rock; one or two steep and very exposed moves must be made here.

A well-balanced and satisfying climb on excellent rock, The Crack is rarely serious

and never brutish; an elegant succession of interesting pitches makes it a climb for everyone. The outing is infinitely more enthralling, however, if one knows something about the first ascent.

1928: Lakeland climbing was reaching the crest of a wave of exploration. Botterill, Jones and Herford had left a stern legacy that upstaged the depleted efforts of the post-war climbers. But momentum was returning: new crags were being developed, new routes appearing. It was the time for deeds . . .

'It was not that the best men were any better than the giants of the past,' wrote H. M. Kelly, 'but they were more numerous, while the standard of ability among climbers in general had increased enormously.'

Nobody had yet succeeded in bettering the difficulty and seriousness of Herford's great climb, but after a period of middle-grade exploration, climbs of a stiffer standard began to reappear. Moss Ghyll Grooves on Scafell, Grooved Wall on Pillar, and Hiatus on Gimmer, indicated what was possible; one of the next obvious objectives was the prominent crack line near Hiatus.

But the crack was thought to be too difficult to reach from below and too hard to continue. Top-roped investigations of the upper crack were made; despite the discouraging reports that resulted, challengers soon emerged in the persons of A. B. Reynolds and H. G. Knight.

Contemporary Lakeland pioneers often favoured top-rope investigation of hard new climbs. 'No one,' it was said, 'would dare to attempt the climb straight away without having a look from a rope.' But Reynolds and Knight boldly did just that, one warm April afternoon. After some hours of climbing, slowed by the usual route-finding and gardening difficulties and by the need to overcome a slab of rock poised in the crack, they reached The Bower – the ledge in the final corner to which George Bower had been lowered during a top-rope inspection. Unable to find a good belay, Reynolds climbed to just below the overhang and tied on there. By then it was growing dark and, after one abortive attempt by Knight, the pair decided that the crux would not go in the failing light.

Route The Crack, Very Severe, 240ft.
Cliff North-West Face of Gimmer Crag, Great Langdale.
First Ascent A. Reynolds and G. Macphee, May 1928.
Map Reference O.S. Lake District Tourist Map, 1–50,000 Sheet 89 (ref. 273071).
Guidebook F.R.C.C. *Great Langdale* by J. A. Austin and R. Valentine.
Nearest Road Car Park at Old Dungeon Ghyll Hotel at the end of the B5343 Great Langdale road (ref. 285060).
Distance and time from cliff 1 mile/1200ft. Allow 1 hour.
Good Conditions Dries quickly in summer.
Campsites and Bunkhouses Large campsite at the head of Great Langdale. F.R.C.C. Hut, Rawhead (3 miles).
Bibliography F.R.C.C. Journal 1928: *The Crack* by G. Macphee (dealing with early attempts and the first ascent).

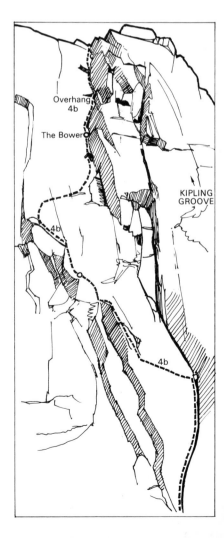

Left: The impressive, but easy, corner/crack that forms the start of The Crack. From this position the leader has to traverse across the wall on the left. *Climber: John Peck*

Right: The second pitch of The Crack starts with delicate moves up a steep slab, before trending back to rejoin the main line. *Climber: unknown*

Ken Wilson

Bob Allen

'The official photographer was here appointed to the position of honorary rescuer to the party, and made speed round to the top of the crags . . . during the forty-five minutes required by the rescuer they admired the sunset over Rossett Ghyll and saw the moon appear . . . However help was at hand and a rope let down from above was used to complete the climb. Such moral support of course invalidated the climb as a first ascent; such is the rigour of the game.'

Graham Macphee's laconic description hardly disguises what must have been a mini epic. The following week, Knight having departed, Reynolds enlisted Macphee for another attempt: 'I was delayed *en route* and reached Langdale at about 4 p.m. While snatching a hasty tea I read a note requesting my presence on the West Side of Gimmer and asking me to bring my Alpine line – the meaning of this ominous message was obvious.'

Macphee hastened up to Gimmer, where Reynolds and the photographer, R. C. Abbatt, were waiting for him. Reynolds led, and the pair made height rapidly. Their route merged with Hiatus for a few feet (a flaw later removed by the more direct mantelshelf pitch) and then the main crack was gained. Reynolds climbed up to a chockstone and made a long thread belay for Macphee, who established himself on the Bower and, facing left, managed to overcome the overhanging section with some difficulty (on the second ascent it was found easier facing right).

'It was a warm day and the second was inadequately protected from falling perspiration . . . "Well anyway The Crack has been led," said the leader, pausing for breath above the overhang . . . the second followed and in the still air from 75 yards was clearly audible breathing steadily through the nose . . . showers of moss and lichen dust filled his eyes . . . in dry weather this might be countered by wearing goggles.'

Macphee's account underlines the fact that at that time The Crack was far from being the polished climb it is today. The first pitch was described as greasy, the mantelshelf as vegetated, and the final corner crack as alternatively dusty, lichenous and damp. On early ascents these difficulties were compounded by the use of hemp rope, the absence of protection and the difficulty of arranging good belays. For obvious reasons, long run-outs were not popular at that time, and virtually any suitable spike was utilized to belay the second man. The first ascent split the climb into nine pitches, whereas now, with runners and 150ft. ropes, three will usually suffice.

Despite the many problems, the climb was not regarded as too difficult. Reynolds, Bower and Macphee made the second ascent a few months later, taking two hours – about par time for a twosome these days. On this occasion the party was followed by two other climbers. Macphee's account of the incident exhibits the contemporary fashion for understatement.

'The two climbers having observed us on The Crack asked if it was any good. On being assured that it might be worth even their attention they proceeded to go up the climb, and I must confess that as interested parties we were rude enough to sit and watch part of their ascent. Our advice, more freely asked as height was gained, must have saved them both time and trouble; but it was interesting to see the nonchalance with which they treated the problems which had given us food for thought . . . The curious slab of rock leaning in the crack below the Bower now lies embedded in the turf at the foot of the climb, having bounced only once in its downward career.'

Macphee concluded by taking what can only be understood as an ethical sideswipe at Central Buttress and Pigott's Climb: 'On this expedition no artificial aids were used – a practice becoming deplorably prevalent even in our homeland climbs. No loops of rope were previously placed at strategic points for use as handholds, stirrups or possibly worse. Not a step was cut, not a piton was driven in, not even an artificial chockstone was inserted in The Crack.'

Ken Wilson

Ken Wilson

Above: The final moves of
the second pitch of The Crack
to gain The Bower. *Climber:*
Tony Greenbank

Left: Looking down
the impressive final pitch of
The Crack. The climber is
surmounting the crux overhang.
Climber: Tony Greenbank.

by Mick Burke

Just to the right of The Crack is a steep buttress of fine rock. Undercut and overhanging at its base, its only obvious line of weakness is a steep groove that cuts its left side. The groove itself peters out at half-height, but a further line of weakness leads across to the right into the middle of the exposed front face of the buttress.

The climb has an interesting history. It was first 'looked at' by Birkett and Muscroft, but the scene that developed was more typical of the sixties than the mid-forties. Arthur Dolphin had a further look, with the aid of a top-rope. He concluded that the route would go, but there would be no protection once the groove itself had been left. A fall from the crux might be well over 100ft.

To do it, or not to do it? Not to do it meant leaving the biggest plum in Langdale to the opposition. So 'twas done: Dolphin and Lockwood climbed Kipling Groove in May 1948. The second ascent passed almost unnoticed: one of the Creag Dhu lads, George Shields, dashed up the route and away. It was so unnoticed that people still thought of doing the second ascent.

The second second ascent caused a lot of controversy. Joe Brown was the leader and he placed a peg to use as a runner: he's reputed to have said that the run-out wasn't justified. The next person to lead Kipling was Pete Greenwood: he thought the peg wasn't justified, so he spat on it and sped on his way without clipping in.

Eventually, Kipling became a trade route for the hard men. But it claimed its victims. Pat Walsh took a big fall trying to exit leftwards from the peg. Paddy Hunt wore through one of his ropes when he lost contact with the rock. I saw one climber fall off the crux three times before he gave up and went home. There was always a good crowd in North West Gully to watch for any action. Even with the peg in place, it was still a 60ft. fall before the rope came tight. Oh yes, a good route, Kipling: good to do and good to watch someone else doing. The Langdale climbers were very proud of it. They used to get very annoyed with anyone who treated the climb badly. With good reason though. There was violence on one occasion when someone

thought it a good climb to do with the aid of a few pitons and a set of etriers. Perhaps there wasn't enough violence: by the late sixties it wasn't unusual to find that the original peg had spawned a couple more.

For someone like myself, who started climbing in the fifties in Langdale, Kipling Groove was *the* route. In Dolphin's own guidebook to the area it was top of the graded list. There seemed quite a big gap between the next to the hardest and Kipling. The only photograph in the O.D.G. bar was of Dolphin on the first ascent. It really was *the* route in Langdale.

I thought, dreamt, planned and plotted K.G. The only thing I didn't do was climb it. I could have got one of the hot-shots to take me up it, but that wasn't the relationship I had with Kipling. I'd been up to climb it once: saved by rain. I'd done the first pitch proper when we did the girdle. Soon I would have to do it. The chance came one Friday night when, after six pints in the Oak, I asked Pat Walsh and Gerald Lund if they'd come and second me on it. Huge roars of laughter – of course they would.

The morning came and we went up to Gimmer. There was no need to read the guidebook: K.G. had been in my mind for too many years.

We arrived on the ledge at the start of the first pitch. A line of tiny footholds leads across a little wall, fifteen or so feet wide. The wall is topped by an overhang: not a bulge, but a clean-cut overhang with a four or five inch crack in the back. I knew it from before. It's too wide to jam your arm in, and there are no holds in the crack. The only thing to do is to use the crack as an under-cling: just step up on to the footholds, lean out on the under-cling and traverse across to the left and bigger footholds. But it's not as simple as it seems. The first foothold is a high step up, especially for a little lad, and particularly as there isn't much in the way of hand-holds. It's a very small, square-cut hold, as well; not too good to stand up on. Pat and Gerald sat there with fixed grins: no help from that quarter. But I knew it would be O.K. – it's just that the footholds are too small. I did it, of course, and traversed across and into

Route Kipling Groove, Hard Very Severe, 175ft.
Cliff North-West Face of Gimmer Crag, Great Langdale.
First Ascent A. R. Dolphin and J. B. Lockwood, May 1948.
Map Reference O.S. Lake District Tourist Map, 1–50,000 Sheet 89 (ref. 273071).
Guidebook F.R.C.C. *Great Langdale* by J. A. Austin and R. Valentine.
Nearest Road Car Park at Old Dungeon Ghyll Hotel at the end of the B5343 Great Langdale road (ref. 285060).
Distance and time from cliff 1 mile/1200ft. Allow 1 hour.
Good Conditions Dries quickly in most seasons.
Campsites and Bunkhouses Large campsite at the head of Great Langdale; F.R.C.C. Hut, Rawhead (3 miles).
Bibliography *Rope Boy* by Dennis Gray, Gollancz, London, 1970 (events surrounding the third ascent).

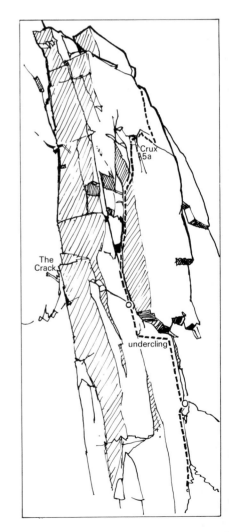

Bob Allen

the groove. It's just that first move; the others, and the twenty feet up the groove, are steep and exposed but on good holds – the climbing one expects of Gimmer Crag. I belayed and smoked while Gerald came across. No trouble for him; he's tall. No trouble for Pat either; he just climbs as if he's tall.

The climbing from the belay was fantastic; very steep, but it went well. Somebody had told me that stepping right on to the edge was difficult. I threaded a sling round a chock in the crack. Safe as houses then. It went very easily; the rock seemed as rough as gabbro. It was hard, but so enjoyable that it seemed easy.

Stepping out of the groove and on to the face, you're in another world. Without the groove to give some protection from the exposure, you're just a tiny dot on a big, rough piece of rock. The spectators across in North West Gully are just a clutter of tiny white faces. I began to feel less confident. A couple of steps up and there was the peg. And what a bomb-proof peg – straight into a horizontal crack. I thought I'd better have a rest; I didn't feel tired, but the last bit had been steep. I shouted down to the expectant ghouls to tell them what was happening:

'I'm just going to have a look. Then I'll come back, have a rest, and then do it.'

It actually looked O.K: 'A strenuous arm pull brings a diagonal crack above the overhang within reach followed by a horizontal crack a little higher to the right. The latter is used just to surmount the overhang and then as a mantelshelf, footholds being almost non-existent.'

The climbing was very steep, but there were a few holds to traverse on. Not many though. I began to wonder whether I would get up. After twenty feet I came to the diagonal crack. But there was a slight

Left: The first difficult section of Kipling Groove. One can either move up to the overlap and traverse underneath it by an under-cling, or use the footholds as handholds and make a few dynamic wall moves to reach the same point.
Climber: Dave Cook

snag – I couldn't reach it. There were side pulls, but they were for leaning to the left and I wanted to reach right. Then there was another difficulty: the wall to the right was undercut, so I couldn't bridge across. I went back to the peg for a rest and a think.

'Right, I'm going up this time. Pay it out nice and easy.' I went back across, but I still couldn't get any nearer than I had the first time. After another half-dozen attempts and shouts of 'I'm *really* going to try it this time', my team and spectators began to show signs of boredom. I decided to try it a little differently. I made the traverse slightly lower, until I was about eight feet below the crack. There wasn't much in the way of hand-holds, but there was a ridge. I laid away on it and after three or four moves I managed to reach the crack – a good one. I moved up then and grabbed the horizontal crack. At that point my feet slipped off, but it didn't matter too much – the hand-holds there are superb. Abandoning the mantelshelf business, I brought my feet up and went crab-fashion rightwards on infrequent, but superb, hand-holds. There were no footholds, but the rock was rough and my feet didn't slip. At the end was a small ledge, where I rested.

The climb was almost done. Another runner, and I moved up slowly. The last thirty feet lead up a steep groove. It's a good crack and there are footholds; really enjoyable climbing above an enormous drop. It's steep, but there are just enough holds, the rock is as good as anywhere in the world, and there are bilberries on the top. What more can you expect?

Below the ledge the rock sweeps away in enormous sheets. I couldn't see the ghouls, they were tucked away underneath somewhere. What a route for people who want to be alone!

Right: The celebrated crux moves of Kipling Groove. The protection peg is in the foreground. The horizontal crack is used to reach the ledge that the climber is hanging from. One can either get on to this by a semi-mantelshelf or continue hand-traversing in a very exposed position. *Climber: Ed Cross.*

Chris Hall

THE LAKE DISTRICT 24 Deer Bield Buttress

by Harold Drasdo

Within their small compass, Easedale and Far Easedale contain nearly all the scenic elements characteristic of the Lake District. Certain qualities of structure and order in the valley's proportions even invite us to imagine an affinity with the flawless landscapes of Chinese painting. And still, in spite of its accessibility from Grasmere and its position in the centre of Lakeland, the dale stays entirely unspoiled. This is perhaps partly because it holds nothing exploitable and so the road hardly penetrates it; and partly because it has no important summit and so escapes the attention of the majority of mountain walkers.

To the rock-climber the valley gives Deer Bield Crag, a sombre little north-facing outcrop with the unusual attraction that pretty well every one of the dozen routes so far achieved turns out, whatever the standard, to be steeper or harder than it looks. Three of these routes, standing side by side, are classics, and they could almost be taken to represent the development of Lakeland climbing: the Chimney, the Crack, the Buttress. The two big companion breaks offered obvious and tempting lines to the first visitors, and the Chimney was taken in 1908. No doubt it was discovered even then that the twin fault to the left was the other side of the same fissure; but over twenty years passed before the enterprising ascent of the strenuous and impressive Deer Bield Crack was made. There remained the low-relief nose between the breaks, a tall many-faceted blade of rock resting against the parent cliff. Up the face of this blade the route of Deer Bield Buttress – 'the first climb in the modern idiom in the Lakes' – was to wrestle a way: but it was to be twenty years again before the successful ascent would be made.

It is really rather unlikely that the thirties saw many attempts upon the Buttress: through these years only a limited number of climbers proved able to cope with the Crack, so there can have been no queues for the more intimidating possibility remaining. But one or two of the experts of the day did measure themselves against it, and one famous and determined attempt was described in the *Rucksack Club Journal*. In Jenkins's dryly entertaining account the

stubborn leader is identified only as 'he' or 'the Tiger'. Certainly the attack was not defeated by lack of equipment, ideas or resolution on the part of the leader, whose manoeuvres included the use, or attempted use, of pitons, inserted chockstones, combined tactics, lassoing, and the improvement of natural holds with a piton hammer. After seven hours of unremitting application, a point some distance up the fourth pitch had been reached when the flake on which the leader was balanced was felt to shift slightly. 'This . . . proved too much even for the Tiger's nerves and he was later heard to utter in a very small voice, "it's a pity I ever came up here . . ."'. So the attempt was abandoned, the tentative line henceforward being promoted in status to the Last Great Problem in the area. And for the rest of that decade, and for the next decade as well, the Buttress waited for the right man.

The right man was Arthur Rhodes Dolphin, who came on 24 June 1951. In more ways than Dolphin knew it was one of the great moments of his life, a point of change beginning the most productive phase of his career and also marking the start of the reshaping of the British climbing scene by other, younger, men.

It is possible that Dolphin had already read the writing on the wall. For a number of years he had played a casual, gentlemanly game with Jim Birkett, repeating nearly everything the great local pioneer accomplished. But his own hardest routes remained to the best of his knowledge untouched, and his place as the Lake District's leading climber seemed beyond dispute. Then, a few months before the success on the Buttress, there came the unexpected ascents of Kipling Groove,* first by Joe Brown and then by Peter Greenwood. There was in Dolphin's character an innocence and candour, communicated as much by his very presence and aspect as by his words and actions (but someone said: 'If ever a man had the mark of doom on his face, that was Dolphin') – and illuminated, too, by a generosity which caused his friends to

* The second ascent was actually made by George Shields—see previous chapter. (*Editor.*)

Route Deer Bield Buttress, Extremely Severe, 185ft.
Cliff Deer Bield Crag, Far Easedale.
First Ascent A. Dolphin and D. Brown, June 1951.
Map Reference O.S. Lake District Tourist Map, 1–50,000 Sheet 90 (ref. 303097).
Guidebook F.R.C.C. *Great Langdale* by J. A. Austin and R. Valentine.
Nearest Road Road junction and car park at Grasmere Village (ref. 333081). The road continues some distance up the Dale but parking is restricted.
Distance and time from cliff 2½ miles/900ft. Allow 1 hour.
Good Conditions Dries quickly in summer or after a strong wind in winter.
Campsites and Bunkhouses Youth Hostel in Grasmere. Various huts and campsites in Great Langdale.
Bibliography Rucksack Club Journal 1936: *Tiger Rag* by J. Jenkins (a highly amusing account of an early attempt). Brief notes in *The Hard Years* (Joe Brown) and *Rope Boy* (Dennis Gray). (Note: Map ref. given in F.R.C.C. Guide is inaccurate.)

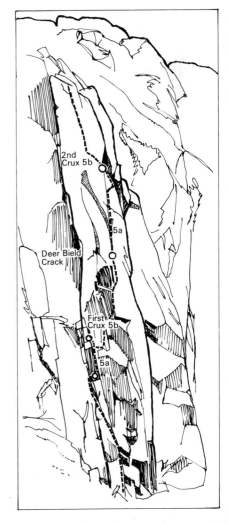

Above: The brutish second pitch of Deer Bield Buttress. *Climber: Harold Walmsley*

defend his memory jealously. But, whatever views he may have held on the place of competition in rock-climbing, it seems unlikely that his huge zest and energy would have allowed him to ignore a challenge to his domination of Lakeland climbing at a time when he knew himself to be actually improving in skill and resources. At any rate, not long after the repetitions of Kipling Groove he went for the best-known problem in the Lakes; and having succeeded he took the unprecedented step of writing out descriptions of the route immediately and presenting them to two of the younger Bradford climbers with the apparently guileless remark that he would value their opinions of the climb.

Dolphin's original description was scrupulously cool and objective. It made no claims for the interest, beauty or severity of the route, giving it the straight VS grading which had to cover the hardest routes in England at that time. It is rewarding to compare that original note with the instructions of the modern guidebook. The first two pitches really amount to a contrived alternative to the start of Deer Bield Crack; the guide now adds the advice that a section

lude in steep grooves leading to the last stance, a very exposed foothold made tenable by a good belay spike. The final problem, 'the second crux', starts with a wild, rather committing lurch on to holds on the bare wall on the left; then straight up, Dolphin's line, where the difficulties are short and sharp, the new guide says; or some further thin moves leftwards to an easier finish, a later solution to the problem.

The route will not arouse too much anxiety in many modern experts. The technical difficulty may be felt to remain of a fairly high order, but it appears likely that Dolphin used only two runners on the whole climb and it is safe to say that today's parties will find a good deal more protection if they feel they need it. The pitches are anyway quite short and the rock is now generally reliable. In fact there can be few safer climbs of this type and standard.

The rest is hindsight. On the very day on which Dolphin climbed the Buttress, the greatest campaign in British climbing history was beginning as Joe Brown made his first route on Clogwyn du'r Arddu. A month later the second ascent of the Buttress went to Peter Greenwood: in one of the most astonishing leads on record, Greenwood climbed the route in stocking-feet during rain, taking the third pitch by the groove alternative and managing somehow after an alarming and sensational fall to collect himself sufficiently to force the exit pitch with the effort of a lifetime. The greatest of Dolphin's later routes were to be realized the following year on Scafell and Bowfell in company with Greenwood: but his death in the Alps was only a further year ahead.

Deer Bield Buttress ranks as one of Dolphin's best half-dozen climbs, but it ought not to be taken as his monument. In a curious way, though, it imitates almost exactly something personal in his style of climbing, an athletic series of transfers and re-establishments between strenuous moves and delicate positions: at the same time it matches a less open aspect of his nature, lonely, separate, puritanical, uncompromising.

of the first pitch is to be laybacked and that the crack of the second pitch is strenuous. Then comes the 'first crux', an easy traverse right, some trying moves up a wall on the edge of a groove, and a brief overhanging section. Dolphin's note admits of no particular problem and the present guide follows him closely, though the description of the same pitch in the Girdle Traverse adds that the wall is climbed with much difficulty and that the overhanging groove which was found to allow a variation to the wall is much more strenuous again. We arrive at the fourth pitch, a pleasant inter-

THE LAKE DISTRICT **25** # North Crag Eliminate

by Neil Allinson

All men dream, and climbers more than most. When Diffs were hard, and Cloggy and the Alps did not exist, I built my dreams – hard, beyond real hope, frightening in their ambition.

Scafell C.B: 'Impregnable fortress' . . . 'Tremendously vertical cliffs'.
Castle Rock of Triermain, North Face: 'Fall by leader or second might leave him in an irrecoverable position' . . . 'Every type of seriousness' . . . 'Intimidating position' . . . 'Steep and dramatic'.
My heart trembled with ambition.

The dreams that drove me on are now long dulled by time; victory is but a memory. They were replaced by others, each in turn weaker and shallower than the last. Perhaps, in the harshness of success, fantasies take on the shape of reality; they need failure to retain their lure. My first dreams, of Castle Rock and C.B., were the best.

Castle Rock of Triermain. The very name is poetic, proud and challenging, and such is its attraction that it drew explorers of unequalled skill and courage: Birkett, Brown, Whillans, Drasdo, Ross, Bonington.

This impressive sugar loaf rises out of St John's Vale barely four miles from the hotch-potch climbing of Borrowdale, but here things are different. To the south the crag is easy and friendly and leans its slabs into the sunshine, but the face to the north is austere, made of sterner stuff . . . and big! Shimmering leaves of summer trees give way to fluting ribs and beetling walls of yellow and black rock. Up here goes the classic North Crag Eliminate, perhaps the best of Castle's harder routes.

The sun shone all that day and the south crag was a pleasant place to be. For us, staff and boys from an outdoor pursuits school, life was pretty good.

With a hard day's work behind them, my colleagues were beginning to talk of 'pub time', but my thoughts were on a different plane. A dream was ripe for plucking. Two hours of light was time enough for North Crag Eliminate: who would hold my ropes?

Now by nature I am a cautious man, but even cautious men can make mistakes. I

made mine that night. You don't run up N.C.E., you climb it; I was set for sprinting.

While Rob (Robin Eggleton, killed at Swanage a few weeks later when a freak wave swept him from the cliffs) acted out the labourer's role and uncoiled the gear, I followed the line of the route with an eye prepared for battle. The guidebook was in Rob's back pocket, the essentials in my head – big groove, pinnacle, yew tree, gangway with big flake – we could still make the pub.

I was never interested in speed climbing, but I was on form that night. The rock still warm, limpet P.A.s cleaved me and crag. I swarmed up with ease and with joy singing in my heart, a runner here and there, mainly for Rob, not me. I couldn't fail. The big groove was nothing but a big groove with holds everywhere except where there were none and even then it wasn't hard.

The next pitch annoyed me because it was short. I'd no sooner left Rob than I was telling him to look sharp and not to hang about, and for one of the great climbs of the Lake District this wasn't all that good.

Christ! It started now. I'd heard tales about the tree, but I hadn't heard that it was *this* thin. 'It's great, man. You climb this tree and pull over the overhang and you're on a fabulous ledge.' Climb this tree? I can climb trees as good as any, and better than most, but this was ridiculous. When I think of trees, I think of things with roots and branches to swing about in and be brave – not something like this, straight out of the womb of Hell with 150ft. of nothing to keep it from its mates below!

I put a runner (for me, not Rob) round the last branch worthy of the name and began a precarious balance upwards, hands hungry for rock always two feet beyond reach. A teeter on the topmost twig exposed my courage to the full, so I rejoined Rob to blow my nose.

Being the kind of sentimental fool who gives climbs a spirit of their own, I screwed up my eyes and sneered to show the contempt I held for that tree. Spitting, to complete the mirage of hardness, I began a more determined gyroscope. Right foot crucified on the nose cone and left foot balanced on a leaf, I began the slow and

Route North Crag Eliminate, Extremely Severe, 250ft.
Cliff Castle Rock in the Thirlmere Valley.
First Ascent H. Drasdo and D. Gray, September 1952; Variation Finish – D. Whillans and D. Roscoe, 1953.
Map Reference O.S. Lake District Tourist Map, 1–50,000 Sheet 90 (ref. 322197).
Guidebook F.R.C.C. *Eastern Crags* by E. Grindley.
Nearest Road A road junction at ref. 318197 on the B5322. A short walk through a plantation leads to the crag.
Distance and time from cliff ¼ mile/300ft. Allow 10 minutes.
Good Conditions The cliff is very steep and stays dry in all but the foulest weather in winter or summer.
Campsites and Bunkhouses Camping is not allowed in the Thirlmere catchment area and it is best to use the Keswick or Borrowdale sites. F.R.C.C. Hut, Salving House in Borrowdale and Youth Hostels in Borrowdale and Keswick.
Bibliography *Rope Boy* by Dennis Gray, Gollancz, London, 1970 (account of first ascent).

Above: The difficult pitch of North Crag Eliminate. The climber has just left the ramp and turned the corner and is hastening to a resting-place. *Climber: Ed Grindley*

delicate upwards stretch towards the sky, beyond which lay my overhang. Furtive fingers groping, I ached for a jug to beat the downward plunge of my courage. I got it! One hand, but worth a kingdom. With holds like these my footwork was immaculate, and a good pull had me swarming up to grapple on more equal terms with the belay ledge. But what a tree!

Now for it – the crux. I'd show this bloody climb the boss and no mistake.

Eyes picked out the details as memory told me what I needed to know. Nip on to gangway, traverse left to great flake, swing round corner on jugs, heave up, belay and away to the pub. Great!

But the nipping on wasn't that easy, and once on I wished to God that I wasn't.

Ian Roper

away from the comfort of Rob's happy grin, and wished desperately that I'd put a runner in the thin crack at the start of the gangway. This was really hard. What the hell was he grinning for?

Twice I moved to the very end of that rocky ripple some optimist had called a gangway, but here the whole crag turned a corner out of sight. It also overhung slightly, with a dreadful and unbroken certainty, to the scree 200ft. below. My error was complete. N.C.E. was a serious and demanding climb and I had approached it with a flippancy that was now all too obvious.

I had to move before gravity could wreak its vengeance. Rob had long since ceased to grin. I knew that Whillans had gone straight up from here; perhaps, like me, he couldn't find the damned flake, but no doubt he was fresh, and he was Whillans. I wasn't fresh, and only mortal, and above looked appalling. I *had* to turn that corner: to hell with the missing flake. My whole future could now be counted in seconds. With strength gone and fingers unzipping from what poor holds they had, I gathered up the little skill and courage left and began the blind moves round that awful corner.

I turned the corner and the rest seemed easy. We laughed at the top as we coiled the ropes and we went to the pub and we were very happy and a few weeks later Rob was dead and I went on to climb sometimes harder and sometimes easier things.

What for? To experience the very things I felt as I turned that corner: to escape the potted, computerized, cellophane existence which is ours in the twentieth century; to play at life's brinkmanship, find freedom and the right to accept a challenge, test oneself to the limit, plumb the extremes of emotion and exhilaration, brain, heart, eyes, strength and balance united in a single purpose – to live like a searchlight of survival searing through the total darkness of failure; to taste the stinging wine of danger, but to sweeten it with the total joy of existence.

That's what life is all about,

That's what dreams are made of.

Gangway? It was more like the road to Hades. Memory has me leaning backwards into space at an alarming angle; even allowing for an extension of the truth, it was a far from comfortable position. By now my fingers knew the awful truth: climbing hard for pleasure after a day of climbing hard for work is hardly in the interests of longevity. I moved further left,

THE LAKE DISTRICT 26 Extol

by Chris Bonington

Extol is rather like Whillans: direct, uncompromising and hard. It goes straight up the centre of Dove Crag, a cliff full of surprises. It's only 300ft. high and looks quite small as you approach it up the easy sweep of Dovedale in the Lake District's Eastern Fells; but once you are on it, it feels big and serious, a fierce contrast to the vista of undulating fells stretching away to the Pennines in the east. The climbing has a brutal character more like that of Wales than that of the Lakeland Fells.

Until 1953 there was only one route on the main face of the crag – Hangover, a line that broke through the overhangs, veering away from the centre of the face. Then, in '53, Brown and Whillans forced Dovedale Grooves off to the left of the crag, a line which, in common with many of their routes, wasn't repeated for some years. The rest of the crag was left alone and Harold Drasdo, guidebook writer for the area, was unwise enough to state that 'the central part of the main cliff presents a challenge unanswerable by unaided climbing'.

Whillans proved him wrong only a year later, when he and Colin Mortlock forced a route straight up the centre of the crag in the spring of 1960. Although Don has not produced as many new routes as Joe Brown, there is a unique quality about most of the lines he has chosen, a quality which stands the test of time; even today many of his routes have retained their reputation for unrelenting difficulty and seriousness. Don has often remarked that he could only become interested in good natural lines up a crag. Extol is one of his finest, and is certainly one of the best routes in the Lake District.

It was indicative of the increased tempo of climbing that it was only two years before Extol had its first repeat. John Lees and I climbed it in 1964, when it had already had several ascents, and it was certainly one of the most exacting climbs we had done. Even the first pitch, up the left-hand side of the slab, had some surprises in store for us. From the bottom it looked quite easy, a struggle through thick jungle up a shallow gully, but half-way up everything seemed to run out: the rock

was flaky and bulged unpleasantly, and we teetered up the chimney with shattered flakes in our hands and tufts of grass underfoot. It was a relief to reach the great shattered blocks at the top of pitch 3 of Hangover.

The wall now jutted above us, gently impending, sprouting moss and grass. It was first necessary to step down across it, swinging on a good jug to the start of a grassy ramp. The wall looked frightening, but went easily. The ramp also was deceptively easy and I ran out 50ft. of rope without really noticing it, to the foot of a steep, holdless groove, described as the crux in the account. There was a good thread immediately below it, and I delicately balanced up; there were no handholds, but the small sloping footholds were just sufficient, and as I reached a resting place on a small ledge I breathed a sigh of relief, for I thought we were over the worst, and began to congratulate myself for finding it quite straightforward; but I was to be sadly disillusioned.

When Whillans completed the climb the groove had been wet and therefore very hard indeed, but when we did it, it was completely dry and the upper part of the climb was by far the hardest. The difficulties just never seemed to come to an end. The line trended slightly to the right up an open groove, bristling with little overhangs and leading straight up to a huge roof. I was off balance the whole time, and though there were plenty of holds none of them seemed in the right place or set at the right angle. Each upwards move was unpleasantly committing, for I felt I should never be able to reverse it once I had started.

Another few tentative moves and I was braced below the roof, leaning backwards in undercuts. Where the hell was the piton mentioned in the description? Nasty little devils were whispering in my ear: 'Put one in now, the peg's been removed.'

But I ignored temptation – apart from anything else, I could not free a hand to hammer in a peg – and reached round the edge of the roof into a narrow V-groove; my fingers curled round a peg. Now at last the difficulties must be over.

A strenuous pull over the overhang, and I

Route Extol, Extremely Severe, 200ft.
Cliff Dove Crag, Dovedale.
First Ascent D. Whillans and C. Mortlock, April 1960.
Map Reference O.S. Lake District Tourist Map, 1–50,000 Sheet 90 (ref. 375108).
Guidebook F.R.C.C. *Eastern Crags* by E. Grindley.
Nearest Road Hartsop Hall at the end of a side road off the A592 (ref. 398120).
Distance and time from cliff 2 miles/1500ft. Allow 1½ hours.
Good Conditions Allow at least four dry summer days.
Bunkhouses and Campsites F.R.C.C. Hut, Beetham Cottage; camping at Hartsop Hall.
Bibliography C.C. Journal 1961: *Entity* by C. Mortlock (account of the first ascent).

Ian Hoper

Above: The first section of the big pitch of Extol. *Climber:*
Chris Bonington

worked my way up the groove, but after a few feet the holds vanished altogether and the only possibility seemed to be a line of narrow sloping ledges reaching out to the left. I cautiously balanced across, hands flat on the rock, the rope pulling persistently at my back, for I had now run out a hundred and thirty feet. The next move was for me the worst on the climb. One had to make a high step on to a narrow ledge, just round the corner, with no handholds at all. It was the kind of problem that would have been amusing on a boulder six feet from the deck; it just needed a bit of 'oomph' and confidence, but at that stage I was sadly deficient in both and unpleasantly aware of the exposure. I couldn't help thinking what it would be like dangling in mid-air at the end of the rope, especially as I had now run out of slings and would therefore be unable to prusik back on to the rock.

I teetered there for half-an-hour, calf muscles beginning to tremble, nerve running out, and then finally summoned up the courage and made the move – a one leg step up, hands outstretched on holdless rock for balance: another two or three thin moves and I was up, full of the wild elation of having stretched myself to the limit; of having climbed one of the most beautiful pitches I have ever encountered.

Above: A more distant shot of the big pitch of Extol with the climber at the foot of the steep groove. *Climber: Mike Mortimer*

NORTH WALES **27** **Gogarth**

by Ian McNaught-Davis

In North Wales it was the era of 'Crag X': the secret crag lying in permanent sunshine, grooves, cracks and overhangs abounding, with just enough holds to make every route an Extreme. At the mention of climbing, conversation in the pub would become guarded:

'What did you do today?'

'Oh, nothing much.' The eyes moved away evasively.

'Where did you go?'

'The weather was lousy.'

'Come on, you've found a secret crag.' Again that shifty look and a move through the crowd to simulate interest in the usual tedious darts match.

Everyone believed that somewhere the ultimate crag was being worked out. Known enthusiasts were grilled at every opportunity, eavesdroppers listened in on their conversations, and occasionally they were shadowed throughout the whole weekend. But as the latest crags were revealed, they turned out to be undersized and overgrown with everything from lichen to loose holds. The 'great' line on the cliff turned out to be 120ft. high, with an exquisite move at 60ft., and it had already had ten ascents. Even Brown was getting disenchanted with the inevitable two-hour flog over a boring moor to visit the latest discovery. Yet all the time the crag really did exist and you could drive right up to it.

Neither Al Alvarez nor myself were really in the game; we were tolerated by the groups more for conversational talents than for innovative boldness at the end of a rope. However, being on the fringe and not taking things perhaps quite as seriously as people thought we should, we were not trusted. We might let slip one word and before you could tie on a P.A., Brown would shake the crag till all the good routes fell like ripe plums, and it was felt that he already had his fair share. So I was quite surprised to find myself going along with Crew and Alvarez to pay the first of many visits to what later turned out to be the greatest sea-cliff in Britain – Craig Gogarth.

I had never previously enjoyed sea-cliff climbing. Cornwall and Swanage, although offering good climbing, seemed to lack some essential ingredient, and I could never understand either my own reluctance to visit them or the unwavering enthusiasm of their devotees. Maurice Herzog wrote that there are five main reasons for climbing mountains – beauty, muscle, risk, adventure and escape. Perhaps a simple test of the value of a crag can be made by applying these criteria. No one would deny that climbing in Cornwall offers beauty, muscle and risk. But adventure? I suppose so, for some. And escape? The climbs are too close to the tourists and too far from the hills for my liking. Yet the sea cliffs of Anglesey offer everything. Adventure comes from even the meanest sea-level girdle, and there is a curiously remote and mountain atmosphere. The climbs are too hard to become overcrowded today, and in some strange way the less than perfect rock adds an element of uncertainty that brings spice to the lowest grade climb.

The sea was calm that day as we roped up; the cliff was white, steep and looked good. The first crack pitch was just right, proving that we were still climbers despite all the booze and laziness. In a word, it was easy; so replete with holds that you could afford to show off your technique. Then Crew traversed across a steep wall, vanished round a corner and the whole climb began to adopt a more serious atmosphere. As the rope tightened, Al became more tense; bulging beneath his ancient, overtight anorak, and kitted up with slings and a hammer that he couldn't possibly use, he wobbled on to the first holds across the wall. For the next ten minutes, a steady stream of curses was broadcast to the desultory group of seagulls, parrots and other winged creatures that flap around the crag. Eventually a culminating 'Shi-i-i-t!' announced that he was either up or off. Since then I have always found that wall hard, and the shallow, overhanging chimney round the corner the easiest of places to fall from.

Crew was really beginning to enjoy himself. He was climbing in one of those moods when nothing seems difficult, with two performers who paid continuous vocal tribute to his expertise. No one fell off the next two pitches, so I suppose they are easy, and we soon found ourselves sunning

Route Gogarth, Hard Very Severe, 360ft.
Cliff Craig Gogarth, Holyhead Mountain, Anglesey.
First Ascent B. Ingle and M. Boysen, April 1964.
Map Reference O.S. Sheet 106, Anglesey, 1–50,000 Sheet 114 (ref. 213836).
Guidebooks West Col *Anglesey–Gogarth* by P. Crew; *Rock Climbing in Wales* by R. James.
Nearest Road Car Parks above South Stack Lighthouse (ref. 206822). A path leads across the moor to the north-east until it is possible to drop down to the end of the upper tier of cliffs on the flanks of Holyhead Mountain.
Distance and time from cliff 1 mile. Allow 20 minutes.
Good Conditions The route is climbable in all seasons and dries fairly quickly. It is not affected by tides.
Campsites and Bunkhouses Various bivouac spots in derelict buildings at South Stack and camping anywhere in the area.
Bibliography Mountaincraft 76 (1967): *The Story of a New Crag* by Ken Wilson (a history of the early explorations on the cliff).

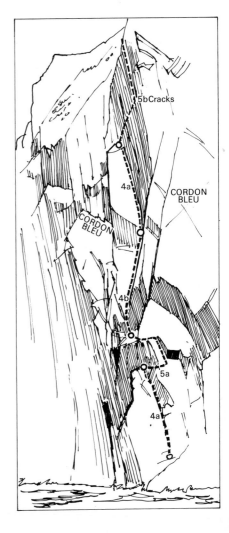

Left: The second pitch of Gogarth. This is one of the more difficult sections of the climb. The route traverses down and across this steep wall and then goes up to gain a corner. *Climber: John Kingston*

Right: The fourth pitch of Gogarth, a delightful Mild VS pitch as a preliminary to the difficult final wall. *Climber: John Kingston*

300ft. above the water while Pete hammered in a peg some way above. His style had changed from flamboyant to hesitant, so we judged that he had run into difficulties. The problem wasn't evident from below. There was an obvious broad ledge, a vertical wall and a delightful looking crack, obviously crammed with holds. We both relaxed, Al puffing at his pipe pretending to take care of the rope; it was clear that the climb was almost over.

The rope tightened and an incoherent screech from Pete sent the gulls flying and launched Al into one of the finest performances of his climbing career. As a sports car enthusiast he has brought to climbing some interesting innovative techniques, and during the next fifteen minutes he used them all. The wall turned out to be overhanging with sparse holds. Al used the Mickey Mouse Move to reduce the problem to insignificance. Hanging from his hands, he ran at the rock below him until the P.A. rubber softened; the minute he achieved maximum stick, he released the Dynamic Leap and became unstoppable. I lay back, awestruck, watching the puffs of smoke billowing from his toes as he kicked, surged and leapt in an astounding series of moves up the wall.

'Shi-i-i-t!' Once again the birds soared.

'Christ!' They swooped over his nodding head as he creamed over the overhang into the crack. It was the most fantastic thing I had ever seen.

The crack was vertical and the holds rattled like old bones, but these problems succumbed without grace to the masterly, muscular technique. Later, alone and unwatched, I followed, stepping carefully on the black rubber skid marks vulcanized on each hold right to the guano banks at the top.

Al summed it all up: 'Second ascent. Not really hard, you've just got to move fast when the rock gets loose.' I'm still trying to work that out.

Ken Wilson

Big Groove

by Richard Isherwood

Before there was a guidebook to Craig Gogarth, people were fairly secretive about the climbing there. I was fortunate, one day, to visit the cliff with Pete Crew and Dave Alcock, and I was shown where Gogarth went. I did the climb as second and surprised myself by leading the hard pitches. I was a bit frightened by the looseness of it all, and by the steepness, but memories of that kind fade very quickly between one weekend and the next.

So, next time I went to Anglesey, with Bob Keates, we thought we'd explore for ourselves; we didn't ask anyone about the climbs. We had overheard something about a line of big holds (Pentathol) going up to the right in the middle of the cliff, but that was about all. It was a hot, sunny day in June and the sea was encouragingly low and calm.

We traversed along at sea level and, sure enough, found some big holds leading up to the right. The line seemed to continue into a series of big corners in the upper part of the cliff. The first bit looked easy, but it proved steeper than I had expected. Our half-hour on the first thirty feet should have been a warning, but at least we were started, and I felt we were really on the crag. The rest of the pitch was easier, moving back to the left across a little slab with some beautifully sharp pockets, and up a groove to a ledge. The rock was black and smooth, spotted with yellow circles of lichen.

When Bob came up, we considered where to go next. A big crevasse led off to the left across an exposed slab into a corner full of bird droppings. This didn't look too hard, but neither did the other obvious line, straight up the big slabby corner above, which seemed to go almost to the top of the crag. We thought we'd go straight up.

Bob led off, grunting and clanking, over a little bulge to another ledge, where a small wall led to the main groove. We hadn't really noticed this wall from below, but it stopped him for so long that eventually he took a belay. After a bit more messing about, I got over it to a resting place. The slabby groove was nearly vertical. It didn't have too much in the back of it either.

I started bridging up the groove, but it was very thin and I had to work it out move by move, coming down for frequent rests at the bottom. That was when I first noticed all the scratches and little scars on the rock, where tiny flakes had broken off. Someone had clearly been here before. Not knowing much about Anglesey rock, I thought a lot of marks meant a lot of people. I guessed it to be a regular route, probably one of the easiest on the crag. I became annoyed with myself for having so much trouble. I tried the groove again, but still couldn't do it.

Eventually, looking round to take my mind off the problem, I saw the peg. It was up to the right in a very steep bit of crag which I hadn't really considered as a way up. However, there it was, and even if it was only someone's abseil point it was something to go for. Goaded by the thought that half the Saturday night darts players in Llanberis had probably been up before me, I made a big effort and got out of the groove, across a little slab and up to the peg.

The position was very impressive; it was all very steep below, right to the sea. It occurred to me that the tide must have come in. The peg, however, was clearly for ascent rather than retreat; it didn't look good enough to abseil from anyway. This groove was steep, but it did have a big crack in it, suggesting protection. So I stood in a sling, laybacked a bit and reached a semi-resting place in the crack. I tried to fix a runner, but decided to go on to a better resting place.

This was my mistake, and it made me very gripped. The crack was not too hard to climb, by wide bridging and jamming, but the apparent resting places were all useless. The bridging soon became so wide that staying in one place was very uncomfortable, and fixing a runner could have led to severe injury. So I had to keep going, further and further above the peg. The crack ended in a flake out to the right, very thin and wobbly-looking at its top and in a very exposed place with no obvious continuation. The alternatives were either to hand-traverse up this, or to get into a smooth little niche on the left, or to fall off. The last possibility was growing more

Route Big Groove, Extremely Severe, 340ft.
Cliff Craig Gogarth, Holyhead Mountain, Anglesey.
First Ascent P. Crew and D. Alcock, June 1966.
Map Reference O.S. Sheet 106, Anglesey, 1–50,000 Sheet 114 (ref. 213836).
Guidebooks West Col *Anglesey–Gogarth* by P. Crew; *Rock Climbing in Wales* by R. James.
Nearest Road The South Stack car parks.
Distance and time from cliff 1 mile. Allow 20 minutes.
Good Conditions Dries quickly. The climb is affected by tides. In calm weather it can usually be reached in all but the highest spring tides but if the sea is rough the climb is best avoided.
Campsites and Bunkhouses Camping and bivouacking at South Stack.

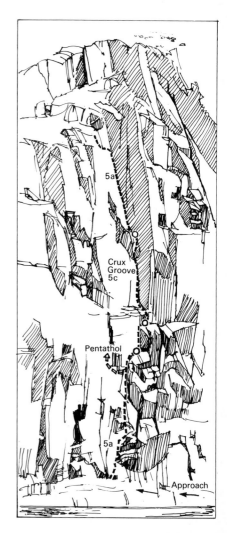

Ken Wilson

John Harwood

Above: The final pitch of Big Groove. *Climber: Chris Perry*

Right: The imposing central section of Craig Gogarth, one of the finest bits of rock in Wales. Big Groove goes up the centre, by the sunlit steps and overhanging walls, and then up the shadowy corner. The impressive impending wall on the right is climbed by The Citadel, Mammoth and Dinosaur, and the sunlit area on the left is taken by equally fine routes like Hypodermic, Pentathol and Jaborandi.

likely, second by second, so I managed to get out of my huge bridge and pulled into the niche, which was so steep that I nearly fell straight out of it.

When I'd stopped shaking, I found that I could rest precariously here. I was now over twenty feet from the last runner – much too far – and I couldn't fix any more where I was; but there were, I thought, some hammer marks in front of me, so I tried to put in a peg. The first of my two blade pegs bounced out and went whirring down into the sea. Fortunately, the second one went in, though only half-an-inch. That had to do. I was becoming very keen to leave the little niche. Reaching high, I found some holds on the next sloping ledge, bridged enormously again, and got into another desperate position. I stood on the eye of the peg, so briefly that it had no time to fall out, and made it to the ledge where I found three pegs. I was pleased that Bob took a long time to follow, even though it was getting late.

He led off up the next groove, which was very lichenous and thin, but full of digging marks. He moved quickly at first, but then he stuck.

'There aren't any more marks. I'm coming down.'

After some argument he belayed where he was and I climbed up to him. I hadn't seen into the groove, so I didn't know what sort of ledge he had – he never said much when he was climbing. I found him standing in some line slings which disappeared into the green, hairy lichen in the back of the groove. I tried not to think about his belays as I climbed over him – I preferred moving to standing where he was. Climbing up on his shoulders, I managed to reach some holds and got a runner in a strange hole in the rock. I went on to a huge jug-handle ledge which I thought must be loose and about to fall. Fortunately for Bob, it was solid; it led out of the groove into a grassy niche, occupied by two young cormorants.

Bob came up, very happy to be out of his slings, and chased the birds up the crag. He scared them so badly that they jumped off, fell two hundred feet in a flurry of wings and learned to fly just in time. He led on to the top in the sunset. It was ten o'clock. We had to be at work three hundred miles away by nine in the morning.

Note: Isherwood and Keates, intending to do Penta-thol, inadvertently followed the line of the considerably harder Big Groove, having climbed the common first pitch. They thereby made an unintentional second ascent. (*Editor.*)

Ken Wilson

NORTH WALES **29** **A Dream of White Horses**

by Royal Robbins

A Dream of White Horses – one of the great names, fulfilling Geoffrey Dutton's dictum that a name should tell you something about the climb or the way in which it was done. One glance at Leo Dickinson's masterful photograph explains it: that great sheet of spray leaping from the sea, rearing from excited waters like a splendid white stallion, and the two figures fastened to the rock just out of reach of the tormented foam. With its whimsical and romantic overtones, the name appeals perhaps more to the American climber than to his British counterpart. A Dream of White Horses. Drummond, who made the first ascent with Dave Pearce, has a talent for verbal imagery, for metaphorical and poetic phrasing. It's not surprising he should produce such a name. But still – A Dream of White Horses – five words! Turgid with subtle meanings. One of the few long names that succeeds. Although I knew nothing of the climb, because of that name and that sensational portrait by Dickinson, it was a route I had to do.

A chill, heavy wind flowed from the North Atlantic beneath dark masses of cloud, not rain laden, but casting showers on the soul, dampening the urge, as we stubbed in tight shoes across the barren, heather-covered crown of Holyhead Mountain. The green sea was agitated.

'Lots of white horses today,' said Whiz.

'Yea, verily,' I replied, suspended in heavy-handed mockery between Shakespeare, St Paul and Zane Grey, ' 'tis a right stam . . . *peed*.'

'You know, you shouldn't try to be clever,' my friend advised. He has my interests at heart. 'You lose points that way. You don't have any judgement about what's clever and what is merely cute. You'll probably put something silly like that in your next article. You're one who should never digress in your writing. The way you ought to write is this: open your story in the middle of a pitch, write about *that* for six pages, and close with the hero (*yourself*, presumably) ten feet higher. Then you might have an article that people would read.'

'Thanks, pal. I'll let you know what's wrong with you too, as soon as I figure it out.'

We were soon at the edge, and I was startled by how sharply the green and brown slope dipped towards the sea. There was a break in the clouds, and the sun flashed on olive sea, and rich, well-watered grass. From the west, a host of albino chargers rushed landward. It was a wind-and-light show and I looked forward to more. The approach was down steep, muddy slopes, the precipice just below. The signals of my mind flashed caution. This wasn't like grit, where one can relax when not actually climbing. On these sea cliffs you can't afford to stumble.

We came across ropes and packs left by others. Whiz was concerned. 'They'll be up to the same thing we are,' he assured me. 'They've just gone down to check out the wind and wet. We can beat them to the ab and get on the route first.'

He talked on in his unique and entertaining fashion, about the likely identity of the others, and about how they didn't know the code for they had parked in the wrong place. Then he digressed to other subjects: political scandals, rock music, architecture, climbing techniques, photography, and the organization and conduct of international mountaineering expeditions. Whiz is an authority on many things. Delivering quick, sometimes harsh judgements, dogmatic, impulsive, abrasive, but often accurate, he is very much alive. So alive that he seems, at times, about to burst with suppressed energy. A weaker man might have drowned that much painful life force in a sea of bitter. But Whiz has it pretty well harnessed. He is irritating at times, but inspires respect, and somehow even a certain affection. But he is a steamroller on the bumpy road of sentimentality, a wine crusher of maudlin grapes, impatient of weakness, scornful of incompetence, not over worried about people's feelings, a skilful and agile polemicist who usually wins. He comes on strong, and sometimes puts people off with his aggressiveness. But he is not impervious to a slight, or to a well-chosen phrase focused upon a weakness. And he is keenly sensitive to the nuances of status, insisting upon his turn in the front seat.

'Let's just whip over and set up the ab,'

Route A Dream of White Horses, Hard Very Severe, 430ft.
Cliff Wen Zawn, North Stack, Holyhead Mountain, Anglesey.
First Ascent E. Drummond and D. Pearce, October 1968.
Map Reference O.S. Sheet 106, Anglesey, 1–50,000 Sheet 114 (ref. 215837).
Guidebook West Col *Anglesey–Gogarth* by P. Crew.
Nearest Road The end of an unmetalled road (ref. 226835) leading from Holyhead Docks to the quarries on the north side of Holyhead Mountain. A track leads over the hill to North Stack.
Distance and time from cliff ½ mile/300ft. Allow 15 minutes.
Good Conditions Dries quickly in all but the coldest weather. At low tide the lower pitch should be added. The Zawn is a wind funnel and this can add extra difficulty to the climbing.
Campsites and Bunkhouses Camping and bivouacking by the North Stack quarries or at the South Stack cafe.

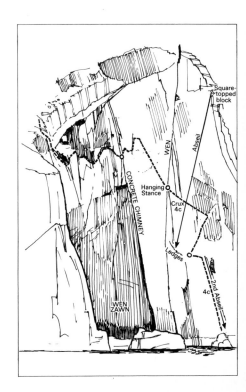

Bob Allen

Left: The long second pitch of The Dream of White Horses. The climber is in the middle of a series of delicate moves leading into Wen. *Climber: Marjorie Allen*

said Whiz, tripping off. But first I wanted to look at the route, so I scrambled down the steep slope. Four climbers were coming up.

'What are you going to climb?' one shouted through the wind.

'White Horses,' I threw back.

'That's what they're doing,' he replied, indicating two figures on the wall, half-way between water and grass. I continued down to a promontory which curved and faced the climb across an impatient, foaming gap. Sea spray was dashing against the wall. What a picture! What a time to be out of film!

Whiz was waving wildly over the shoulder of the slab. I surmised that he desired my presence. I knew he would be thinking: 'We mustn't let those "nods" get ahead of us.' (Except for occasional uses of 'twit' or 'freddie', Whiz, to express disdain, favours words starting with 'n' sounds, words like 'nod', 'gnome', 'nurd', 'nob', 'nibbler', etc.)

I arrived to find him taking great care setting up the 'ab ancs'. A close friend had recently been killed abseiling, and Whiz didn't want to go the same way. Nor did I.

'This is a dangerous place,' I said, clipping to the 11 mm runner he had looped over a sturdy block and backed up with two more anchors.

We were now directly above the copulating waters. Whiz threaded the ropes through his brass figure-eight, and was off. The place provoked in me the same feeling I get descending to the notch of the Lost Arrow Spire in Yosemite, with the prospect of falling into the Arrow Chimney. In such places, the recurrent theme of abseiling, that one's eggs are all in a single basket, comes home with special force prompted by the hideous aspect of what one would fall *into*.

I dulfered to Whiz who was waiting on a narrow, irregular ledge, just the sort that someone, someday, will fall off. 'Just look,' he said in a jocular tone, 'at that tangled and barking ocean.' I missed the allusion to Yeats, but his metaphors seemed *nearly* right. The route properly started 70ft. lower, but as the water was only 60ft. down we had to forego the pleasures of the first pitch. We were on Wen Slab. 'Slab' in this case doesn't mean low angle, for the rock averages about 80°, and is vertical or overhanging in many places. It is a slab in that it is a single slice of compact rock, one wall of a zawn. A zawn is a yawn in a sea cliff, the bottom filled with water.

The outside wall of this zawn is a promontory which juts into the sea and curves towards the south, a sort of pillar the top of which is directly across from, and half-way up, Wen Slab. This pillar is a natural bridge. The waters in their ebb and flow have surgically cut a tunnel through the pillar in an attempt to isolate it and transform it into a sea stack.

Through this tunnel the waters burbled and boiled, forming a counterpoint to the larger boiling flow from the natural mouth into the ocean. I was struck by the savagery of the place, the frothing and sucking, the wind blowing, spindrift flying, the water churning and surging on to the cliff, and the surges breaking and leaping up the wall to hang like lace curtains while slipping back into the sea. Aphrodite, they say, was born of sea foam. But this was a rough sort of love, this mating of water with rock. It was elemental, and affected me as do thunder-storms or raging blizzards. I loved the fearful violence of it. In the clash and dash of water, the thundering and pounding, the crashing, breaking din, there was great power, but no evil. It gave pleasure similar to boulder trundling, but touched one's emotions at a deeper level.

I turned my back to the sea and started climbing, moving vertically, following a crack on the right side of the slab. It was steep, but not difficult. All the same, I slotted a wedge, and continued up on toes and fingers. The rock there is good for climbing: it doesn't have holds everywhere, but might have holds anywhere. In this respect it is like the rock in the Lakes or the Welsh mountains, but it isn't granite. Such rock offers very good face climbing, but is comparatively rare in the United States. Most of the climbing in the U.S.A. is on 'young' granite or sandstone, and generally follows crack systems. But even in the Shawangunks, where there are few vertical cracks, the complexity of this sort of British rock is lacking. In the Shawangunks there is a certain predictability about what lies ahead. This is not true of places like Craig Gogarth, a fissirostral sea cliff, where it is very difficult to tell from fifty feet away whether a passage is easy or impossible. Or from even closer than that.

I was 40ft. above Whiz. At that point the route traverses left two-and-a-half pitches straight off the cliff. I started, aiming for a crack 50ft. away. There was nothing obvious. A solution had to be found for every foot of progress. The route wasn't going to yield to an aggressive approach. I advanced, tentatively, and the rock revealed some of its secrets. I made further advances, careful but firm. And the rock again yielded, unfolding more, exciting me, raising my hopes. There was a bit of a struggle, a setback, a renewed onslaught, and I broke through, confident now and eager for success. But I was stopped cold. False hopes; the damning disappointment of hoping too soon. The next bit was difficult. Should I take a chance and push forward? No, I would have to find the key. I was almost ready to give up. I considered it. But what would Whiz think when I admitted that I couldn't handle this bitch?

Where *was* the fire? It was cold on the shady slab, with the constant cold wind and the water running down over the holds. The climb was proving cold and contemptible, leading me on, acting easy, then closing the door in my face. Rebuffed, I knocked again. My eyes scanned the rock, noting every detail. I could take a high line or a low one in an effort to traverse to good jugs and a crack. I chose the low way and descended a bit, fingers feeling the rock, sensitive to every minute variation of texture and contour. I had to be careful, for I was now committed. There was an awkward piece before reaching the crack. I had to restrain myself, to hold back from lunging to escape the tension. But I was getting sick and tired of fiddling around. Finally I found the key and moved into the crack, and up a bit, to a belay where I was to spend the next hour suspended from two chocks and a spike.

I took in the rope. 'O.K. Come on up.'

Left: The second pitch of The Dream of White Horses during the first ascent. *Climbers: Ed Drummond and Dave Pearce*

Above: The impressive final pitch which traverses round the crumbling back wall of Wen Zawn. *Climber: Trevor Jones*

Bob Allen

He came up neatly, not fast, but controlled and competent, and soon reached me.

'Found that troublesome, did you?' he asked.

'Rather,' I admitted. 'But good. Real rock-climbing.'

'I led that last time,' he continued, 'and I dare say I found it a sight easier than you did.'

'That's nice,' I responded. 'That's why I come to Britain, you know, to ease the inferiority feelings of you D team men.' Whiz always insists he's strictly D team. He's kind enough to classify me as B, so it greatly pleases him when he climbs better than I do.

'Well, there's a lot to be said for age and experience,' said Whiz, encouragingly. 'But I've yet to learn what it is.'

Leaving these words of 'whizdom' to rattle around my head, the mountain Herr grabbed the next lead. It was a classic. I longed for my camera. Whiz followed a flake which ran up left, offering good grips, but little for the feet except friction. It was vigorous climbing, different from my tippy-toe balance lead. The protection wasn't brilliant, but he made quick work of it, and then took a long while arranging his belay anchors. I like that sort of care.

I followed the flake up and then descended a bit to Whiz's belay and took a gander at the last pitch. I would not have guessed it went *that* way. It looked like rubble. But not so much rubble, because rubble implies angularity; it was more like Dalinian rubble, rubble gone soft like Dali's watches, rubble which had melted and then refrozen, a great dripping morass of melting vanilla ice-cream refrozen in its slopping and plopping descent into the sea. Frozen magically hard. It was uncanny the way some force had cemented those sand grains. First it was sand, then sandstone, and then it was heated and squeezed into super-sand-stone: quartzite. Picture the outer walls of a sandcastle which a wave has overrun. The soaked edifice crumbles and melts, but in this case it was caught in mid-melt and rehardened into an extremely durable battlement.

The traverse proved a rare treat. I climbed slowly, savouring it. Whiz gave me pointers on double rope technique. Above, the rock overhung, forcing a leftward passage. It overhung below as well, so much so that an unroped climber, slipping from the traverse, would fall 200ft. directly into the water and perhaps escape serious injury (!?). I finished in dazzling sunshine, hot in a heavy sweater. Before disappearing up the grass to a belay niche, I looked back along the double ropes across the crumbling wall to Whiz, who had been enjoying my enjoyment of the rock. It was spectacular, and the rays bouncing off the white rock made me squint. White rock. White horses. This route will be a classic.

Whiz walked up the green hill and took off the rope. We coiled it and packed our gear.

'Let's go,' said Whiz, his eyes suddenly lighting up with boyish enthusiasm. 'I know a great place near here for trundling.'

We rushed off, eager for more tumult, forgetting in our haste to retrieve the runner and karabiner we had left for the dreadful abseil.

Leo Dickinson

109

by Nick Estcourt

Around the time when the Gogarth new-route bonanza was just getting under way, but information was still in very short supply, I paid my first visit to Anglesey. Only having the vaguest idea of the whereabouts of the crag, let alone any routes, I drove to South Stack car-park and started looking. Naturally enough, the first thing I did was examine the South Stack cliffs, and of course the first view I got was of the Mousetrap zawn from the bottom of the steps leading to the South Stack lighthouse.

In those days, it was the sort of thing no one would have dreamt of climbing: we 'knew' that anything looking like Mousetrap was for looking at only. Most of all, it is the texture of the crag that is unique: alternate layers of soft and hard rock, the softer rock eroded away by wind and sea so that the folds and faults are shown in high relief. This structure was like nothing else I'd seen anywhere. The veins of hard rock had been bent and crumpled so as to resemble corrugated paper more than rock. Along each bend and fold in the strata stood rows of seagulls; great white streaks of guano hung down from the more crowded areas. From the steps, the line of weakness followed by Mousetrap is invisible, and it appeared that the cliff would be both difficult and unpleasant to climb.

Several years later, when Pete Crew and Joe Brown did a route up this cliff, I was as surprised and impressed as most people. The combination of horrifying first-ascent photos and gossip about looseness all helped to keep people away from the route. Although the South Stack crags are covered in climbs now, Mousetrap represented a breakthrough at the time it was done. It was followed by a brief period when people positively revelled in looseness: instead of boasting about how good or how hard a route might be, they dwelt on how loose and how serious it was.

Now, five or six years later, some of the routes seem quite different, much more friendly, and not really all that loose. One wonders how much this is due to the cleaning up of the routes and how much to the changing attitudes of the climbers. Obviously a bit of both.

My first direct confrontation with Mouse-trap itself came on a warm Sunday in 1971. Other teams were moving unobtrusively towards the zawn and, sensing competition, Ken Wilson and I raced down the lighthouse steps to beat them to the start. The result was six panting climbers arriving at the foot of the climb in quick succession. There was some feverish uncoiling of ropes. Brushing aside my claims on the first pitch, Ken launched himself on to the rock and claimed first place in the queue. A crafty move, this, as he later admitted, for though the first pitch appears horrifying, leading it leaves the fourth pitch, the crux, to the other climber. Ken's rapid start slowed considerably as he climbed up to the hard section. The problem is to descend a dusty scoop and make a big step across a vertical wall to gain some unique curving chimneys. The traverse is protected by a peg, placed by Brown on the first ascent. This is welcome because a fall would result in an exciting pendulum and, apart from the peg, the protection is not too good. Having reached it, one has to wriggle up the first chimney until it seems best to swing dramatically out and round into the next one. The climbing isn't very hard, but the rock looks rather dubious and one has to be very careful to distribute one's weight in case one of the holds snaps unexpectedly. Ken worked up these chimneys and, after some apelike swings on gargoyles, disappeared from view. With the second party hard on my heels, I followed. I found that the stance was an unexpectedly large ledge, which was gratifying because the next pitch looked hard. It took several minutes to work up the courage to make the initial pull on a very wobbly handhold. Having done that, I climbed up a very steep but juggy wall and gained the bottom of another dusty scoop, this time a vertical one, hemmed in by an overhanging rib. On the first ascent, Pete Crew climbed directly up this scoop, but Brown, seconding, decided to have a look round the overhanging rib and discovered that by swinging round it was possible to climb easily up some enormous holds. I fixed a runner on Crew's peg in the scoop and then made the dramatic swing round the rib. Sure enough, there were the holds and the next 20ft. was

Route Mousetrap, Hard Very Severe, 420ft.
Cliff Mousetrap Zawn, South Stack, Holyhead, Anglesey.
First Ascent J. Brown and P. Crew, October 1966.
Map Reference O.S. Sheet 106, Anglesey, 1–50,000 Sheet 114 (ref. 203823).
Guidebooks West Col *Anglesey–Gogarth* by P. Crew; *Rock Climbing in Wales* by R. James.
Nearest Road The South Stack car parks. At high tide abseil down the spur between Mousetrap Zawn and Red Wall and at low tide descend to the Zawn from the Lighthouse steps. The cliff should be avoided during the nesting season (Feb.–August).
Distance and time from cliff 100 yds. Allow 1 minute.
Campsites and Bunkhouses Campsites and bivouacs by the South Stack car parks.
Bibliography C.C. Journal 1968: *The Boom Years* by Ken Wilson (brief reference to first ascent).

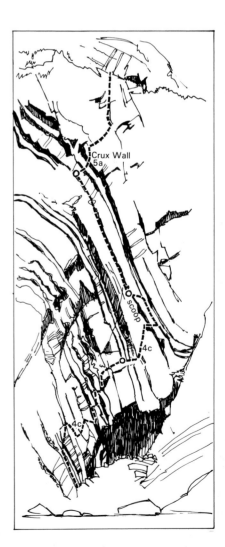

Ken Wilson

really incredible country, more like a structure put in a zoo to amuse monkeys than rock: vertical or overhanging rock with great hollows several feet deep, providing hand and footholds. Then, after a quick move back left, you arrive at a small stance near the bottom of the slab. Ken rushed past and bounded up the slab, his Adam's apple and jaws proclaiming the quality of the route. After about 100ft., at the top of the slab, he spent some time getting a belay fixed, mumbling about the lack of good anchors, and when I joined him I had to admit that I had seen safer places. The ledge was fairly sizeable, but the weird collection of flakes and loose pegs he had assembled looked decidedly spooky. This was unnerving, because the next pitch looked very steep and hard. A red wall towers above the slab, and there appeared to be few good places to rest for about 40 ft. I set off. Ken was whimpering about runners so I got some on, but I was getting more engrossed in the climbing which was now really solid and steep. The compact red rock of the South Stack cliffs is usually the best, although the holds are less frequent and smaller than elsewhere. That was what it was like here and it made for a fine pitch, completely different in character to the lower section. Bold finger pulls and swings were in order, whereas no such rashness could be contemplated below. Just as my arms were beginning to feel the strain, the wall eased off into another dusty groove, which soon steepened up and forced me to make some energetic laybacking and bridging moves. But nothing was too hard, the position was superb and the sun warm, and I completed the pitch without mishap. I lazed in the sun while Ken came up. Occasionally there would be a yell of delight as he did one of the good moves. A few minutes later we were both jumping up and down with delight, amazed at how good a climb it was. The following party arrived almost at once and joined in the raving. Mousetrap may not be the fearsome monster it was once thought to be, but it is certainly one of the great classics of Wales.

by Les Holliwell

Few climbs warrant the pretentious appellation 'The', yet here it is apt. A groove gouged out by geological accident to inspire and dominate a major crag, it does not disappoint.

Llech Ddu, a huge, gable-shaped crag, is situated at the head of the remote Cwm Llafar. The setting is impressively rugged, in striking contrast to the undulating green hills that encompass the cwm. This is a lonely place, away from the thronged, sun-blessed cliffs at the road-side. Uninviting and even repulsive on first acquaintance, it is one of the least known Welsh crags. Heavily clad in vegetation, invariably wet, and bristling with mossy overhangs, it demands respect. The Groove, magnificent and unmistakable, cleaves the highest and most continuous buttress.

How 'Mo' Anthoine and Ian Campbell must have enthused at the prospect of this superb route! Any new climb is a unique challenge, but few can have equalled this five-day epic for suspense and excitement. Loose rock, copious vegetation and the inevitable wet constituted infinitely more serious hazards than the technical difficulties involved. Nowadays, even for those with an intimate knowledge of the cliff, it is difficult to imagine the conditions that then prevailed. This was only the second climb to tackle the awesome central section of the cliff; it was also considerably harder than the classic Central Route, itself a milestone in the crag's development. Beyond the third pitch retreat is far from easy, and the commitment made by a team that had little knowledge of what lay ahead must have been considerable. Modern protection, familiarity, and the network of harder routes in the vicinity, enable us now to make a dispassionate assessment. It is a route of modest technical involvement, qualifying for its grade by virtue of its length, excellence and position, a combination seldom surpassed.

The approach is best made from Gerlan, above Bethesda. An ill-defined path from the local waterworks wends its way through small fields typically walled with stone. Soon, these give way to open country, and a more distinct track contours the broad, glaciated valley above Afon Llafar. The going is comfortable and there is a rare peace to imbibe. Rounding a bend, one is suddenly confronted with the crag. Denied the sun, its northern aspect is black and forbidding. The Groove is seen to the right of centre; it takes the Pinnacle, a huge flake which is not immediately recognizable as such.

The initial pitch is a slim 8oft. groove leading to a broad terrace and a comforting tree belay. It has intrinsic merit, but is really only a means to an end. It is, however, deceptively steep and technically more demanding than appearances might suggest. The crux, at two-thirds height, is protected by a peg that few will spurn. Above the terrace is an open groove, lying back, or so it seems: but this is yet another deception. The groove is invariably wet and not well protected. It constitutes the crux in all but perfect conditions. Delicate bridging leads to a bulge which is awkward to surmount. At fifty feet an uncomfortable belay niche is reached, beneath an overhang. Descending slightly to a line of flaky jugs, an exposed traverse of forty feet gives access to the base of The Groove, which is ascended for a few feet. The belay, in slings poised above the void, is in a position such that a nagging feeling of insecurity is hard to suppress. The magnificent line of The Groove rises above for 13oft. It has all the ingredients essential to make a good climb great – it's a masterpiece. Clean, sound, nowhere desperate, it nevertheless leaves the outcome always in doubt, with each move apparently more difficult than those below. The final section of the pitch lies back a little and a well-appointed grassy belay platform on the left edge contrasts perfectly with the enclosed groove. The final steep wall is climbed on good holds, and manages to minimize the inevitable anti-climax. A wide crack above is uninviting.

The interest is well maintained throughout, and the line is natural, with no easier options even from the broader terrace. This climb deserves wide acclaim and is definitely a 'must' for the potential hardman and competent 'plum-bagger' alike.

Route The Groove, Extremely Severe, 300ft.
Cliff Llech Ddu, Carnedd Dafydd.
First Ascent J. Anthoine and I. Campbell, 1961.
Map Reference O.S. Tourist Map to Snowdonia, 1–50,000 Sheet 115 (ref. 665636).
Guidebook C.C. *Carneddau* by L. R. Holliwell.
Nearest Road A minor road on the south side of Gerlan above Bethesda (ref. 634662). Follow the road past a farm and work up through marshy fields to Cwm Llafar.
Distance and time from cliff 2 miles/1000ft. Allow 1 hour.
Good Conditions Allow several days of dry summer weather.
Campsites and Bunkhouses Camping and bivouacs below the cliff or near Ogwen. Huts in the Ogwen Valley or the Llanberis Pass.

Left: The second pitch of The Groove. *Climber: Laurie Holliwell*

Right: The main pitch of The Groove seen from the ledge at the top of the first pitch. The awe-inspiring Great Arête, first climbed by Ed Drummond and Ben Campbell-Kelly dominates the scene. *Climber: Al Wright*

Les Holliwell

Tony Riley

NORTH WALES 32 Cenotaph Corner

by Peter Crew

Standing at Pont-y-Gromlech, the focal point of Llanberis Pass, it seems as if you are completely surrounded by crags. Probably the most impressive, on account of its steep and clean-cut features, is Dinas-y-Gromlech, in the centre of which is a huge smooth corner. This is Cenotaph Corner, or *the* Corner as it is more familiarly known to Welsh *habitués*, probably the best known climb in Wales if not the whole of Britain. It is a paradox typical of climbing that a single pitch of 120ft., on a 200ft. crag only ten minutes' walk from the road, is one of the most important routes in a major climbing area. For the past twenty years, since its first ascent by Joe Brown, Cenotaph Corner has occupied a unique place in Welsh climbing; even today it is still regarded as the yardstick by which an up-and-coming young climber measures his progress.

Climbing in the Pass is very recent, starting in the 1940s with Menlove Edwards. Little is known about early attempts on the Corner, though many must have been tempted by its obvious attractions. Peter Harding and his friends were turned back from the first hard section at 20ft. in the late forties. In his monumental guide to Llanberis Pass in 1950, Harding gives dire warnings of things to come: 'The Cenotaph Corner is still an unclimbed gap, throwing out its challenge. There is no doubt that, with sufficient ironmongery and few scruples, this corner could be ascended. The last word is chosen specially. Some day the call will prove too strong and the Cenotaph will lose much of its virtue.'

The first ascent of Cenotaph Corner marked the beginning of Joe Brown's career and the start of a new era in the history of British rock-climbing. Brown describes an attempt and the eventual ascent in *The Hard Years*, with a minimum of fuss and emotion – probably the way he climbed the route. On his first (?) attempt he reached the niche, using some five pegs for protection and dropping a peg hammer on to his unfortunate second. The pegs were removed and his second lived to tell the tale. On the actual ascent it seems that the biggest problem was placing a good peg in, or above, the niche; although

Brown states that the peg remained there for eight years, Mike Harris quite clearly describes placing the pegs on his ascent in 1958. It appears in fact that Brown used four pegs on the first ascent, in two groups of two; these were quickly rationalized on subsequent ascents to the standard two pegs. It would be interesting to know whether Harding and his contemporaries considered that the Corner had been 'ascended' or 'climbed'.

Cenotaph was probably the original 'last great problem' and there is little doubt that its ascent by a young and unknown working-class climber caused a stir amongst the establishment. Certainly Cenotaph was one of the cornerstones of the huge myth which surrounded the activities of Brown and the Rock and Ice for the next eight years or so. The early leads of the Corner were all made by Rock and Ice members, the first by an outsider probably being that by Hugh Banner. Even in 1959, the golden year when the youth of the next generation cut their teeth on Brown's myth, it was still possible, sitting by the camp fire in the Grochan field, to enumerate the ascents and the names of those who had made them!

Despite all the tremendous developments in climbing during the past twenty years, Cenotaph still holds a certain mystery and fascination for climbers of all types. It is the ultimate ambition of the climber in his thirties who never quite made it; it is still an almost essential prerequisite in the repertoire of any young hard man. The Corner must have had more ascents than any other climb of comparable grade; it has been climbed in rain, sleet and snow and/or in boots or nails quite regularly; it has been soloed several times and is frequently claimed to have been climbed 'without' the pegs – whatever that may mean. This is the kind of treatment reserved for only the greatest of climbs!

Looked at clinically, without any of the attendant myth and background, the climb itself is a little disappointing – indeed, many routes of the same length and similar features are dismissed as mere outcrop climbs!

The foot of the Corner is reached by

Route Cenotaph Corner, Extremely Severe, 120 ft.
Cliff Dinas-y-Gromlech, Llanberis Pass.
First Ascent J. Brown and D. Belshaw, August 1952.
Map Reference O.S. Tourist Map to Snowdonia, 1–50,000 Sheet 115 (ref. 630570).
Guidebooks C.C. *Llanberis North* by P. Hatton; *Rock Climbing in Wales* by R. James.
Nearest Road The A4086 at Pont-y-Gromlech (ref. 630566).
Distance and time from cliff ¼ mile/700 ft. Allow 20 minutes.
Good Conditions The climb is a drain and needs a day or two to come into condition after heavy rain.
Campsites and Bunkhouses Good campsites, bivouac boulders and huts in the Llanberis Pass.
Bibliography *The Hard Years* by Joe Brown, Gollancz, London, 1967 (account of first ascent); *Rock Climbers in Action in Snowdonia*, Secker and Warburg, London, 1966 by Cleare and Smythe; C.C. Journal 1959: *Revelations* by Mike Harris (early ascent).

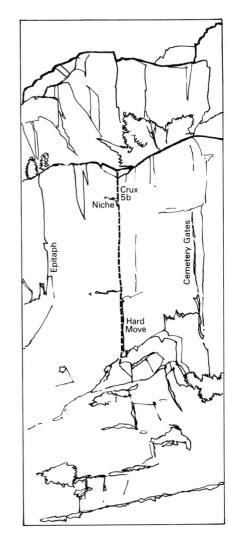

John Cleare

100ft. or so of simple scrambling. The sloping area of bare rock, which was once a series of grassy ledges sporting two or three trees, is a grim reminder of the number of feet which must have passed this way. Looked at from this angle the walls soar vertically upwards, seemingly impossibly smooth – second men watching their leaders' progress must beware of neck cricks. Closer inspection reveals the unique character of Cromlech rock – the sharp-edged pocket-holds in abundance, and an ample corner crack for jams and runners.

The features of the climb revolve around the width of this corner crack. At 20ft. it closes briefly, forcing a dynamic move to good holds above – this is where many attempts fail and there is often a raggle-taggle of slings obscuring the best thread runner. The first 70ft. or so are fairly straightforward – move up, find the best resting position, relax, runner on and start again. A common tendency is to go too fast, using up strength vital for the upper sections. In the middle of the pitch is an excellent resting place, providing you like standing on one foot. (If you are not happy here, don't do the Girdle Traverse which uses this foothold as a stance.)

Above is the wide section of the crack, some 20ft. high, closing at the famous niche. In the early days the key to the climb was the position of the large chockstone. If this was low in the crack, getting into the niche was desperate, but for many years now the stone has been high enough to stand on whilst finding the crucial undercut finger-hold. If the peg is not in position, one can savour the difficulty of the first ascent – normally it is grabbed with little compunction and it must have saved many a possible fall from this point. The niche is a unique 'resting' place, with left cheek and right foot in opposition and a view straight down between your legs to a critical second man.

Above, the crack is very thin for 10ft. or so and strenuous laybacking and bridging follow, helped by varying degrees of pulling on the pegs, to a standing position one move below the top. This is where fingers start to uncurl as the courage is plucked up for the final lunge for the jugs on the left and the safety of the horizontal world above.

Two views of Cenotaph Corner. The left-hand photo shows the leader on the comparatively straightforward middle section of the route, and the right-hand shot catches him on the crux moves above the niche. *Climber: Rusty Baillie*

John Cleare

NORTH WALES **33** **Diagonal**

by Brian Wyvill

In Welsh climbing circles, fashion dictates not only the amount of knee exposed in wearing breeches, but also the popularity of different cliffs and areas. The Llanberis Pass, which started to become popular in the early thirties, presents two sets of cliffs, each with its own character and history. For me, the sombre nature of the crags on the south side invests them with an enticing mystique which I cannot resist.

Nearest to the road is Dinas Mot, 'Fortress of Mot', guarding the northern tip of Crib Goch's north ridge. Its dripping wings hang open, drawing the eye to the magnificent central 'Nose', a smooth trapezoid slab jutting out between the overhanging bulk of the wings as though shaped, tilted and propped against the mountainside by some Olympian geometrician. At first sight, the uniform purity of this massive slab is broken by only one line of weakness, a straight and bold groove up the centre. This line, the Nose Direct, was first climbed by C. F. Kirkus in 1930.

In 1931 came two more difficult and serious routes: Western Slabs, up the slabs to the left of the gully separating them from the west wing, and West Rib, a vague weakness nearer the cliff's centre.

Activity on the cliff then relaxed until Arthur Birtwistle and G. F. Parkinson set off to repeat West Rib in August 1938. Having only Kirkus's vague route description, they climbed a slanting line from left to right across the centre of the Nose, unwittingly creating Diagonal. The route had a blatant boldness, full of character and technicalities: a marvellous balance climb, a wandering line hopefully challenging blank slabs, untainted by crack or terrace. Every foot of ascent is hard-bought from the cliff in exchange for technique.

Diagonal was put up during an era of balance climbing and it epitomizes the period. Long, poorly-protected run-outs and technical difficulties make it a good HVS even by modern standards; it shows clearly what commitment on a climb is all about. In more recent times, its purity and protectionless character have made it a soloist's prize.

My own encounter with Diagonal came in 1972. One warm June morning, I emerged from beneath the Mot boulder to find the sun, a rare visitor to this north-facing crag, full on the face. The Nose was illuminated in all its inviting splendour, and I was able to trace the line of Diagonal. A few prominent features stuck out from the surrounding expanse of bald slabs, the most eye-catching being a rectangular block, about 15ft. high, glued securely to the centre of the face. Its right-hand edge has been cut acutely to produce a bottomless 'V' chimney, a possible stumbling block to a climber.

Having roused my companion Jon Britten, an American, we made for the start, a devious rightwards traverse from the left corner of the crag. Inexperience led me to the wrong traverse line, above the undercut base of the Nose. An exciting half-hour of tenuous moves on widely spaced and minute holds brought me to a recess beneath a wet overhang, twenty feet below the bottomless chimney. Jon soon joined me on this poor excuse for a stance, mumbling about runners to protect seconds on a traverse. He viewed the chimney with trepidation.

There are two ways of reaching it: straight up to the left of the overhanging base of the block, then round below it across a blank slab; or over to the right – not so hard, but with poorer protection – entering the chimney with a 'long reach on a good flake'. Jon chose the latter. Twenty feet up, he stopped to explain in his own Wild West way that he had no protection, that he was gripped out of his mind, and that he couldn't reverse what he had just climbed. I shouted encouragement, and after some colourful idiomatic Americanisms he entered the chimney by a peculiar move, wormed his way up and disappeared left to a belay at the top of the block.

I'm ashamed to say my performance on this pitch was of dubious worth. Every move seemed harder than the last, and I couldn't gain entry to the chimney by Jon's peculiar method. Jon's comments on my parentage and nationality didn't help, but a healthy yank (forgive the pun) on the rope took me into the chimney. I was angry, desperate and scared, but fortunately the chimney succumbed to my efforts at

Route Diagonal, Hard Very Severe, 240ft.
Cliff Dinas Mot, Llanberis Pass.
First Ascent A. Birtwhistle and G. F. Parkinson, August 1938; Direct Finish – P. R. J. Harding and A. J. J. Moulam, May 1946; soloed by J. Griffin, c. 1954.
Map Reference O.S. Tourist Map to Snowdonia, 1–50,000 Sheet 115 (ref. 627564).
Guidebooks C.C. *Cwm Glas* by P. Crew and I. Roper; *Rock Climbing in Snowdonia* by R. James.
Nearest Road The A4086 at Pont-y-Gromlech (ref. 630566).
Distance and time from cliff ¼ mile/300ft. Allow 10 minutes.
Good Conditions Although the cliff drains quickly it can stay rather greasy in cold weather. Warm or windy conditions are needed to dry the cliff quickly after rain.
Campsites and Bunkhouses There is a good bivouac boulder below the cliff. Camping, huts and bivouacs in the Llanberis Pass.
Bibliography Cambridge Mountaineering, 1961: *Ten Minute Interval* by Stuart Crampin.

Ken Wilson

Ken Wilson

wide bridging and a few moments later I was with Jon on a neat little stance. It was up to me to find a way off. I prevaricated by pointing out a figure thrutching up Cenotaph Corner, and musing on my own 'historic' ascent when I managed to get off route! But Jon was not to be distracted, and I was goaded into action.

Over to the right was a line of vague footholds. Jon gripped the rope encouragingly, squatting quietly on the stance like a poorly-fed budgie. The valley, too, had gone quiet; the atmosphere was still and tense, the silence almost solid. I started the traverse. It was only a few feet, but every movement of a limb unbalanced the others. Reaching a rest position at the base of a shallow scoop, I paused to try and place one of our precious nuts at foot level without bending down. Eventually, after a series of strange contortions, I engineered it into position. To prevent the nut being lifted out, I had to keep the rope slack, thus increasing the distance of a potential fall.

Now I had to climb the scoop, a bridging problem, on holds several magnitudes too small. Feeling Jon's eyes on the rope, I didn't dare move down, but instead made a decision of commitment (which means keep going or fall off). The tension in the atmosphere increased. Suddenly, in contrast to that silent, blank area above, came a shattering, angry peal of thunder. My first thought was, 'Good, I can retreat without shame', until I remembered that there was no retreat. Lightning flashed with neon brilliance. A tottering move took me even further up a blanker and blanker section of slab. Was I wandering into a void, away from the true line? The rain hadn't come yet; speed was necessary, yet a tiny error would be enough to tip the balance.

An awkward mantelshelf on the right, a quick move, and the void was over; I could rest at last on a tiny ledge. Fear of the impending onslaught of rain sent me swinging boldly on a curious pocket to reach good holds above; the angle eased, and the scoop passed. The rain held off, to Jon's relief; he came up the pitch at a rate which baffled me, and settled on the stance with a loud belch.

The top pitch, a steep, sometimes dripping crack, is a variation added by Harding and Moulam in 1946. We had heard that it was technically easier than our earlier trials and I pointed Jon at it, thinking we were almost home. A few moments later he retreated, aided by Newton's Laws, and announced that I was better at brutal cracks. Unfortunately this wasn't entirely true, but eventually I got up to a resting place after Jon had shouted at me. Exhausted by my struggles, I suggested that he should try again, but his reply was unprintable. Cursing under my breath, I swung up into a neighbouring crack on the right, making use of an illegal sling to reach the finishing jugs. Finally, with great relief, I pulled over the top, only to fall some way down Western gully – perhaps not the subtlest way of finishing this astonishingly good route, the climax of the balance-climbing era.

Above: A more distant shot of the second pitch showing its isolated position on the front of The Nose. The leader has climbed the scoop and is just completing the difficult mantelshelf move. *Climbers: unknown*

NORTH WALES 34 The Grooves

by Jim Perrin

The Grooves on Cyrn Las is a great, and typically Welsh, rock-climb. Cyrn Las lies high above the Llanberis Pass, providing a focal point to the magnificent mountain scenery of Cwm Glas. The approach to the cliff is up a hillside green with sphagnum moss and strewn with great boulders; high up on the left are the red screes of the North Ridge of Crib Goch, closer at hand the glistening black wall and streaming water of Craig Rhaiadr. The path follows a stream cut through a hump of grassy moraine; as you breast this, Cyrn Las suddenly takes on its full stature, a gathered permanence towering above the level bed of the cwm. It is a huge and solitary cliff: grassy ribbed slabs on either side bound the dark clefts of Schoolmaster's Gully on the right, and Great Gully on the left. Between the two, and above 300ft. of broken rock, is a single great buttress; stratifications in the rock sweep up to the right, and produce the huge holds which are so merciful a feature of the steeper sections of the cliff; a heavy, leaning rib and groove structure to the left helps to give an impression of enormous height and authority.

The Grooves takes the obvious disjointed line of grooves on the right-hand section of the main buttress. It starts from a heathery terrace reached by scrambling up the broken lower rocks. The first pitch is a fine groove of 120ft., awkward at first due to a damp and sunless little overhang where all the holds slope disconcertingly. But it soon relents to an enjoyable hundred feet of steep jamming and bridging up to a grassy bay. A short wall behind leads to the main feature of the climb. A steep and slabby groove runs up for perhaps thirty feet to abut against a hanging rib. It is obviously hard. The continuation of the groove runs up left of the rib and is disturbingly hidden from view. The slabby groove is hard; the cracks are narrow and shallow and the angle uncomfortable. Moving into the bottom of the hidden groove proves difficult, and the view ahead plucks at your courage. The crack is straight, mossy and green, with an overhang after a few feet. Rotting and frayed slings abound, adding fuel to the fires of anxiety. But the pitch is honest: it is hard, sufficiently so to tax

one's arms and make the heart race, but it's not malicious. There is nothing that is not obvious; you struggle and sweat and the crack smiles impassively, but only the weak are spurned. At the top, a huge ledge of heather and bilberry, best savoured in late summer when the fruits are ripe, adds to the general air of well-being and solidity about the climb.

The wall above, the cliff's top tier, over-hangs alarmingly. Just to the right a huge corner gives the start of Banner's Over-hanging Arête finish. Still farther right, a green and evil corner signifies one of Allan Austin's excursions, infrequent but note-worthy, into the mythology of Welsh climbing; it looks a very hard and un-pleasant piece of climbing.

The Grooves itself proves a little demure again hereabouts. Its finish is hidden round a corner to the left, luring one back towards the centre of the crag. A little ledge leads round the corner, giving access to an exceptional degree of exposure and an extremely steep groove; the Great Buttress route unexpectedly emerges from the abyss at this point. The little groove above has holds which more than compensate for its angle: big slings draped over them make the exposure bearable. But the holds give out all too soon and, tired, you have to lay-back over that awesome drop, and stretch and strain up to a hold at the very tip of your fingernails. Lunge up a bit and it's in your grasp. Your knees scrape up a slab and with a little more effort it's all over, the drop gone, the climb behind you.

More boulders, brown grass on the hill-side behind and the train on the ridge above, tearing up the silence. The basaltic sills of Clogwyn-y-Ddysgl and the cloud louring; so much rock plunging sombrously into the shadowed valley, so many inton-ations of grey in one's mind. The Grooves is a great climb; honest, hard, strenuous, yet somehow straightforward, well-integrated; one feels weary but satisfied.

Route The Grooves, Extremely Severe, 370ft.
Cliff Cyrn Las, Cwm Glas, Llanberis Pass.
First Ascent J. Brown, D. Cowan and E. Price, September 1953; Overhanging Arête – H. I. Banner, 1959; Right-hand finish – J. A. Austin, 1959; First solo ascent (via Overhanging Arête) by A. McHardy, 1968.
Map Reference O.S. Tourist Map to Snowdonia, 1–50,000 Sheet 115 (ref. 615559).
Guidebooks C.C. *Cwm Glas* by P. Crew and I. Roper; *Rock Climbing in Wales* by R. James.
Nearest Road The A4086 at Blaen-y-nant (ref. 623570). A path leads directly to Cwm Glas from this point.
Distance and time from cliff 1 mile/1300ft. Allow 45 minutes.
Good Conditions Allow at least three dry summer days after bad weather.
Campsites and Bunkhouses Camping at Blaen-y-nant or in Cwm Glas. Huts and bivouac boulders in the Llanberis Pass.
Bibliography *The Hard Years* by Joe Brown, Gollancz, London, 1967 (brief first account); *Rock Climbers in Action in Snowdonia* by Cleare and Smythe, Secker and Warburg, London, 1966.

Ian Roper

Above: The start of the second pitch of The Grooves. Having made a few hard moves up, the leader has to make this short traverse to reach the foot of the main groove which is followed on strenuous jams. *Climber: unknown*

Right: The first pitch of The Grooves. The leader has just surmounted the difficult initial overhang. *Climber: unknown*

NORTH WALES 35 Great Slab/ Bow-Shaped Slab

by Peter Crew

Anyone visiting Cloggy for the first time is recommended to leave the path some way above Halfway House and to cut straight across the moor towards the crag. In this way, on climbing the slight rise to the top of the lakeside moraine, one is suddenly confronted with a magnificent panorama of the cliff. This is the best viewpoint for the West Buttress, soaring above the dark lake, with the splendid expanse of Great Slab, flanked by similar but much smaller counterparts. The moods of Cloggy, like those of any great cliff, are unpredictable and infinitely varied, but on a less than perfect day with shrouds of mist floating across the top of the buttresses there is always a tremendous air of foreboding.

The foot of the West Buttress is a steeply rising rake with a band of broken rock above, which overhangs from a few feet on the left to twenty or thirty feet on the right. There are few breaks through this formidable barrier; none are easy, and certainly the most elegant is that used by Great Slab. Unfortunately the upper reaches of the slab are disappointingly broken and grassy; over the years it has become the practice to link the start of Great Slab with the main pitches of Bow-Shaped Slab, which forms a direct and natural line up the cliff.

Bow-Shaped Slab arose from a premature attempt on White Slab; its start is thus far to the left, rather wandering and not particularly pleasant. The main section follows the delicately bow-curved recess sliced from the left-hand side of Great Slab. This provides two superb long pitches of roughly the same standard as the Great entry; the combination of the two is, simply, one of the finest slab climbs in Wales, at any standard.

Great Slab was, of course, the original route of the West Buttress, and its first ascent by Colin Kirkus was a remarkable feat of Extreme climbing on grass, with which the route was covered: '. . . Most of the (first) groove is occupied by the Green Caterpillar . . . An acre or two of pasture is followed until it is possible to reach the line of paddocks running across the face to the left . . . The fields are gradually going under the plough . . .' Bow was a completely different proposition and it held out

against all attempts until 1941, when Menlove Edwards laid siege to it, climbing the route on his third try. The crucial section of the climb is the leftward traverse on to the Bow itself. Edwards took a low line which involves long reaches for poor holds and has rarely been repeated.

Bow was first mentioned in print shortly afterwards, in Edwards's 1942 guide to the crag. It was graded 'Vb': 'The only difficulties, however, are well protected'. This guide, incidentally, is interesting for being one of several temporary guides produced around this time which tentatively experimented with a numerical classification for Welsh climbs. The experiment appears to have been quickly forgotten and numbers never found their way into the proper guide. Of the other ten routes in the guide only Sunset Crack was graded any easier than Bow, so it must have been something of a shock to the pundits of the time when no one else could climb the pitch. The second ascent was not made until 1948, by which time the climb had become something of an obsession with the leading Welsh climbers. Perhaps the most remarkable story to emerge from this period is that about 'Scotty' Dwyer and Dick Morsley, when Dwyer found the easier higher traverse and Morsley refused to follow. Apparently they each continued to the top of the crag, Dwyer on Bow and Morsley on Great, linked by their 200ft. of hemp!

The first moves of Great are as hard as any on the climb, so the doubtful leader will soon find out whether or not his nerves are up to scratch. There are various ways of crossing the first smooth slab: low, high, or both. All are equally awkward. A confident leader will dispense with the obvious runner high on the right, as removing this can make life hell for the second man, who is faced with a huge pendulum if he falls from here. Once across the slab there is a comforting flake crack in the long shallow groove which is now empty of the infamous Green Caterpillar. This can be taken pleasantly on the left arête or direct up the crack to a small ledge at about 100ft. The ten feet above are quite tricky, but good holds soon arrive and lead to the cave stance at the foot of the Bow itself.

Route Great Slab/Bow-Shaped Slab, Very Severe, 500ft.
Cliff West Buttress, Clogwyn du'r Arddu, Snowdon.
First Ascents C. Kirkus and G. MacPhee, June 1930 (Great Slab section); J. M. Edwards, J. Cooper and G. F. Parkinson, September 1941 (Bow-Shaped).
Map Reference O.S. Tourist Map to Snowdonia, 1–50,000 Sheet 115 (ref. 599555).
Guidebooks C.C. *Clogwyn du'r Arddu* by P. Crew and H. I. Banner; *Rock Climbing in Wales* by R. James.
Nearest Road A minor road leads from the Llanberis Mountain Railway Station to Hafodty Newydd (ref. 588578).
Distance and time from cliff 2 miles/1300ft. Allow 1 hour.
Good Conditions The climb is well drained but still needs a few dry days after bad weather unless conditions are very warm or windy.
Campsites and Bunkhouses Camping by the lake below the crag or in the Llanberis Pass. Huts and bivouacs in the Llanberis area.
Bibliography *Let's Go Climbing* by Colin Kirkus, Nelson, London, 1941 (first ascent account); *Samson* by Sutton and Noyce, Published privately, c. 1960; *The Black Cliff* by Crew, Soper and Wilson, Kaye and Ward, London, 1971; Mountain 8, *The West* by Paul Nunn (an appraisal of the climbing character and problems of the West Buttress slabs).

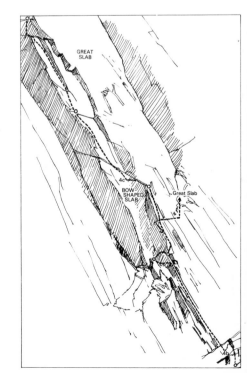

131

Ken Wilson

The route keeps with Great for part of the next pitch, up the pleasant ridge on the right, continuing to an airy stance on the edge of the Bow. There are now several pegs here, despite a number of adequate natural belays. This is the start of the crucial traverse – the objective being the grass ledge across on the left. The original route goes horizontally left and up to the ledges, all horrible moves and slightly irreversible. Instead, climb up until your feet are in the break and shuffle across the bulging slab (or overhanging wall, if you are feeling gripped) to good handholds. Then take a series of delicate steps down to the left and back up again to the ledges. This is all beautiful climbing, to be taken slowly and savoured.

The real difficulties are now over and all above is pure joy. A word of warning, however, to spare a thought for your shaking second and place some runners for him – they are not much use, but would stop him swinging over the edge on to Narrow Slab! The next pitch follows the narrow strip of slab under the encroaching overhangs until you are forced out over a slight bulge to enormous holds and the stance at the very top of the Bow. This is a superb viewpoint from which to watch the antics of others on the East Buttress routes. The final easy slabs are for picking up carefully in cramped feet, or for a wild rush to the sunshine and warmth on the other side of the crag.

Left: The first pitch of Great Slab. The difficult start crosses the square slab under the overhang at the foot of the picture. Having completed that, the climber can enjoy over a hundred feet of delightfully exposed climbing. *Climber: unknown*

Right: The crucial traverse of Bow-shaped Slab. The leader is making the delicate downward moves. *Climbers: Rowland Edwards and Peter Crew*

NORTH WALES 36 Vember

by Tony Smythe

A climb is as personal to the man who climbs it as a pair of shoes, and if one person's shoes pinch there is no reason that the next man's should do so. One therefore offers one's experience of a well-known climb doubtfully, hoping that the critical climbing reader will realize that from the point of view of an anthology you can't really put together a collection of climbs – only climbers.

My two ascents of Vember were made over ten years ago; that is, in 1961. My approach to the climb was traditional in that I found myself seconding the route, and then a few weeks later led it, which was a considerably more meaningful experience. I put my cards on the table immediately: I found the route very hard indeed, and since it came after months of instructing at Plas-y-Brenin, when I climbed every day and almost every evening, it was as hard a route as I am ever likely to achieve.

I called it a well-known climb, but perhaps, in spite of its fantastic reputation and appearance, there has never been a queue to climb it. Ken Wilson tells me: 'Vember still stands up very well as one of the harder early Brown routes and one of the most stupendous lines in Wales. Although many of the newer routes are very fine, hardly any of them really come into the top level of quality – perhaps one or two on Anglesey, but that is all. I remember when you did Vember it was considered to be one of the more reasonable Brown routes, but now only Black Cleft and Woubits Left Hand get done less.'

Plenty has been written about the magic of Clogwyn du'r Arddu. This great cliff seems to exert a powerful hold on the imagination of even the most unimaginative climber. The formula combines the superb simplicity of the vast syncline folds, the forbidding atmosphere of the north-facing, water-streaked six hundred feet of rock, and the pervading greyness and silence. The only sound you associate with Cloggy is that of the wind blowing round the cold vertical edges. The place must get some sun in the summer, but you don't remember it. You almost feel the crag needs to be psychoanalysed to rid it of some of its inward-looking melancholy.

The East Buttress, though no more impressive than the West, is more brutal: 300ft. of fantastically steep, bubbly, diamond-hard rock. From Sunset Crack to the Corner, the cracks are frightening and uninviting; as climbs, the walls between them are triumphs of mind over matter. The Pinnacle, on top, has a multitude of routes that I have always considered less important: all that activity up above is rather bothersome to the true East Buttress man, partly, I suppose, because he thinks somebody might pull a load of choss on to him.

Vember is about half-way along, where the buttress is tallest. It has only really got two pitches, but it is as big in character as almost anything on the West Buttress. Its position is incredible – just to the right of the Great Wall, and just to the left of Curving Crack, which in its own way is one of the finest climbs in the British Isles.

When I seconded Gunn Clark, somebody said it was the twelfth ascent. Gunn was from the wrong background and was perhaps too sensitive to have been one of the greatest climbers, but his dry analysis of a situation, his self-honesty and wry sense of fun attracted everybody who climbed with him. He looked good on rock, and technique counts for a lot on Vember.

So there was Gunn, bridging like a ballerina up the first long shallow crack, and then bridging on up the second pitch, which is so darned steep you couldn't see how he could stay on like that. When I climbed Cenotaph with Gunn, he bridged up that. He bridged up everything.

Desperation. Is that my only memory of my climb with Gunn? No – Gunn's elegance and eloquence lifted one out of such a commonplace state. Faithfully copying his technique, I enjoyed the millimetric precision of the tiny holds, but I was acutely conscious of the rope in front of my nose. Seconding Vember was enthralling gymnastics, but meaningless in terms of research into one's inner self, which for me has always been a more important part of British rock climbing. This can only be obtained by leading.

So, a few weeks later, I arrived at the foot of the climb a second time. In the

Route Vember, Extremely Severe, 310ft.
Cliff East Buttress, Clogwyn du'r Arddu, Snowdon.
First Ascent J. Brown and D. Whillans, October 1951. A. Birtwistle led the first pitch in 1937.
Map Reference O.S. Tourist Map to Snowdonia, 1–50,000 Sheet 115 (ref. 604554).
Guidebooks C.C. *Clogwyn du'r Arddu* by P. Crew and H. I. Banner; *Rock Climbing in Wales* by R. James.
Nearest Road A minor road leads from the Llanberis Mountain Railway Station to Hafodty Newydd (ref. 588578).
Distance and time from cliff 2 miles/1300ft. Allow 1 hour.
Good Conditions Allow three dry summer days after bad weather; even then the Drainpipe Crack can still hold water.
Campsites and Bunkhouses Camping by the lake below the crag or in the Llanberis Pass. Huts and bivouacs in the Llanberis area.
Bibliography *The Hard Years* by Joe Brown, Gollancz, London, 1967 (first ascent account); *Rock Climbers in Action in Snowdonia* by Cleare and Smythe, Secker and Warburg, London, 1966.

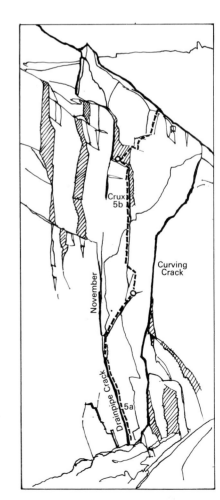

Ken Wilson

interval I had been reflecting a good deal on how much better, or worse, I was going to climb on the sharp end of the rope. Usually I climb better – after all you have to, to survive – but on a climb where the barriers are intensely psychological you can easily find yourself climbing worse.

There were two others on the rope, both women – Denise Evans and Jo Scarr. It never bothered me to climb with girls. I was perfectly well aware that they were not going to hang on to the rope so well if I fell off, but that was a thought I was eager to suppress. Anyway, I was so big-headed that I climbed better with girls. And in any case, the protection on the first pitch of Vember is so terrible that it doesn't make much odds who's standing at the bottom holding the rope.

As usual, it was a cold grey day, although the sun may have been shining elsewhere. After the usual messing around with equipment and donning P.A.s, there was the circus-balancing on boulders, on clothing, on coils of rope – on anything to keep the feet dry. There was a hard move stupidly near the ground, just like a boulder problem – you have to shut out the fear of things like this happening higher up.

Twenty feet . . . forty feet . . . still no blasted runner. It all becomes deadly quiet when you know, and the watchers know, that a peel is going to mean a broken neck, or just a broken leg if you're lucky. But I've seen people fussing so much about runners that they've almost lost the will to climb. I forced myself not to worry about runners because I knew there weren't any for 70ft. I balanced from point to point, a succession of moments of elation as I realized it was working. The concentration was intense – nothing existed except the interplay of hold, muscle and gravity, all computing together, with the nervous tension flowing and ebbing as each move was made.

Before I got the runner on I was asking myself for the thousandth time: how could I put myself in this position? – as I suppose a volunteer must ask himself as his platoon advances towards an enemy line. I reached for the discipline to control the sweat, which itself could cause disaster by greasing up the holds. Then I got the runner on, a lovely

little thread, although the edges were a bit sharp. But then I don't fuss about things like that. I'd sooner have a good thread than a poor, rounded spike. The climbing machine like Brown will tell you that a runner is only as good as its breaking or dislodgement strain; but a lesser mortal like me, whose propulsion often depends on the psychological security of a runner, gets a primitive satisfaction out of threading a piece of rope into one hole and drawing it out of another. You conceive the mountain having to be pulled away first – you reject the idea of the runner failing.

Bridging up that first long groove of Vember, you are fully aware of how much you are depending on what has gone before: the P.A.s that squeeze your toes, the strong nylon rope that slips through the runner underneath, and above all the gradually-evolved attitudes and techniques that have made such a climb relatively a commonplace. Climbing a Brown route, I thought of Brown and how little he had to lean on ten years earlier. And Arthur Birtwistle too: to have led this pitch in 1937 must have required a special kind of philosophy. For a man climbing so far ahead of his time, not many electrical circuits could have stood between rational judgement and a despairing, suicidal impulse.

The pitch couldn't be rushed, that would have been fatal. The meticulous, thoughtful bridging went on and on, the white blobs of faces becoming detached far below. Tiny things on the rock were interesting – a speck of quartz, a blade of grass, an insect. Sometimes on a climb I have looked at an insect and wanted to change places with it.

At last I pulled on to the seemingly enormous turf promenade that divides the two main pitches. It must have been awful for Denise waiting so long, getting so cold and demoralized, but I was too busy screwing myself up for the next pitch, the hard one, to worry too much about her. She was very light, so I knew that one way or another I would have a second on the ledge. An unjust thought – she climbed it like a cat.

Those grassy ledges on Cloggy are somehow unique. Usually they don't slope, but unless they are growing actually on top of

Tony Riley

136

rock the whole thing can slowly detach itself, with the noise of a velcro fastener. There's usually time to search around for something else to put your feet on; it's only worrying if you're not actually belayed.

The thin crack of November shoots up the wall to the left, a line that Brown and his mates were contemplating even as they were busy with Vember in 1949. Vember was finally conquered in October 1951, six years earlier than November. But the fact that Vember was one of Brown's first routes on Cloggy means little, and the leader quailing at the foot of pitch two is not reassured by the knowledge that the maestro himself came hurtling off the crux move on a wet day before the route was finally vanquished. Legend has it that two strands of the rope parted in that peel, and it is interesting to speculate how the history of Cloggy's climbs would have been written had the third strand gone as well.

You get a kind of start with the second pitch by having a definite point to aim for – a small ledge about twenty feet up. From below it looks good enough to have a rest on, but this hope is dashed; after wedging and clutching up the crack underneath, one finds that the ledge is sloping and the rock above bulging. You can get a solid runner on, but I couldn't rest, and my fingers felt very strained.

On another day I perched in Curving Crack and photographed Trevor Jones in a sweat-soaked yellow vest leading Vember, with Peter Hatton following after rain had begun. It was a grandstand view of two men wrestling with a RURC – a realized ultimate reality climb. From Curving you get a better idea of what sort of climb Vember is than when you are actually on it.

When I was too tired, or too frightened – I forget which – to stay on the sloping ledge any longer, I started up. Ten years is a longish time to remember a place clearly, but I shall always remember The Move. The shallowest of chimneys with an appalling exit. Experience told me to use my right buttock on the right wall and to use my left foot as a kind of scraper to scrape myself upwards. The scraping surface was a patch of pale grey rock, so smooth and friction-free that a P.A. slipped from it pathetically, like a dying animal kicking its last. I could see what I had to get – a little spike just out of reach.

The position was so precarious that I made no attempt to lasso the spike with a sling. I eased myself up, like a champagne cork rising and, a whisper before popping, I had the spike.

I think Denise had been getting very worried, but now I was *communicado* again and I started busily understanding the case, because I needed a second on the grass ledges above, underneath the final fiendish little wall below the top gallery. Then, feeling like a drop of pure condensed Hallelujah Chorus, I ambled up to the grass.

Extremely Severe, Exceptionally Severe – I've never known the difference. But let no one try to kid me that Vember is 'only' Hard VS! It must be one of the great climbs. Even the name is nice – it almost rhymes with Rembrandt, and is every bit as much a masterpiece on rock as the immortal Dutchman's portraits on canvas. It is a climb that lives in my imagination long after most other mountain days of the same vintage have become blurred memories.

Left: Starting the second pitch of Vember, where a short layback crack allows the sloping ledge to be gained before the main difficulties start. *Climber: Al Wright*

by Ed Drummond

'You've just got to climb it now.' That was all the man said: Boysen slipping quietly off to climb. Seal cold in my shorts I was feeling a little blue. Below us Llyn du'r Arddu flashed black glass. On the line of the mountain the toy tiny train crept, its gasps of steam signalling like heartbeats.

'Come on lily legs.' Crew didn't like to be kept waiting; it was him holding the rope.

Above me the wall beamed gleamy with rain, bald as a whale. Easter Sunday 1967. I gulped to see there was a line; my pub outboast still stoodered. This wasn't funny.

A paraphernalia of cameras, wormy ropes, comments, draggles of steel krabs, oh, and a talisman rurp I'd hidden in the pocket of my shorts; he said I wouldn't need any pegs. The camera shot me in black and white, glossing over my burning cheeks. My knees were news in wild Wales. Boysen was slinking up his route on velvet feet.

On blunt finger-tips to a jingle of krabs, I footjigged the first wall to the small overhang. 'That's as far as Banner got,' floated up. I can rest up there thought I, peering, manteling.

I could not and, mouse nervous, I not-rested for an hour, Crew spearing me from below. 'I didn't have a runner there.' But I did, after an hour, and then I rose again. Ten feet. There was a quartz break and I took one too and looked around.

I could just make out Llanberis smudged between hills; woman and child would be up now asking where I was. Below me a delighted Pete was blowing advice to a numbed Boysen. Above me was a peg; with an open eye. If I could poke my finger in, he certainly wouldn't be able to see. If I had a ten-foot arm.

I lift up to the left, 'Clements fell off that way,' bless you sir – a five-foot arm – my fingers start to finger the slippery dimples, toes walking backwards. A ten-foot arm.

Then he tells me he moved right, 'then a quick layback and then up to the peg.' I note the connective; he didn't say a quick layback up *to* the peg, so what happens when I get to that 'and'? Climbers arriving below would ask how long I'd been there. I felt established as a kind of gargoyle. Stuck.

A five foot arm suspension bridging your life in your hand at three foot arm I don't have to fall

off Solesstickonicenice. Made it, snug as a nut, my *doigt* in the peg. While I'm not-resting at the peg he tells me he used it. I'm getting to like him.

Now you're big enough to fly, jugs come lovely, hands full of rock up I go like a slow balloon, pink knees bumping up after me. Two rusty pegs peep; 'That's as far as Brown got.' Uncle Joe beams at me from his advert and Pete sounds a long way away.

Now once upon a ledge in the middle of Great Wall I sat on a jammed half arse and dangled. A tidal wave of rock swelled out all around. Above me a twenty-foot groove groped to a slim bulge; above this straggled a ragged crack. Where this began was a tiny sling, waving to me. Suddenly hungry I took off my sock and lowered it on the slack to the deck where someone put a block of my dates in which I pulled up to suck. For a while. I'd turned cold. While someone else held the rope Pete ran on the spot for warmth. Climbers below moved off home silent as fish.

I was delighted now to bridge, push, flow, no runners since the ledge, warmer. The little sling was trying to reach me. Boysen, perched, smoking, watching.

The bulge slid into my arms, frigid with cold. It was staring me in the face. Thirty feet above a runner, only noholds here. Sixty feet is long enough to see where you're going. The noholds in front of my eyes float up, slowly. First you see them, then you don't.

P.A.s on wheels I move quickly, fingers whimpering. The little sling stops to tickle my chin and I put a krab on it and hum. One thin nut on eyelash tape. Then I put my foot in the noose.

Down I glide, invisible, in the lift, and slip among the staring crowd on the street. He's still up there. He must be holding on to something. Then he moves jerkily. Suddenly no one is talking, upturned white faces eating the sight alive. You blink and stop breathing. He stands in the sling. 'This is like cracking a safe,' he yells. We look at each other. He's all right. I'm all right. Pete shouts something up.

Now the crack grins for two sweet nuts. Elephants bounce past trumpeting. I would like to put my fingers in its mouth, free as

Route Great Wall, Extremely Severe, 200ft.
Cliff East Buttress, Clogwyn du'r Arddu, Snowdon.
First Ascent P. Crew, May 1963 (it rained, so the second did not follow); Arête Finish by A. G. Cram and P. Scott, May 1966.
Map Reference O.S. Tourist Map to Snowdonia, 1–50,000 Sheet 115 (ref. 604554).
Guidebook C.C. Clogwyn du'r Arddu by P. Crew and H. I. Banner.
Nearest Road A minor road leads from the Llanberis Mountain Railway Station to Hafodty Newydd (ref. 588578).
Distance and time from cliff 2 miles/1300ft. Allow 1 hour.
Good Conditions Allow two days after bad weather. The route is well drained but the easier, upper section can remain greasy.
Campsites and Bunkhouses Camping by the lake below the cliff or in the Llanberis Pass. Huts and bivouacs in the Llanberis area.
Bibliography The Black Cliff by Crew, Soper and Wilson, Kaye and Ward, London, 1971.

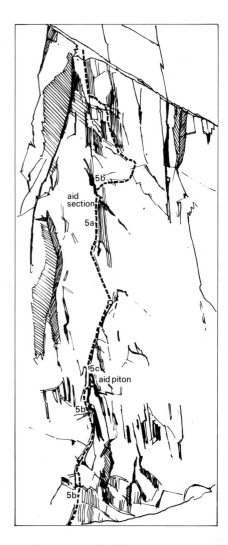

air, but I'm saving that for a sunny day. Then the crack shuts up and it shut me up until he said there was a peg behind a hidden flake to the right. After that parabola there's just a human sucker move with a ledge after, just lying there waiting for you to stand on it. Pancake hearted I plopped a fist in five feet above, just as my feet skedaddled. I'm not usually lucky.

It was too late for him to follow now, and I sat chilling, the silly rurp still in my pocket, while he abseiled down to unstick my runners. 'Well done Scream,' he's said. Five years ago. He was still in love with that wall. Lovely boy Crew, arrow climber. Wall without end.

Left: The first pitch of Great Wall at the point where a difficult move allows the climber to reach the piton. *Climber: Ed Drummond*

Right: The second pitch of Great Wall, with the climber on the free-climbing section just below the point where the jammed nuts have to be used for aid. The climber is doing the route in one run-out, but nowadays most teams take a stance at half-height. *Climber: Ed Drummond*

NORTH WALES **38** **White Slab**

by Peter Crew

White Slab embodies most, if not all, of the qualities of a great rock climb and in its own peculiar way is the most typical and the best of the slab climbs on Cloggy. From a distance, and to the tutored eye, it stands out clearly – a thin, tenuous streak, nestling elegantly amongst its ruder neighbours and forming the centrepiece of the sheaf of ribs and slabs on the left of the West Buttress. The slab narrows at half-height, so that from a distance it looks like an elongated hour-glass. In detail the route is intricate, continually changing in character and style as it oscillates in a rather unsatisfying way from the pure line. But in a sense this is the climb's strength as well as its weakness. An ascent of White Slab involves small sections of five other routes, both old and new, giving shades of glories past or hints of deeds to come. It is a traditional climb in the best sense of the word.

Like most truly great climbs, White Slab was well known and tried for many years before its first ascent. Early attempts included those by Menlove Edwards/John Barford and Jock Campbell/David Cox in the 1940s, both of which resulted in other climbs being discovered. David Cox could possibly lay claim to the first ascent – though from the comfortable depths of an armchair in the Officers' Mess of the Llanberis Army Camp! The practical result of a *vis-à-vis* confrontation with the rocks was far from the armchair dream, but Sheaf Climb must have been more than adequate recompense. Peter Harding tried too, presumably during his extensive work on the Llanberis 'bumper fun' guidebook. The first peg on the arête of the slab is a testimony to his eye of faith and to the strength of the psychological barriers not yet broken down.

The campaign against White Slab opened in earnest during the ascendancy of Brown and the Rock and Ice. An early attempt in 1951, when the first long slab was climbed, was fortuitously recorded for posterity by a certain John Edwards of Barmouth who was taking his little known series of photos of the crag. The problem at this point was to re-establish contact with the slab after the diversion into Ghecko Groove. There is some contention as to who finally solved the problem, but the solution – the lasso pitch – is well known. The problem lay fallow for some years due to expedition and other commitments, and although Brown had made most of the running, his presence on Mustagh Tower left the field open for his fellow members in the Rock and Ice. The story is well known: Whillans declared his interest in the route and was burnt off by an impatient Moseley.

For several years, White and Bloody Slabs were regarded as the ultimate – the big blank slabs of the myth-making machine. Banner, on an early ascent, was observed stationary on the crux for nearly two hours. Jack Soper correctly surmised that if anyone, even Banner, could stand there for so long, then there must be holds. Armed with this revelation, and with Austin's 'Little Black Book' (of descriptions), Soper and Dave Gregory made the first 'incognito' ascent. The effect was quite remarkable and by the following summer, 1960, White had become an established trade route for aspiring hardmen.

The climb has since suffered indignities of the worst kind. It has been done as an Alpine training route in under two hours, it has been soloed several times and even women have led it. It is now dying a slow death through being smothered by countless rubber soles and stripped to the bone by foreign pegs.

The first pitch is a masterpiece of route-finding. A small shattered pillar gives access to a long horizontal traverse along the lip of the overhangs. The various tempting and futile possibilities above, marked by battered pegs and tatty slings, have been the downfall of several renowned figures and should be ignored. The pleasant crack pitch of Bow-Shaped leads to the foot of the first slab, at the base of the Hour-Glass, where the climb starts in earnest. The pitch up the edge of the slab, starting by Linnell's Leap, is a beautiful exercise in alternately delicate and strenuous slab climbing. The holds are all there and the protection is good, but the lack of any ledges and the exposed positions give a disproportionate feeling of insecurity which is difficult to overcome. The crux is moving right and upwards from the large spillikin by a kind of semi-layback on polished holds.

Route White Slab, Extremely Severe, 535ft.
Cliff West Buttress, Clogwyn du'r Arddu, Snowdon.
First Ascent R. Moseley and J. Smith, April 1956; variation to third pitch and Cannon Hole Exit by H. I. Banner in 1959; variation to Cowboy pitch by J. A. Austin in 1959; modern way of doing the fifth pitch by J. H. Deacon in 1959. Soloed by C. Phillips in 1969.
Map Reference O.S. Tourist Map to Snowdonia, 1–50,000 Sheet 115 (ref. 599555).
Guidebooks C.C. *Clogwyn du'r Arddu* by P. Crew and H. I. Banner; *Rock Climbing in Wales* by R. James.
Nearest Road A minor road leads from the Llanberis Mountain Railway Station to Hafodty Newydd (ref. 588578).
Distance and time from cliff 2 miles/1300ft. Allow 1 hour.
Good Conditions Several dry summer days after bad weather.
Campsites and Bunkhouses Camping by the lake below the cliff or in the Llanberis Pass. Huts and bivouacs in the Llanberis area.
Bibliography C.C. Journal 1945/6: *A Great Wall of Rocks* by John Barford (early attempt); *Don Whillans* by Whillans and Ormerod, Heinemann, London, 1971 (events surrounding the first ascent); *Snowdon Biography* by Winthrop-Young, Sutton and Noyce, J. M. Dent, London, 1957; *The Black Cliff* by Crew, Soper and Wilson, Kaye and Ward, London, 1971.

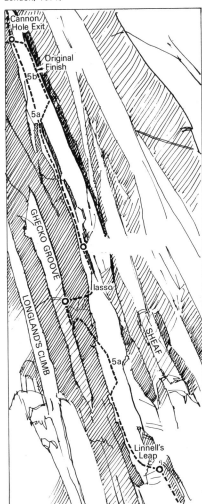

Unfortunately this is spoiled more often than not by the presence of uncalled-for metal. Above, the slab is steep and very blank, but a fortuitous traverse leads easily round to the left into the secure recesses of Ghecko Groove.

Now comes the cowboy pitch. From a precarious position on the arête one can just make out a hand-sized spike across the blank slab. This is lassoed – on the first attempt, by the lucky or skilled, and never by the doomed. An exhilarating swing across on the rope leads to the easy central section of the Hour-Glass.

The final slab disappears up over a bulge on the left skyline. Short staccato moves between well-spaced holds lead delicately to a lonely peg. The easy jugs straight up are a modern soft option. Traditionalists move right and struggle up the greasy groove; masochists and sadists with corpulent seconds are recommended to follow Banner through the Cannon Hole.

Unfortunately the climb ends here, squeezed out to nothing between the slabs of Longlands and Narrow, but a fitting end is the neglected direct finish to Longlands, across a razor-sharp rope-cutting ridge and up the loose unprotected chimney overhanging the Black Cleft. This can provide a real shot in the arm for jaded addicts.

Left: The first pitch of White Slab showing the second man making the difficult traverse above the overhangs. *Climbers: John Hartley and Clive Horsfield*

Top right: The big slab pitch of White Slab, where the route gains the edge in a magnificent position. *Climber: John Hartley*

Bottom right: Half-way up the big slab pitch. At this point the route traverses back into the centre of the slab and follows a slight crack by semi-layback moves. *Climber: Dave Alcock*

NORTH WALES 39 Slanting Slab

by Dave Cook

Like the folds of a fan, the slabs and ribs of Clogwyn du'r Arddu's West Buttress open in geometrical splendour above the steeply rising Western Terrace. This feature is a geological banana skin on which the whole complex rests, slumped against the sober stump of the Boulder, still slightly drunk from its volcanic orgy.

The result, in rock-climbing terms, is a collection of superlative slab and groove lines, with their natural entries torn away by this *en masse* displacement. Climbers have avoided the problems created by this rhyolitic caesarian in two ways. Most of the older routes made long traverses from the left to reach the grooves above. More recently they have lanced directly on to the slabs. The overhangs above the Terrace may be big, loose and intimidating, but they are not relentless. In a few places, lucky combinations of fallen rock provide entries, as in the cases of Great and Bloody Slabs, making possible routes of rare dignity.

Between these two routes a huge wedge of cliff lay untouched. Pete Harding's West Buttress Girdle had crossed the upper section in 1949, but lower down an Eldorado of character-packed rock beckoned. In July 1955, Don Whillans, accompanied by Vince Betts, climbed on to the slabs with two pegs for aid, and worked out a superb natural line slicing through this bristling complex. Although other explorers have followed him over the roofs, Slanting Slab remains the most authoritative statement of bold route-finding made on the cliff in modern times.

The central assumption of the current numerical grading system is that it is possible to divorce the technical difficulty of a climb from subjective feelings arising from its position. On Slanting Slab this assumption founders. Atmosphere, position and 'feel' are all. Further up the Buttress, John Streetly's Bloody Slab traces a similar sort of side-stepping line. Its crux, not well protected by modern standards, is a full grade harder than anything on Slanting, yet its impact is a whisper beside the latter's roar.

Even as you crouch in slings on the eaves of the slabs, only twenty feet from second, thermos flasks and solidity, the exposure begins to snap at you. Once over the lip, the snap becomes a snarl, as the sandwich of slab, constricted between the undercut base and the long roof that pushes the line away to the left, merges into the open face.

The traverse line crosses a grass patch, says the guide; but lose any illusions you may have about picnics. In the words of some Prussian, 'grass climbing is rock climbing by other means'. A step up a rib takes the line on, via a further traverse, to the grassy shelf on which the belay is taken. Flimsy protection offers little consolation to leader or second, and this rib is the crux. As a climbing detail it is not memorable, but as a personal mind-exploder I will remember it until my dying day.

The ropes rustled leftwards to Dave's stance, somewhere round the corner. Slings, detached from their pathetic connections by the tugs, rattled like an overhead wireway in a big store.

'How hard?' I shouted.

'As hard as Sickle,' came the reply.

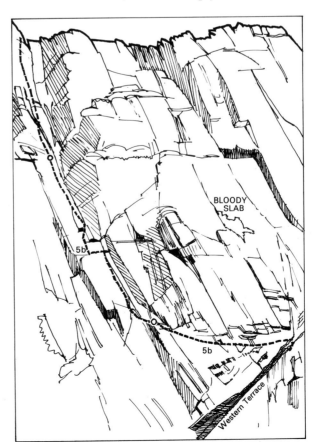

Route Slanting Slab, Extremely Severe, 420ft.
Cliff West Buttress, Clogwyn du'r Arddu, Snowdon.
First Ascent D. Whillans and V. Betts, July 1955.
Map Reference O.S. Tourist Map of Snowdonia, 1–50,000 Sheet 115 (ref. 599555).
Guidebooks C.C. *Clogwyn du'r Arddu* by P. Crew and H. I. Banner; *Rock Climbing in Wales* by R. James.
Nearest Road A minor road leads from the Llanberis Mountain Railway Station to Hafodty Newydd (ref. 588578).
Distance and time from cliff 2 miles/1300ft. Allow 1 hour.
Good Conditions Several dry summer days after bad weather. Completely dry conditions advisable.
Campsites and Bunkhouses Camping by the lake below the crag or in the Llanberis Pass. Huts and bivouacs in the Llanberis area.
Bibliography *The Black Cliff* by Crew, Soper and Wilson, Kaye and Ward, London, 1971.

Adrenalin, associations and memory jostled into battle with my cool. Of course the move wasn't that hard, but when I came to do it I felt as if I was carrying a rucksack loaded with position and history. 'But we just want the technical difficulty; forget about everything else.' Don't make me laugh: on the 120ft. of Slanting's first pitch, 'everything else' is the technical difficulty.

Pitch two is paradise gained. Although this awe inspiring 180ft. is wonderfully complex, its variety is within an overall line dictated by one of the great leftward-facing corners that divide the West Buttress. The seriousness of the start, whose keynote is danger, has gone. In its place is a more generalized mountaineering seriousness of an altogether more acceptable nature. Whillans's route-finding achievement thunders in your mind as you swing from slab to slab, from crack to groove. The runners drop into place with satisfying regularity, and the sustained HVS climbing does not rear up in any sudden anger. It is a pitch to wonder at; a continuous erogenous zone of climbing sexuality on a cliff noted for good experiences.

All great routes become encrusted with layers of mythology, and the whole aura and life-style of those associated with them. In the early 1960s, when I did the climb, this fatty tissue lay heavy. Today, the splendidly precocious irreverance of modern attitudes and the ever more sophisticated protection techniques may have cut the climb down to size, but the muscular frame that lies beneath still assures a rating in the big leagues for Slanting Slab.

Left: The first pitch of Slanting Slab, with the climber half-way along the traverse. *Climber: Lew Brown*

Right: The same pitch from a different viewpoint, capturing less of the detail but more of the atmosphere of this impressive climb. *Climber: Lew Brown*

Leo Dickinson

151

by Richard Isherwood

Castell Cidwm is such an attractive crag that it is surprising it wasn't developed years before 1960. It sits in a beautiful valley, it dries out quickly, it's not too far from the road, and it's very steep with plenty of holds. This last description doesn't apply to all the climbs, but some of them are sufficiently 'juggy' to give exciting climbing without too many hard moves. The best of them, and one of the best small-crag climbs in North Wales, is Dwm.

The south-east face of Castell Cidwm is a longish wall overlooking a steep stream bed. As you face it, the wall slants down from the left, roughly parallel to the stream bed, then turns a slight angle away from the stream and runs into a slabby ramp bounding the main cliff on its right. At the angle, the lowest point of the main crag, the cliff is highest and perhaps also steepest. Low down, this angle is just a vague rib, but higher up it juts out into a spectacular prow, cut by a curving groove. Dwm climbs into the groove and thence up over the prow.

Cidwm, although only a small crag, is impressively steep, particularly when you reach the foot of the rock. From the start of Dwm, you crane your neck to see the line, until you find you can see more comfortably facing outwards from the cliff. The first pitch starts at the toe of the crag right below the final groove, and leads left, then right, up a snaky crack which must be ten degrees over the vertical. Fortunately, the holds are huge, and the main danger lies in going up too fast and forgetting the runners. The crack leads to a sloping ledge with a peg belay, from which the ropes hang free.

The belay ledge is almost directly below the corner, but you can't see it as there is an overhang immediately above. The route goes out to the left, fairly easily at first, to a little ledge where you can fix a big thread runner. From here, for those with strong arms, the girdle traverse of Castell Cidwm breaks out to the left along the ledge and over the first of many overhangs. Dwm goes the opposite way, almost horizontally to the right across apparently overlapping slabs to a patch of bright green grass in the corner.

Overlapping slabs they appear to be,

until you step off the ledge. Then you realize they are little walls, and it's all out of balance. This section is climbed mainly on side-pulls and pinch grips, and needs working out. Some work it out wrong, and find themselves back under the overhang, level with the stance but six feet out from the rock. However, with the right combination it's not so bad; you move across, up to some apparently loose blocks, and further across into the corner at the top of the little tongue of grass. From a distance, this grass has the appearance of a pleasant stance, but, like the overlapping slabs, it proves deceptive. The stance, just two footholds in the corner, is so small that you are well advised to stand in a long sling if your companion is not too fast. Again the rope hangs free; you can't see the foot of the climb.

The third and final pitch must have been the crux when the route was first done, but very early in its history it suffered the same degradation as many other crux pitches. It starts as a more or less vertical corner, but soon curves away to the right as a very steep, smooth slab under a big, stepped roof. The crack between the slab and the roof is a natural seepage line and seems always wet.

It's thirty or forty feet under the overhang to the end of the nose, and Joe Brown climbed it with three pegs, which must have been hard. It seems now to be permanently pegged with five or six, making the overhang almost entirely artificial, easy but spectacular. You swing along, with the odd hand-jam bridging the gap between pegs. The slab below the overhang is smooth, often wet, and very holdless, and it narrows towards its end so that the lip of another overhang is below your feet. Where the pegs end, a very fine and extremely exposed move leads round the end of the overhang into a short chimney on the very tip of the nose – not desperate but hard enough, in that position, to make you stop and think, and some indication of what the pitch must have been like in its virgin state.

Ten feet up the chimney, hardly clear of the overhang, the climb ends as suddenly as it started, and you're out in the deep springy heather on the top of the cliff, in another world. For 180ft., Dwm packs in a lot of climbing.

Route Dwm, Hard Very Severe, 180ft.
Cliff Castell Cidwm, Mynydd Mawr.
First Ascent J. Brown and H. Smith, March 1960.
Map Reference O.S. Tourist Map to Snowdonia, 1–50,000 Sheet 115 (ref. 550553).
Guidebooks C.C. *Cwm Silyn and Cwellyn* by M. Yates and J. Perrin; *Rock Climbing in Wales* by R. James.
Nearest Road The A487 Caernarvon/Beddgelert road just south of Llyn Cwellyn (ref. 568540). A forestry road leads up the west side of the lake to the crag and parking is sometimes allowed in the farmyard at the entrance.
Distance and time from cliff 1¼ miles/300ft. Allow 30 minutes.
Good Conditions The ridge is sheltered and quick-drying in its lower half, although the top pitch is often wet. Allow one good day after bad weather.
Campsites and Bunkhouses Camping just north of Beddgelert or in Nant Gwynant.
Bibliography *The Hard Years* by Joe Brown, Gollancz, London, 1967 (brief account of the first ascent).

Ken Wilson

John Cleare

Left: The second pitch of Dwm, where the route moves back to the right across the overlaps. This is generally considered the most difficult section of the climb. *Climber: Chris Bonington*

Above: A view of the front face of Castell Cidwm with Llyn Cwellyn in the valley below. This viewpoint forms the basis for the diagram on the previous page. *Climbers: Chris Bonington and Rusty Baillie*

Right: The artificial section on the final pitch of Dwm. The climber is about to enter the exit chimney. *Climber: Eric Jones*

John Harwood

by Jim Perrin

Tremadoc – a long line of grey cliff slanting up from dark woods of dwarf oak, flat green fields beneath, an old estuary reclaimed. Clear western light and beyond the embankment sandflats stretching out into Cardigan Bay; the sea, something of the mystery of Wales. To the south and east line upon line of hills fading away to the merest suggestion on the horizon, their names a soft cadence which contemplation whispers round the silence of their form: Cader, Rhinog, Arenig, Moelwyn, Cnicht; a pastoral setting, colourful, calm. And the cliffs friendly, rough-rocked and comforting; the climbs a swarm of pitches over the sun-warmed rock, people everywhere upon it. Gymnastic anonymity is the hallmark of the average climb at Tremadoc – a myriad pleasant routes; the miracle is that it should possess one which is truly great.

The Milestone Buttress, leaning and knife-cut clean down to a torn wilderness of overhang and bloodied rock, swathing blades and fanged flakes in majestic disarray; here Vector finds its improbable way. Climbed by Brown in 1960, Vector rapidly acquired a huge reputation. Trevor Jones, attempting to second the first ascent, found himself dangling ten feet away from the rock, and was lowered down to spread his ample gospel amongst the climbers of Wales. Leader after leader plummeted from the crack of the top pitch; an inscrutable, smiling crack slipping across the lip of the overhangs, it established for the climb a devastating psychological advantage; of having a strenuous crux right at the top after a great deal of hard and technical climbing.

So from Brown, old master of the fifties, came the technical yardstick of the sixties, the test-piece for climbers aspiring to express themselves in a new technical idiom. A hard climb, bold yet safe, intricate yet uncontrived, a pointer to the mood of an emergent generation. And above all a climb of great beauty, of scintillating movement and exquisite situation, self-expression sculpted to natural lines and a piece of magisterial rock-artistry.

Not that you feel this, stumbling up muddy boulders, past mossy trees and over rotting leaves to the dank flake at its base;

nor gazing up along a single tenuous line pieced together into its hostile face.

Vector is a climb for technique, without which nothing; even its first and easiest pitch is a technical delight. A little groove to start, sharp layaways and high-footing it on to a convex slab where the holds lead in a semi-circle of delicate sufficiency to a dark short groove above, and the first uncomfortable stance beyond. The next is the crucial pitch and so you know from its very start. Desire here is the strongest concomitant to success. A good flake at shoulder height: move on it high, hand and foot on it both and the right foot splayed out in some sloping distance; tiny finger-holds to straighten on and stretch so far to a single good hold at the extremity of reach. A swing and skipping feet to smooth the lurch across, and suddenly those fingers scream the first signs of strain: on up a thin bulging finger crack climbed with the force of fear till the arms sink to deep jams; a little farther and the Pinnacle nestles between your thighs, a huge runner for the heaviest sling. Rest and be thankful for that's a steep wall beneath.

There is a certain nightmarish quality about the rock above; the crux area, hanging over your head, a great curved blade of rock, thin-edged, fretted, rust-coloured, the Ochre Slab; a strange name for an overhanging groove. Hard to leave the Pinnacle behind, a body-lean, kick round into balance and teeter upwards, hand groping for a long rounded hold; a treacherous, unwashed ally, grease-spattered from this roasting spit of a crux. Tiny footholds, aching calves, a move to be made. Vector on a hot day, hands sweating and feet agonized in the confines of P.A.s, has brought me closer to my technical limit than any other route. A breathless move up, convulsive, the tiniest footholds; an excruciating hand change, layback, bridge, and you're on the Ochre Slab at an old bent peg. Nothing more beautiful. The ropes swing out and down, far into the rock, the slab hugely overarched by roofs, and the thinnest groove slipping past them to lose itself beneath the largest. How many interpretations of that little off-balance and edge-of-nowhere groove. Delicacy, elegance,

Route Vector, Extremely Severe, 250ft.
Cliff Bwlch-y-Moch, Tremadoc Rocks near Portmadoc.
First Ascent J. Brown and C. E. Davies, March 1960; soloed by A. McHardy in 1969.
Map Reference O.S. Tourist Map to Snowdonia, 1–50,000 Sheet 124 (ref. 578407).
Guidebooks C.C. *Snowdon South* by C. T. Jones; West Col *Tremadoc Area* by P. Crew and A. Harris; *Rock Climbing in Wales* by R. James.
Nearest Road Car Park at a filling-station just west of the cliff on the A498 Beddgelert/Portmadoc road.
Good Conditions The climb is very sheltered and rarely gets wet (except the last few moves and the start). Avoid very hot days as sweat makes the climb harder.
Campsites and Bunkhouses There is a barn at Bwlch-y-Moch Farm and camping in the fields at the top of Craig Pant Ifan.
Bibliography C.C. Journal 1963: *Lazy Men's Ways* by Allan Austin (entertaining account of an early ascent); *The Hard Years* by Joe Brown, Gollancz, London, 1967 (first ascent account); *Rock Climbers in Action in Snowdonia* by Cleare and Smythe, Secker and Warburg, London, 1966.

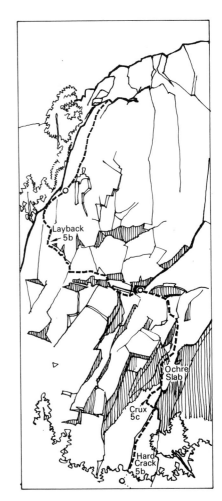

Layback
5b

Ochre
Slab

Crux
5c

Hard
Crack
5b

in stepping through on the limits of adhesion to its outer rib; desperation in a layback, fear strung to a rounded, fingertip edge; or an ungainly straddle to subdue its shy demeanour, all lead to a shaky hold on which to rest body and mind. To the left a peg beneath the overhang, and a crack leading left for slim fingers, the toes outstretched to a moist tongue of slab on the lip of the overhangs. A last biting move round into a dark, cramped hole, sturdy pegs in its dripping recess.

The top pitch is well-nigh perfect: out again to the thin interstices of the overhangs, and over the first one with amazing, joyful ease on a huge hold. A slab; a rough, airy slab, all enclosure behind and but one barrier of overhang above. A little step, delicate, down, the very edge of air; an anxious move up to an antique peg of massive steel, and on the left that final crack, leering and beckoning round the corner of the overhang. Hard to start, bridging on rounded ribs and undercut jams, reaching out so far to the edge of the crack, the world falling away beneath; and it's good, you go, layback, the fingers draining of energy, a sense of urgency as the crack runs out. Fingers claw-like on the left wall, a final hard move, pulling free that heavy body from a vortex of air. And then all beneath, two hundred feet of perfect movement behind. The climb itself: a short climb, a small cliff, crowded, not of the mountains; yet each move imprinted indelibly on the mind, each a perfect cameo; epiphanies of the possible, epitome of a great climb.

Left: The crux of Vector, where a strenuous move has to be made up on to a slippery, sloping jug below the Ochre Slab. *Climber: Baz Ingle*

Right: The moves above the protection peg on the Ochre Slab. *Climber: Dave Alcock*

John Cleare

Almscliff Crag, Yorkshire

The Girdle Traverse of the North-West Face

by Dave Cook

Route North-West Girdle, Hard Very Severe, 200ft.
Cliff Almscliff Crag, Yorkshire.
First Ascent A. Dolphin, J. Cook and J. Ball, 1944.
Map Reference O.S. Sheet 96, 1–50,000 Sheet 104 (ref. 268490).
Guidebook Y.M.C. *Yorkshire Gritstone* by M. Bebbington.
Nearest Road A minor road from Huby to Rigton, two villages close to the A658 Harrogate/Bradford road about five miles south-west of Harrogate. Park on the north-west side of the cliff.
Distance and time from cliff 200 yds. Allow 3 minutes.
Good Conditions The crag is very exposed to bad weather but dries quickly.
Campsites and Bunkhouses No huts or camping but there are bivouac boulders below the crag.
Bibliography Mountain 19: *The Sombre Face of Yorkshire Climbing* by Dave Cook.

'God! I hate this strenuous, boring pile of boulders': not the comment of a state farm inmate confronted with his rock-pile, but the regular groan of a West Riding enthusiast making yet another visit to his favourite local outcrop. Don't be misled. Most fans save their really choice abuse for their local team, and climbers are no exception.

In fact this little fortress-like lump, overlooking a great green sweep of Lower Wharfedale, is one of the very best of the Northern cliffs. On its turreted walls tower some superb natural lines (as well as some very unnatural ones), and in the jumbled gymnasium at their feet a sub-culture of bouldering thrives. A free-climbing tradition, stretching back to the 1890s and incorporating some of the meanest mind-blowers ever climbed on outcrops, keeps the rocks as clean as the west winds that blast them.

So what's news? The same could be said about a score of Pennine cliffs. We're talking about superlatives in this book. The whole North-West Face of Almscliff is a superlative, of a style and grandeur matched by very few gritstone buttresses. This is the land of the natural line, and the Girdle Traverse is no exception.

By 1943, Arthur Dolphin had led first ascents of Z Climb, Overhanging Groove, Great Western and Crack of Doom, and was prospecting the Girdle line as the next logical step. A year later he accomplished the first complete crossing; it is typical of his legendary generosity that he invited the partner-less John 'Pug' Ball, who had not even inspected the problem, to accompany him and John Cook. They were impressed. What was Ball's reaction? In the guidebook historical notes, Allan Austin describes his achievement in doing the climb as last man, 'on sight', as being 'among the greatest exploits on gritstone'.

I don't know if 'Almscliff Eric' Lilley was conscious of this precedent when he agreed to do the route with me, but his garb suggested that he wished to honour Ball's achievement in some appropriate way. As his normal HVS footwear – curly-toed 'Hawkins Walkins' – were being mended, Eric was wearing basketball boots, with the white plastic toe-caps thoughtfully removed

'in case they crept on the tiny holds'.

Now on the Girdle every step is a move, so much so that the guidebook length of 200ft. seems unbelievably short. The climb is so packed with rich incident that it seems twice that length. There is no gentle lead-in. The Traverse line is reached by climbing most of Z Climb, a route on which the feet become progressively more redundant each time you do it. Eric had done it many times: I saw arms doing a version of the butterfly stroke up the first overhang, and then a racing crawl up the steep crack beyond. These are the first jams of the route, and their abundance is indecent here. Before long we'd be grunting for them.

Dolphin's Z Climb turns sharply off the crag to the left, but the Traverse continues up Eric's free-style lane. The crack becomes wider, too wide. Leaving those jams behind is almost as wrenching as moving out of etriers: you end up fingering tiny craters to swing into the lolloping slotters of good old Central Climb.

To reach me, Eric aped his way along a horizontal crack to arrive in the great cave of Parson's Chimney, the first part of his mission successfully accomplished. His toes had not yet touched rock.

But on the chimney right wall, he needs them. A balancy sidle on to and up the rib, and then it's all systems go again along another handrail. The contrast is as ecstatic as raw grape-fruit followed by hot black coffee. But now . . . hallowed ground: Frankland's Green Crack, an incredible lead for the early 1920s, and still a checker fifty years later. We only touch it long enough to thread an ancient nut, before the first really technical climbing of the Girdle, out of the gaudy bilious green of the cleft on to the detached pinnacle known as the Pulpit, as all such pinnacles seem to be. Nothing wild, just a tasty little two-step like half a hundred gritstone cruxes at everyone's favourite standard (that happy land at the top of the VS grade), before the grips really start.

This dropping detour on to the Pulpit is the weak point of the route, but what's a few feet among friends? Eric, displaying a guile beyond his tender years, lashes himself in the good stance at the top of Long

Ken Wilson

Chimney, and points me at the pitch that no one wants to lead, across the top of Wall of Horrors, a climb which for a long time was arguably the biggest lead on grit.

A big roof canopies the first fifteen feet: awkward arm-draining moves, a computer programme of sorties and returns ('just to be confident that I can get back'). Confrontation with the moment . . . commitment . . . a cliché, but such occasions aren't unique, they're all sickeningly alike. It hangs for a long moment, and then falls at a rush. Fast moves across blunt holds; then you can stand without strain. Still twenty feet more to the cave of Great Western, but you know you've done it. Words bubble out. A dangerous moment: in post-cruxal ecstacy you never know what you'll say.

Last pitch, and anti-climax. But this is ridiculous. On what other climb would a leap down the overhanging crux of Great Western, a fifteen-foot hand traverse into a marvellous roofed corner, with a classic lurching exit up Crack of Doom, be so relegated? It's a fairy-tale ending to a great route.

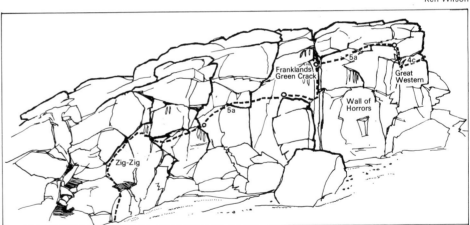

I had to lend Eric my shoes so that he could walk down to the road. Toes apparently play a bigger part in his walking than in his climbing. As we crossed the fields down to the Harrogate bus, I told him of Pug Ball's feat in crossing the Girdle without previous inspection. He was unimpressed. 'Depends what he was wearing,' he said.

161

Kilnsey Crag, Yorkshire

Main Overhang

by Dave Nicol

The Yorkshire Dales contain some of the greatest depths of mountain limestone in the country. However, the more impressive pieces of rock architecture usually conceal themselves in narrow, water-worn gorges or folds in the rolling fells. The exception is Kilnsey crag, the most accessible of all the big outcrops.

Rising only a few hundred feet above the wide valley floor, the crag still manages to dominate a large part of upper Wharfedale. It is seen at its best on a cold winter's morning when the mist hangs low over the river, covering the dry stone walls and flat green bottom-lands. As you drive along the winding road from Grassington to Kettlewell, the great overhang of Kilnsey comes suddenly into view. Arched over a short green pedestal, it resembles the ram and bows of some titanic Mediterranean galley, abandoned by its oarsmen and left to drift in a spectral sea. On such a morning the view from below is intimidating; the lower impending walls, darkly streaked with bitumen, lead to the petrified cornice of the overhang. The winter rains percolate into fissured rock and drain through the roof, their droplets falling far out from the undercut base.

The overhang has always been a well-known landmark. It was a popular target for the hikers and youth-hostellers of the twenties and thirties, who tried to hit it with stones. Doubtless the occasional climber passed by, but the overhang never assumed proportions greater than those of an academic problem. During the thirties, clouded tales drifted out of a troubled Europe. It appeared to many that the rank and file of the Fascist climbing world had mobilized for an all-out assault on the last unclimbed bastions of the Alpine front. Their chief weapon was the piton, first used in the Eastern Alps before the First World War.

Few climbers in Britain understood the real significance of these ascents, which sometimes necessitated the use of an 'artificial' technique. None were equipped to overcome Kilnsey's thirty-foot roof, even if it had occurred to them to attempt such a technically unfamiliar problem.

By the beginning of the fifties, British climbers, now largely unaffected by tra-ditional attitudes, were visiting the Alps in ever-increasing numbers. It soon became clear that hard Alpine ascents were possible for many, and there arose a need for somewhere to practise artificial techniques. Pennine limestone, shunned by the climbing establishment because of its 'treacherous' nature, was to provide the perfect medium for rehearsal.

Yorkshire had an early tradition of aid climbing. The long crack at the entrance to Ilkley quarry was pegged before 1947. Probably the first to drive pitons in earnest into Kilnsey's limestone were Harold Drasdo and Keith King. On returning from the Alps in 1952, they attempted a line to the right of the overhang. An errant girl-friend carried the news to the Rock and Ice, who soon came to look. Joe Brown climbed the incipient diedre below the widest part of the roof, and various other attempts were made over the next few years. However it was the technically advanced Ron Moseley who was to make the breakthrough.

In 1957, Moseley climbed the overhanging corner to the right of Brown's line. He commenced an alarming hanging traverse of 120ft. across a subsidiary flake below the roof. Weekend after weekend he returned, climbing a few feet further and then retreating down a line of fixed ropes. 'It looked just like Moby Dick,' said a contemporary. Like Ahab, Moseley, although tormented by doubts, pursued his quarry with an obsessive vigour. Belayed by John Sumner, he finally triumphed after an exhausting eleven-hour session. The following year, Hields and Hirst made the connection between Brown's diedre and the roof crack. This became the most logical and least terrifying way of climbing the route. The original line fell into disuse and the so-called Direttissima became the most famous artificial climb in the country.

In the same year, Robbins climbed the North-West face of Yosemite's Half Dome and the new Europeans probed the last overhanging walls of the Dolomites. In comparison, when viewed through the objective tunnel of fifteen years' perspective, these vacillations on Kilnsey perhaps seem a trifle ridiculous. But it should be remembered that Moseley and his companions,

Route Main Overhang, A3, Severe, 250ft.
Cliff Kilnsey Crag, Yorkshire.
First Ascent R. Moseley, J. Sumner, F. Williams and A. Knox, March 1957; direct way (route described) R. Hields and R. Hirst, 1958.
Map Reference O.S. Sheet 90, Wensleydale, 1–50,000 Sheet 98 (ref. 973680).
Guidebook Y.M.C. *Yorkshire Limestone* by F. Wilkinson.
Nearest Road The crag overhangs a minor road. Parking possible on weekdays but inadvisable at weekends.
Good Conditions The route is climbable in virtually any weather.
Campsites and Bunkhouses Camp at Malham or bivouac under the cliff.
Bibliography *The Hard Years* by Joe Brown, Gollancz, London, 1967 (account of early attempts).

John Cleare

Above: The first pitch of Kilnsey Main Overhang.
Climber: Peter Crew

just like Robbins and Brandler, were tackling the greatest and most unfamiliar problems readily available to them at the time. In an uninitiated climate of opinion, a few hundred feet of limestone can weigh as oppressively as two thousand feet of vertical granite.

The climb is likely to remain a classic, although most of the aura has gone. To appreciate fully all its components one should have climbed it at least eight years ago. It was traditional to sleep beneath the overhang between the still warm cow pats (this is a favourite shelter for a variety of beasts of the field). Although light-headed from a night in the nearby Tenants' Arms, one was very aware of the depressing area of

horizontal rock above, a feeling which current accounts and descriptions did little to dispel. In the dank half-light of the Pennine dawn, the undercut first few moves were a stomach-wrenching affair; a few free moves and then it was up and gently out, over the blackened cord threads and heroic chunks of iron: not the silent methodical shuffle of the tape-dangling modern, but a more thrashing upward thrutch, held in place by a straining second. At 90ft. the leader reached a footledge and tied on to a reassuring battery of pitons. A frightened coupling at the stance and a new figure swung out for the long reach to gain Moseley's crack. Most aspirants had their secret weapon to overcome this, the

'technical crux', meat-hooks or wire coat-hangers and fifi hooks being the most popular.

The toes were balanced gratefully against the subsidiary bulge, with the fine crack leading out diagonally to the bolts on the lip. A strange position this; though logically only a rope-length from the ground, it was like nothing one had ever experienced before. A vigorous series of moves and one was back to a more familiar world and a stance on the edge of nothing. The last pitch was anticlimactic though harder than it should be, but the excitement was over. Baffled, the Sunday tourists drifted back to their cars on the road below and the bottleneck slowly dissolved.

No longer is the overhang a test-piece, but it is still the touchstone of limestone aid climbing. In the evolutionary sense it is as remote from the chrome-molybdenum subjugated neo-horrors of Strone Ulladale and Berry Head as is *Eohippus* from the modern horse. Because of its uncompromising structure it can never suffer the ritualistic cleansings of the free climber. Neither is it fated to become a meaningless piton ladder. It remains a monument to a few exploratory years, to a lonely figure with a red and white rope, and to the days when a hundred feet of limestone was an adventure that lasted all weekend.

PENNINE AND PEAK OUTCROPS 44 Carnage

by John Porter

Carnage, a Barley brothers' creation, is a poor man's allegory of limestone climbing and, in a small way, of all climbing. In the space of two short pitches, blacks and whites, goods and bads, and exclamations both declamatory and defamatory on the nature of climbing swell the head and slow the body. Like any determined pilgrim, the climber on Carnage must first overcome the diabolical to obtain the ethereal white upper reaches.

On the journey to Malham, we debated whether to climb or picnic. Having put the matter to the vote, it emerged that I would be among the climbers while others vanquished themselves on booze. One has to console oneself at such times with reflections on the beauty of nature and the follies of mankind.

North of Skipton, the country changes from the domination of grey gritstone outcrops to a rolling landscape of white, first seen in the long limestone walls that break over the dales like white-caps on a sea. Small scars of bedrock begin to emerge from the hillsides, and finally Malham, like a frozen wave, slants into view at the top of a rise.

We parked on the top of the right flank and descended through sheep pastures to the horseshoe amphitheatre of Malham. The cove below is filled with trees and tourists, and a small stream that wanders from the base of the main wall. This wall is the centre-piece, 300ft. high, creased on its lip by a stream-bed from which a waterfall once plummeted.

The cove is a Roman stadium in reverse, for the spectators watch from the field while the climbers perform in the galleries. On the main wall, daring young bolt climbers practise their sport. Hardcore, psychopathic American bolters, hands in pockets fondling drill bits, would stop perplexed at the base of Malham, shaking their heads in dismay at the thought of three such climbs on one cliff. But bolt climbs exist in every country, and there is room for them; where there's not much room, as in England, it's better to concentrate them. Here, in Malham, is British climbing's skeleton in the closet, and appropriately it shares a place with the fossils of billions of other skeletons from some primordial sea. Those who find no consolation in this should remember that some famous climber must once have said: 'Ethics are for those who begin to lose patience with their own aesthetical drive'.

But I digress. We stood beneath the right flank of the crag, some of us sorting hardware, the others slowly becoming oblivious to both the beauty of nature and the follies of mankind. The right flank is the mistress of the main wall. The best free climbs at Malham are there, but she is a selfish piece of rock, and most mortal climbers are hard put to it to get off the ground. And so to Carnage itself. It starts not far from where the right flank joins the main wall. The exposure begins almost before you get off the ground, since the floor of the cove is 150ft. of high-angle field below. Geoff had won the toss, so I got the first pitch.

In defiance of the facts, the memory serves up black as the colour of this pitch, for that matches its nature. Twenty feet up steep grass, at the base of a leaning wall, the climbing begins. There is an obvious shallow scoop above the first wall. If you try to climb straight into it, handholds are dispensible. Objecting to the particular flake on which you are about to suspend yourself, you can throw it away and try its neighbour. But this is not the way to start.

A few minutes of tottering non-progress brought John Syrett over from the picnic to point out the obvious move right! The wall still leans, but the holds are sounder. The move is unpredictable enough to activate those inner scales which balance the body's upward progress against the probable softness of the landing below. My arrival on the first ledge above the difficult start brought a call from John: 'That's it! You've done the climb.' Puzzled, I was considering returning to the picnic in triumph until the impossibility of reversing came to me, along with Geoff's protests. His pitch was the supposed crux!

So, left and into the shallow groove, and up this to the first protection. Now, the dark, grotty nature of the wall is forgotten for a moment on a beautiful traverse left, small holds for the hands appearing just in time. At the end of the traverse, a legal peg

Route Carnage, Hard Very Severe, 120ft.
Cliff Right Wing, Malham Cove, Yorkshire.
First Ascent A. and R. Barley, 1965.
Map Reference O.S. Sheet 90, Wensleydale, 1–50,000 Sheet 98 (ref. 898640).
Guidebook Y.M.C. *Yorkshire Limestone* by F. Wilkinson.
Nearest Road A minor road leading from Malham village up to the right of the Cove (ref. 903638).
Distance and time from cliff ¼ mile. Allow 5 minutes.
Good Conditions The cliff is a suntrap though it can be very windy near the top. The climb dries fairly quickly.
Campsites and Bunkhouses Camping at Malham.

Left: The difficult mantelshelf on the second pitch of Carnage. *Climber: Roger Baxter-Jones*

167

and another shout from John: 'It's all over now. You're there.'

Wondering how many more times I'd have to complete the climb before reaching the top of the first pitch, I started up towards a large tree emerging from a crack in the vertical wall. Sure enough, at the tree, with the tone of a priest assuring his audience that they were buying a piece of the true cross, John let me know it was 'all over'. Bush-whacking up through the overhanging vegetation, I discovered that this time it was true. Sweating profusely to the delight of a million midges, I settled myself down in the cave and took in the dull end of the rope.

The dull end was soon the sharp end. Geoff presented only a momentary diversion from the insects before he disappeared over the lip of the cave leaving three slings floating like banners from the peg. The rope moved out quickly from the pile and, with an occasional hoot of delight, Geoff sped to the top.

Soon it was my turn. I pulled into the slings and looked up to see what all the chortling had been about. A milk-storm of rock! Here was real joy ahead. Hanging from the first good hold, I unclipped the slings from the peg and hurried on. The pitch absorbs you while you're on it and leaves you little to remember but a feeling of delight. Up left for a bit, good stoppers, the climbing balancy but not too difficult, the holds in the right directions. You reach the peg and the rope begins to insist that you go right, but the climbing goes straight up to where a right-facing corner and a bulge meet below the infamous mantelshelf.

It's tiring now, steep, and the mantelshelf is the sort of move you can easily balls up, pushing down on the right hand, or should it be the left? . . . half on, half off . . . stretching to reach small side pulls up on the left . . . and when you're up you wonder if it would have gone better on the other hand . . . the other foot? Now you can traverse right where the rope waits hanging down the final corner. A series of horizontal jam moves, kiss'n cousins of many a grit-stone climax in the neighbouring south, but not to be expected on limestone and, for an American, not to be expected at all. Finally, the rope leads straight up, and in a few moves the meadow on top is under foot.

Superb! Coil the ropes and down to the wine past sheep that lift their heads and stare with concentrated stupidity.

Stanage Edge, Derbyshire

Right Unconquerable

by Jim Perrin

In retrospect, Stanage is for me the focal point in that Golden Age we all once knew when we first came to the hills; a pastel-sketched mood of mellow remembrance, the Eastern sea-board of the Peak, west-facing over wave upon wave of moorland edge. Brown peat and purple heather, the rock so softly red in evening sunlight filtered through the smoke-haze of distant, unseen industry. So much beauty in those smoke-bruised sunset skies: violets and purples and violent reds, sometimes the Northern Lights flickering columnar over Bleaklow and Kinder, flanked by the glow of vast cities below the moorland night.

A time past, when the rocks stood about unknown to us, and eager and lustful we explored their every intimacy, climbed until the failing light veiled the crags with shadow and widowed them into night; and tired we would gather bracken golden from the slopes to sleep in sandy caves, our hands lacerated by the crystals of many a crack savagely fought. Early days, early struggles, our blood on the rock as an inextricable bond of friendship about which we built the flesh of our climbing career. The smoke-blackened surface of the rough rock, grouse croaking away and the fresh smell of wet bracken on a June morning; these are the reality of the place. Great nebs worn by the wuthering wind into stern, harsh forms. Rough rock, wild wind, and the reality of the place.

Gritstone has its own form of consciousness: quite simply, it possesses the finest and purest free-climbing ethic in the world. Every new wave in British climbing has gained its initial momentum from gritstone's wild and prehensile freedom of attack. The keynote of gritstone climbing is aggression: the climbs are short and steep; characteristically they deal out inordinately large quantities of pain and fear. Torn hands, scraped knees, strained arms and a dry throat are all in a gritstoner's day: the cracks in particular are armed with vicious teeth. They have about them a degree of static malignity which demands an equal display of controlled temper to overcome them. It's not that climbing on gritstone is more difficult than climbing on other forms of rock, it's just that the defences are

more systematically designed to disconcert: rounded holds, rough bulging cracks, and an overbearing angle; you just have to get used to them.

Stanage is the great crag; four miles long, and with over five hundred climbs. It would be impossible to get a concensus of opinion on which one is typical, let alone best. There are probably fifty climbs as good in their own way as the Right Unconquerable. But this one exemplifies the gritstone approach, and historically it stands at the beginning of an era, the last of the great cracks of Stanage to be climbed, and the first of Joe Brown's great gritstone climbs.

Brown and Stanage! Mohammed and Mecca and many subsequent prayer-mats. In 1947 came the seventeen-year-old Brown to the mountain long revered of his elders, and climbed it in unfaltering style, a rope attached to make the feat respectable. Since that time the climb has come to stand in much the same relationship to gritstone climbing as Cenotaph Corner to climbing in Wales; it is not so much a test of technique as one of approach, an initiation into the attitude of the harder climbs.

Relatively short, fifty feet more or less, it takes an overhanging flake crack running up the face of an otherwise remarkably smooth buttress. Round to the left it has a sister who leads you on gently but clams up at just the wrong moment. She gave in a little earlier but isn't really as good, doesn't allow of the same freedom of movement and hasn't quite got the character of her right-hand twin. Possibly she requires a little more technique, but then climbing on grit is a physical thing.

There is a common start, a short crack which most people fall off before they realize they're not going to run up it. A step right and she stretches out above you. The first straight section of the crack is easily climbed, before the way is sealed by the base of a jutting flake. Above lie step upon step of overhanging flake, thirty feet and the crux at the top. A decision to be made and not lightly because that's a long way to go on ever-weakening arms and what little courage is given to Man; if you want it, you have to fight for it. Hunching

Route The Right Unconquerable, Hard Very Severe, 50ft.
Cliff Intermediate Area, Stanage Edge, Derbyshire.
First Ascent J. Brown, 1947.
Map Reference O.S. Peak District Tourist Map, 1–50,000 Sheet 110 (ref. 240843).
Guidebook B.M.C. *The Sheffield–Stanage Area*, edited by E. Byne.
Nearest Road A minor road below the crag just west of a road junction at ref. 238837.
Distance and time from cliff ¼ mile/300ft. Allow 10 minutes.
Good Conditions The Edge is very exposed to any bad weather and very windy. It dries quickly however.
Campsites and Bunkhouses Campsite at North Lees Hall (ref. 234832). C.C.'s Bob Downes Hut at Froggatt and the L.U.M.C. Hut at Grindleford.
Bibliography *The Hard Years* by Joe Brown, Gollancz, London, 1967.

your body fearfully beneath the flake, reaching high and out one-handed, suddenly you go, swinging right up on to the flake, huge layback holds, hooked hands, the crack sometimes closing, occasioning little shuffles rightwards, awkward hand-changes, anxious moments, racing up the flake to where the top layer juts disturbingly, and all the time on your arms, moving fast. If you do the climb at all, you do it quickly.

The top is rounded and frightening; you haul yourself over on flat hands in exultation. A race against failing strength and breath, fighting all the way, serious, yet an absolute joy in movement. The gritstone essence, living it fully over a few feet of rock. Let them never be so short, for me there are no better climbs in the world.

Left: Laybacking on the Right Unconquerable at Stanage Edge. *Climbers: Geoff Birtles and Bill Beech*

Right: Right Unconquerable, near the end of the layback, where it is necessary to move to the right before making the final difficult moves back left. *Climber: Jim Perrin*

Bob Keates

PENNINE AND PEAK OUTCROPS **46**

Valkyrie

by Nat Allen

Froggatt Edge is the prominent rivelin gritstone escarpment that is seen to the east as one leaves Calver on the A622 Grindleford road. For many years it was one of the gritstone edges forbidden to the climber. But after the war, when restrictions on open country were relaxed, climbers slowly began to filter on to the crag. However, with the exception of members of the Valkyrie M.C., very few returned, the rest perhaps being repelled by the abundance of unclimbed and obvious possibilities.

But 'The Valkyrie', a group of young climbers and hard walkers from the Derby area, did return, to pioneer the majority of the routes on the edge, and to undertake the task of compiling the first guidebook to this area. Froggatt Edge now ranks amongst the most popular crags in the Peak District.

1948 was a dampish summer; at Idwal a group of the Valkyrie, having had more than their share of rain, reached the end of their holiday and set off for home and work, leaving behind Wilf White and 'Chuck' Cook to climb for a further week in the company of two Manchester climbers with whom the group had struck up a friendship. The arrangements to see the pair again, for a return bout on gritstone, were left in the capable hands of Wilf White.

Some weeks later we met the 'Mancunians' at Froggatt Edge. The motley crew that turned up was led by the tall fellow and his little mate that we had met in Wales. Friendly banter was exchanged over a brew, until we set off on a guided tour of the edge – it was 'Slim' Sorrel's and Joe's first time in this area. Soon, it was the short, north side of Froggatt Pinnacle, the little-climbed centre-piece of the Edge, that had everyone grappling with the bulging rib of Henry Bishop's Original Route and Pinnacle Face. Then we moved down the gulley and gazed up optimistically at the south and west faces as they were then – sixty feet of unclimbed gritstone.

The west side clearly interested Joe, and later, after patiently watching the abortive efforts of our best men, he amazed the gathered assembly by pulverizing the

oblique crack that splits the lower wall of the pinnacle, finally reaching a ledge in what we have all come to accept as the Joe Brown style.

It was not until one weekend in the Spring of 1949 that 'Brown' renewed interest in the pinnacle climb. He moved smoothly up the crack which he had demolished the previous year, then, instead of moving leftwards, traversed right to the ledge on the nose. Wilf White joined him on the stance, then with surprising ease Joe proceeded slowly and methodically to solve the problem of the upper section. A remarkable lead for the period.

The route, Valkyrie, is the classic excursion of Froggatt; it combines all that is found in gritstone climbing: cracks, traverses, airy stances, bulges, mantelshelves and a slab, with the added kick of the rope-down descent of the north side.

To climb the deceptively easy looking Oblique Crack is a fairly strenuous business. Good hand jams aid progress to a foot-ledge in twelve feet. The move back into the crack is awkward, with the now poorer hand jams, and it is difficult to hold the body from twisting out of balance. When the horizontal fault is reached and a semi-resting position is gained, a nut runner can be arranged, the quality of which depends on the luck of the nut chosen. The traverse right brings the belay ledge at chest height. Reasonable hand-holds assist the awkward landing where chockstones behind the block give good anchorage for the belay.

The second and more serious pitch starts without incident. However, the bulging nature of this section soon makes itself felt, and once again protection is not good. There seem to be two methods of reaching the sloping ledge above on the arête. The old-fashioned way involves semi-finger-jamming in the three-foot crack with the right hand, reaching the nose with the left, and transferring the balance until a semi-mantelshelf can be made. The other way is to ignore the crack and move up on two reasonable hand-holds. The leg can be wedged in the fault below the nose, and the ledge reached. Mantelshelf the ledge and ascend the easier-angled slabby rib above to the summit.

Route Valkyrie, Hard Very Severe, 65ft.
Cliff Froggatt Edge, Derbyshire.
First Ascent J. Brown and W. White, 1948.
Map Reference O.S. Peak District Tourist Map, 1–50,000 Sheet 119 (ref. 248765).
Guidebook B.M.C. *The Sheffield–Froggatt Area* by E. Byne.
Nearest Road The B6054 ½ mile south of the Grouse Inn in laybys at ref. 254776.
Distance and time from cliff ¾ mile. Allow 15 minutes.
Good Conditions Very exposed to winds and bad weather but dries quickly.
Campsites and Bunkhouses Campsites in Calver and North Lees Hall near Stanage. C.C.'s Bob Downes Hut below the crag and the L.U.M.C. Hut at Grindleford.

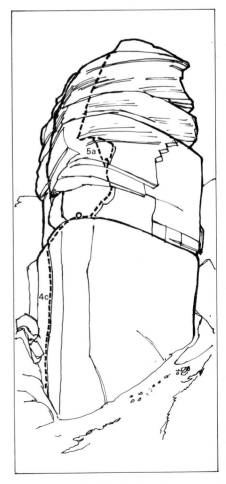

Left: The first pitch of Valkyrie where the route moves right on good jams in a horizontal crack.
Climber: Jim Perrin

173

Ken Wilson

Left: The second pitch of Valkyrie. Some steep moves above the stance allow the ledge to be reached with the hands and then gained fully by a precarious mantelshelf move. *Climbers: Jim Perrin and Martin Jackson*

Right: Approaching the difficult section of Elder Crack (*see following chapter*). Climber: Geoff Birtles

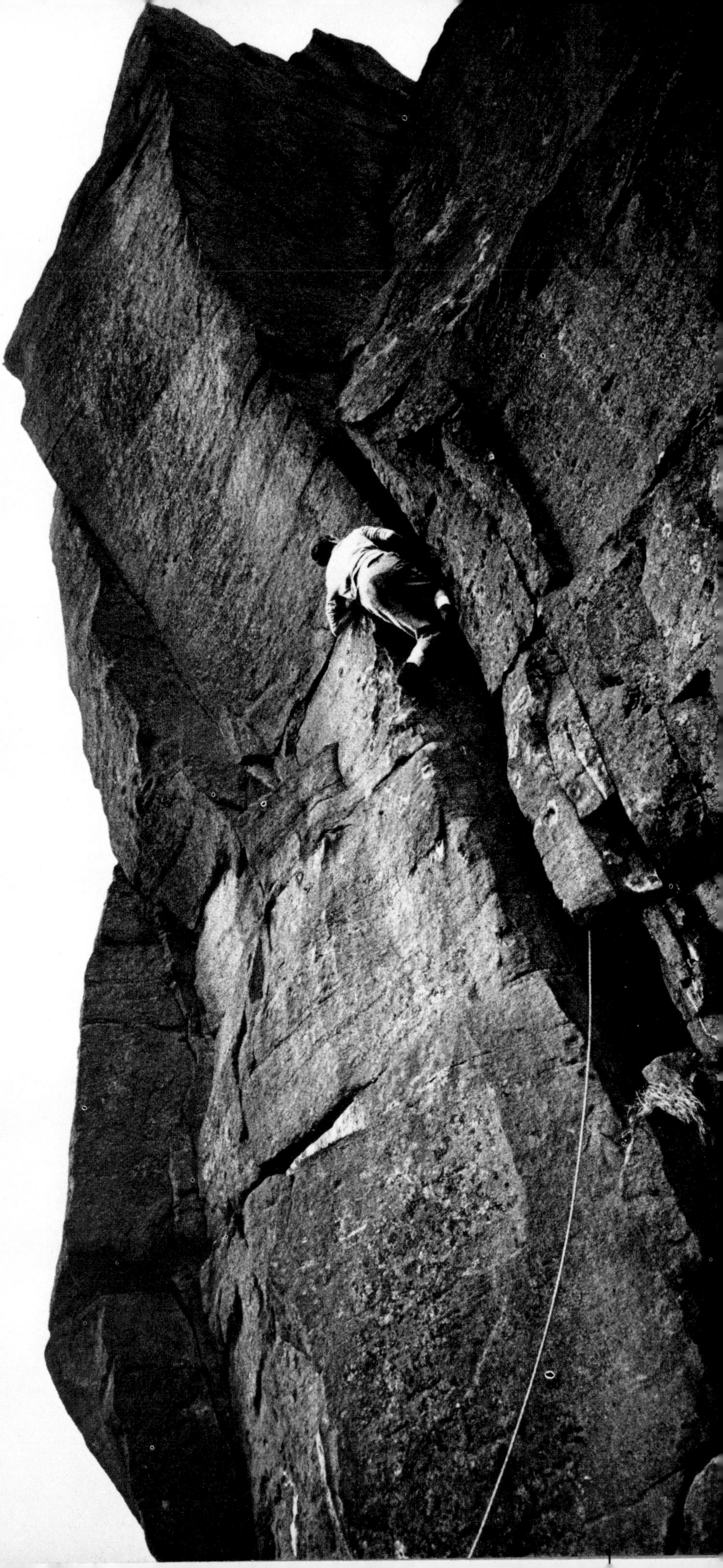

Bob Keates

Curbar Edge, Derbyshire

Elder Crack

by Geoff Birtles

Route Elder Crack, Extremely Severe, 70ft.
Cliff Curbar Edge, Derbyshire.
First Ascent J. Brown and party, 1953.
Map Reference O.S. Peak District Tourist Map, 1–50,000 Sheet 119 (ref. 258752).
Guidebook B.M.C. *The Sheffield–Froggatt Area* by E. Byne.
Nearest Road A minor road leads off the A623 through Curbar and over the Curbar/Baslow escarpment. Park in laybys at the top of the hill (ref. 261748) and walk along the Edge.
Distance and time from cliff ¼ mile. Allow 5 minutes.
Good Conditions Exposed to winds and bad weather but dries fairly quickly.
Campsites and Bunkhouses Camping at Calver and Stoney .Middleton, huts at Froggatt and Grindleford.
Bibliography C.C. Journal 1958: *Red Rose on Gritstone* by Allan Austin (discussion of the harder Derbyshire Gritstone climbs).

There are plenty of excuses for failing on Elder Crack, but few for not trying. Its seventy feet make it the longest route on the whole Froggatt–Curbar escarpment, and it is the best looking of all the cracks: a dog-leg cocked provocatively above the road to Curbar Nick. A short walk up to the Edge discloses to the experienced eye that the major difficulties lie in the middle twenty feet, a crux-and-a-half of the Joe Brown special category that makes you think he had something secret under his vest. But alas! His biggest feature is his grin. So who grins on Curbar Crack?

By the summer of 1950, Brown had been demobbed from the army after spending months sleeping twenty hours a day in the back of a store-room somewhere in Singapore. According to the little man himself, he came out bursting with energy: 'It was just as though I had saved up all that sleep.' Come the autumn and civilian Brown was fast picking off nearly all the best lines left on the Eastern Edges. Elder Crack was one of those that fell in the fall of 1950 – almost a non-contest against the Baron in his prime.

I talked to Brown about the first ascent.

'You did it, didn't you?' I asked.

'Yeh!'

'Who did it with you?'

'Can't remember.'

But he could remember a small elder tree low down in the crack and long since extinct.

'It says in the old pink guide that it was VS,' I said.

'Well it is, isn't it?' he replied.

So I changed the subject.

Elder Crack is now graded Extremely Severe; some consolation for the effort. The guide says: '. . . the overhang is climbed facing left . . .' More fool you. It is much easier facing right.

The overhang is more of a bulge in the crack-cum-chimney, not wide enough to climb inside when it really matters, nowhere narrow enough for a rosy hand-jam. The lower section is relatively easy at about Severe; no need for draggy runners here. This leads to the widest part of the crack beneath the crux. Here, lucky leaders find the broddling stick *in situ*, enabling a runner to be fixed. I took it there in 1964 to thread a

small natural chock deep in the back of the crack. (The alternative in those days was the then standard one-inch square nut from the railway line at Hathersage.) On that occasion I climbed the crux to within reach of the sloping resting ledge, but was so exhausted that I slithered back down the crack and popped out of the bottom. The runner held, almost disintegrating the small chock, and the next time I went back it had, significantly, gone. Nowadays you just hook one of those fancy wedge-shaped things on the end of the stick and plop in a stopper. Dead is the great pebble-threading craft.

With the security of a good runner, approach the bulge with legs splayed and undercut holds. Don't be tempted into jamming in the right knee; you only have to switch later on. Try it if you like. More awkwardly reach up with the left arm for a flake high up inside the crack on the right wall, lean back and bring up the left knee to jam. Look, no hands! Too late now for misgivings. You need a special gritstone technique here, the Gritstone Udge; a fairly select move, too rare for Pete Crew's climbing dictionary. It is used only when there are no handholds and no footholds, and the only way forward is to . . . udge up a bit. The classic three points of contact are abandoned, as a dozen points consolidate into a thrutching mass. You get your left arm jammed across the crack, left buttock and left knee inside, right leg scratching outside and right hand pinch-gripping the square outside edge. Then you kind of swim. And up you go.

A friend of mine once got into this position, quite pleased at his first XS knee-jam. Then he discovered that his knee was truly jammed and he couldn't move. At this point one is virtually supported by the knee and, as everyone knows, all you have to do is take the weight from above, straighten the leg by bringing the foot upwards into the back of the crack, thus narrowing the knee and so on and so forth. But this lad was a journalist and 'You can't tell them buggers nowt!' So he fell off.

The trouble with the swimming bit is the rope, which jams between the leg and the crack: put the knot front or back and it still jams, put it on your right hip and you

chance being flipped upside down if you fall off, so the knot goes on the left hip as the lesser of two evils.

After udging for some way there is a hold on the left, somewhere out in space behind you; this can be used by means of a half-nelson to emerge from the crux on to a sloping resting place. There is a good chockstone here which is well worth it for first-timers. The crack above is much easier, but the arms are tired and a dozen layback moves lie ahead, with occasional grasps inside the crack for hand-jams that never appear. If you get to the top, you know you've climbed a gritstone crack. Then you can grin.

Somebody once mocked that gritstone climbers jam up blank slabs . . . How else?

Right: The crux of Elder Crack. *Climber: Tom Proctor*

Cratcliffe Tor, Derbyshire

Suicide Wall

by Paul Nunn

Route Suicide Wall, Hard Very Severe, 90ft.
Cliff Cratcliffe Tor, Birchover, Derbyshire.
First Ascent P. R. J. Harding and Miss V. Lee, May 1946.
Map Reference O.S. Peak District Tourist Map, 1–50,000 Sheet 119 (ref. 228623).
Guidebook C.C./B.M.C. *The Chatsworth Gritstone Area* by E. Byne.
Nearest Road The B5056 Bakewell/Ashbourne road at a road junction (ref. 229619).
Distance and time from cliff ¼ mile/200ft. Allow 5 minutes.
Good Conditions Steep and fairly sheltered, thus frequently dry, but once wet it can retain lichen for some time.
Campsites and Bunkhouses Camping at Dudwood Farm, just down the side road by the parking spot. Huts at Froggatt, Grindleford and Buxton.
Bibliography *High Peak* by Eric Byne, Secker and Warburg, London, 1966 (account of the first ascent).

Top right: Cratcliffe Tor with Suicide Wall on the extreme right. The Bower, with its massive tree, is under the prominent overhang to the left of the wall.

Bottom right: The steep crack behind the flake half-way up the second pitch. *Climber: Jim Perrin*

Unlike most gritstone edges in Derbyshire, Cratcliffe Tor is isolated and compact, the largest of a series of romantic, tree-studded tors of massive bouldery gritstone which outcrop west of the Derwent. The steep, clean-topped walls are shrouded in trees below and characterized by a blocky structure which creates long horizontal creases and wiltingly blank interior walls. Hidden behind an ancient yew, a hermit's cave is ill-protected by a rusting metal fence, and the south-easterly aspect of the place makes it both pleasant and somehow warm and intimate.

A hundred-foot wall dominates the east end of the cliff. Plumb-vertical, sprouting hardy trees at its base and a pattern of awkwardly distributed cracks above, this wall was for many years the outstanding challenge of the crag. A narrow crack escapes from the trees and leads diagonally to the Bower, a shelf below a beetling overhang. The Bower sports a massive tree which has seen countless abseil retreats. No crack escapes direct from there to the cliff top. Instead, a fierce flake descends the upper wall to fade out a few feet away in an apparently smooth short section of grainy gritstone.

The Bower itself was reached by a Severe route as early as 1922 by Fred Pigott and Morley Wood of 'Cloggy' fame. Above, the overhang blocked all access to the upper wall, while the horizontal crack leaving the Bower's east corner offered few holds and less apparent possibility of progress. Doubtless others looked, but Frank Elliott, leader of the nearby Unconquerable, top-roped the exit from the Bower

in 1933. It appears that this bold pioneer was unprepared to lead it, and it was not until 1946 that Peter Harding led the wall after a top-roped inspection and some gardening. He was accompanied by Veronica Lee, who must have been a considerable female gritstoner for those days.

Suicide Wall remains a serious undertaking, especially if the lichen, stimulated by mist or rain, makes the usually rough rock at all slippery. A gritstoner's climb *par excellence*, it is varied, steep, strenuous and unrelenting, and yet never outstandingly difficult. A deceptive tree-swarm over the initial bulge leads to a niche below more serious climbing. A running belay here might prevent impalement on the barer branches of the gnarled trees below. The narrow, slanting crack above is a hand-grinder and lacks footholds, so that it frequently draws blood. It leads quite quickly into the edge of the Bower, which provides a belay and a good place to recoup one's energy for the rigours of the upper wall. It also enables the leader to reassure doubting seconds, for the wall above is entirely out of sight round the overhang to the right.

The shelf is left by a swing on horizontal hand-jams, placing the climber in a bridged position below the smooth section which cuts him off from the cracks above. A delicate and perhaps committing step up is not so difficult as it appears, but in summer nettles growing from an exiguous crack could end up in the leader's face.

Above, a sharp flake is best taken boldly on jams and layaways until a central niche is attained. A dwarfish resting position becomes possible here.

The final flake looks formidable and, by rapidly widening beyond jamming width, prevents aged gritstoners from avoiding abhorrent laybacks. Again, a quick bold approach is probably preferable in order to reach excellent jams and jughandles like battlements, which allow an exhilarating final swing over the top for those with excessive remnants of energy. Most climbers accept such gifts gratefully, as arms tire, ropes begin to snag and the second snoozes indifferently, neutralized and blinkered in the Bower below. But then his turn is yet to come!

Right: The same point as that on page 179. The alternative way of climbing the flake is by a bold layback. *Climber: Geoff Birtles*

Left: Having traversed out of The Bower the climber is starting the difficult section of the second pitch. *Climber: Jim Perrin*

Bob Keates

by Nat Allen

Route Chee Tor Girdle, Very Severe, 650ft.
Cliff Chee Tor, Cheedale, Derbyshire.
First Ascent C. Jackson and J. Atkinson, 1964.
Map Reference O.S. Peak District Tourist Map, 1–50,000 Sheet 119 (ref. 124733).
Guidebook C.C./B.M.C. *The Northern Limestone Area* by P. J. Nunn.
Nearest Road At the Railway Inn (ref. 138731) on the B6049 Tideswell/Blackwell road. Follow the old railway or the dale itself.
Distance and time from cliff 1 mile. Allow 20 minutes.
Good Conditions The climb is very sheltered and stays in condition longer than other Derbyshire Limestone routes.
Campsites and Bunkhouses Camping near Blackwell or at Stoney Middleton. Eldon Potholing Club Hut at Spring Gardens in Bakewell.

Chee Dale is that stretch of the Wye valley that runs from a point three miles east of Buxton, on the A6 Bakewell road, to a bridge on the B6049 in Miller's Dale, on the Tideswell road. Chee Tor is the half-way point on a footpath which, if followed from the Buxton end, provides the climber bound for the Tor with striking views of some of the most spectacular limestone architecture to be seen in the area. The curtain-raiser is Plum Buttress, one of the finest cliffs in Derbyshire. This escarpment, seen on the right, ends on the long wall of Moving Buttress, returning into the prominent Runyon's Corner. The next crag to appear as one walks down the narrowing dale is Two Tier Buttress, which bears a strong resemblance to Chee Tor. Some 200 yards further, Nettle Buttress is passed. Then a footbridge is crossed to the correct side of the river for our climb. The second footbridge is not crossed; the track along the right bank is taken until the fine expanse of Chee Tor comes into view. The Tor may also be approached by the disused railway line and its tunnels of dubious construction. This way is slightly quicker, but it does not have the aesthetic value of the more scenic river path.

Chee Tor attracted the attention of a number of early wanderers and writers. In the nineteenth century, James Croston, author of *On Foot in the Peak*, described the mighty Tor . . . 'as seen rising in solemn grandeur, lifting its hoary head in awe and majesty, to a height upwards of 300 feet'. But, despite these and other excusable comments, climbers were not attracted to the dale.

The appearance of Graham West's *Limestone Guide* in 1961 revealed the extent of the exploration and achievements made on the Tor by his band of limestone pioneers. West himself had led Alfresco, and Malcom Baxter had a free-climb, Doggone Groove, at the right-hand end of the crag. In November of the same year, armed with the knowledge gleaned from this book, Colin Mortlock, Pete Hutchinson and Lyn Noble paid a visit to Chee Tor. This predominantly North Wales team ascended Mortlock's Arête, and the scene was set for further development. 1963/64

were busy times for the crag, and most of the classic lines were climbed then by teams from all areas, with no special group making Chee Tor its preserve. A visit of this type was made in late August 1964 by the established Stoney Middleton team of Chris Jackson and John Atkinson, already foremost in the ranks of the Cioch Club's new route addicts.

The pair started to traverse the crag from the right-hand end. The first couple of pitches turned out to be so straightforward that they began to think the climb must already have been done. Odd pitons appeared here and there, all associated with the plumb lines that crossed the fault. Two peg runners were employed to safeguard the hard section of the fifth pitch, but in the main the protection was in keeping with limestone traverses generally, with a wealth of superb thread runners appearing. The next hard pitch had *in situ* an old wood wedge with a hemp sling, which tempted Chris Jackson to use it for a crafty hand-hold. Without warning, it plopped out, giving the leader a gripping moment whilst avoiding parting company with the rock. He recovered, and the pair continued with the final fight through the brambles, having won what must certainly be one of the most celebrated traverses on limestone.

Some weeks later, Joe Brown and John Amatt crossed the girdle, using similar tactics to the Cioch pair and making what they thought to be a first, instead of the second, ascent. This received some publicity, and is wrongly recorded in Eric Byne's book, *High Peak*.

Having arrived at the right-hand end of the crag, the climber can either start the girdle by walking on from the right, above the lower tier, to a point above Doggone Groove, or he can make the ascent of this climb as a very worthy starter. Doggone Groove is the first real line: a crack and good holds lead to a sapling runner; a steeper wider crack is then utilized to a widening, while soil dribbles down from tree roots above. A short spasm of 'tot grovelling' leads to belays on the fault line. From here, the 'Good Book' says two 8oft. pitches for the next section; I prefer to take it in one, 150ft. of rope being adequate. The

Right: The fourth pitch of
Chee Tor Girdle just before
the rounded arête.
Climber: Tony Watts

Doug Scott

first part is pleasant slabby climbing. Beyond a recess a steep wall is descended, and good side-pulls lead down to a welcome foot-ledge. After moving back up the fault, a step is made round into a tree-filled bay, with a comfortable belay. The next bit of the route is on steeper ground. Good hand-holds and thread runners lead to the now-exposed and usually damp last thirty feet or so, the difficulties usually being found where the fault line closes up. The magnificent yew tree growing from the crack provides the best belay; the pedestal on the left is now poorly protected, for the overpegged rock hereabouts is unstable. This sad trend of robbing permanent peg belays will surely prove the ruination of some limestone climbs.

From here the route looks really good. What can be seen of the horizontal fault doesn't look as though it should present the climber with any desperate problems. The wall below is 'plonk on' vertical; above our heads is an almost continuous roof with an unbroken headwall.

Carrying all the long slings we have for oversize threads, we find the first bit is more difficult than it seemed from the belay. The footholds are high and an awkward corner has to be crossed to gain a delightful sequence of traversing moves out to the resting place on the rounded arête. Stock is taken here: the drop is beginning to pull at our heels, and the way ahead looks gripping. Once round the corner visual contact is lost, so a last cheery word is had with the patient second. Clipped into a welcome peg on the left, with claws sharpened, it is necessary to descend slightly away from the friendly fault, which has more or less closed up. Down

on the wall in this increasingly superb position, it is reachy and tiring. Regaining the fault line, it is a relief to catch hold of the big pockets as the larger crack reforms. Hereabouts the footholds are either too high or at full stretch. The first nook is not a good place to stop, but further on there is a more comfortable though far from spacious eyrie that is good enough. In the 'Good Book' the way ahead is aptly described as 'a strenuous hand traverse', and it looks it. We have a great open corner to our left which has to be crossed, and you might say that from here we are in for some fun and games.

Gingerly, the pleasantly difficult but not too strenuous hand traverse is made to the corner, where a glance back to the belay reveals the situation on this superb white wall. The crossing of the left wall gives one final problem, and a feeling almost of sorrow when one realizes that *that's it!* . . . the end of a couple of hundred feet in a climber's paradise of good holds and airy situations.

The continuation of the traverse is something of an anti-climax, bringing nothing more than a fight through brambles and vegetation. A more fitting finish can be made at the ash tree belay by abseiling down the impending wall that has provided the exposure for the last few hundred feet of climbing. A final flourish and a fitting finish.

I have done the Chee Tor Girdle a number of times in varying conditions and could never tire of such a climb. Classics in any area are always a must, and this one is no exception.

Cheedale, Derbyshire

Sirplum

by Paul Nunn

Cheedale's cliffs remained almost unexplored until the late 1950s. Harold Drasdo had climbed the gritstone-like crack of Stalk, on Plum Buttress, but most of the subsequent climbing had been unambitious. There was a certain wariness about bigger, steeper bits of limestone, particularly after the spectacular fall enjoyed by Gordon Mansell when he was attempting the unclimbed bulge which later became the Big Plum. In this atmosphere, Gray West's ascent of Big Plum seemed like a breakthrough, although it was really only a matter of catching up with normal limestone practice elsewhere. For a time it seemed that Plum Buttress would remain a pegger's paradise, and subsequent climbs like Tony Howard's Victoria served to emphasize the fact.

Yet many a nosy climber, groping his way along the bisecting rake below the overhangs, must have cast his eyes across the bulging wall on the right, where black roofs meet the vertical in a jumble of small overhangs and undercut grooves. Images of that wall when it was virgin include not only these long-familiar features of an impressive climb, but also a black-cowled, six-foot flake, poised in the very middle, ominous in its obvious insecurity. Not that most climbers were likely to have gone so far as to imagine themselves clinging to such a tottering missile, for the wall itself appeared so steep and fierce that it did not require this stern guardian to give it a nightmare quality in those imagination-ridden times.

By dint of persistence, a little ambivalence of mind regarding the extent to which it would go free, and that subtle mixture of myopia and imagination which first ascensionists of hard climbs require, Bob Dearman sorted it out; and the vogue for Sirplum swept through the local *habitués* as a natural aftermath to the intrigues which always surrounded new climbing activities in those times. Only the sourest of critics could carp at the excellence of the route and the boldness of its first ascent.

Grass and wild flowers creep across the promenade which was once a railway through the Wye Valley. It is a reversion symbolic of new priorities and characteristic of the double-edged nature of so-called

progress. The dodging of trains was the most death-defying feature of climbing in this area until the late sixties; tunnel-walking escapes, when the valley path flooded on winter nights, provided the pinnacle of sensation, as one leapt from the path of an oncoming monster in complete blackness, or cowered, nose in water, between the sooty walls and the roaring wheels. That particular excitement has gone, and one can only conjure up the spooks of trains and tunnelling navvies on black night retreats. At the same time, this once noisy valley has reverted to the peace lost during the last century. And yet, as one walks into Chee from the west, the gargantuan and irremediable destruction wrought by the quarrying companies, carving out a limbo of dust, mud and ugliness from a gentle, rolling limestone upland, is so painfully apparent as to make anyone who has known this country well retreat into near despair. The peace of the Wye and the minor modifications brought about by the railway companies seem both Lilliputian and fragile in contrast.

The transition from mass peggery to quieter, athletic free-climbing seems a suitable accompaniment to the locomotives' retreat. Sirplum once looked as if it should be an aid climb, but it never really became one despite the four or five pegs originally used as aid or protection. As for the climbing itself, it works a gentle and tantalizing escalation upon the aspirant. Relatively solid, white, lower walls provide alternative routes to the rake, where one can be weakened not only by a large block behind which a supposed leader may attempt to hide his shame-filled face, but by the lateral rake which offers an enticingly easy and flower-strewn route to the pub and ennui, a variation which may seem singularly attractive on closer inspection of the steep black bulge above.

Confidence alone is hazardous here; the incautious leader, anxious to dangle the statutory twenty feet of rope before his first runner, could miss a rusty piton about which a small loop may be draped. Although no longer respectable as aid, this is useful as a runner. A few grasping arm pulls, some swinging up and shuffling of the feet, and

Route Sirplum, Hard Very Severe, 180ft.
Cliff Plum Buttress, Cheedale, Derbyshire.
First Ascent R. Dearman and R. D. Brown, 1963.
Map Reference O.S. Peak District Tourist Map, 1–50,000 Sheet 119 (ref. 115726).
Guidebook C.C./B.M.C. *The Northern Limestone Area* by P. J. Nunn.
Nearest Road An unmetalled road leaves the A6 Buxton/Matlock road at Topley Pike and curves down into Cheedale. Park at the railway bridge (ref. 116727) and walk along the bed of the old railway.
Distance and time from cliff ¼ mile. Allow 5 minutes.
Good Conditions The crag dries quickly and the valley is sheltered. The route is climbable in all seasons.
Campsites and Bunkhouses Various Youth Hostels in the area and the C.C.'s Bob Downes Hut at Froggatt. Camping locally or at either Stoney Middleton or Calver.

Tony Riley

Tony Riley

Above left: Plum Buttress in Cheedale with climbers on the comparatively easy first pitch of Sirplum. *Climbers: Pat Fearnehough and Rod Valentine*

Above right: The big pitch of Sirplum. *Climbers: Bob Dearman and Bob Toogood*

Right: On the big pitch of Sirplum just beyond the position of the climber in the previous picture. *Climber: Henry Barber*

one is led to the first fresco of jugs and a protection piton.

Seductive jugs lead left, with an occasional rattling complaint, to the plinth from which the guardian flake was once levered, groaning and crashing into space. It provides a pleasant chapel of rest, with runners above. Stepping out and up, over the quite big overhangs below, can be quite alarming if one looks before making the bold moves which lead to apparently even less friendly territory. At this point the climb begins to

give a little, providing a man-thickness thread which could be embarrassing to the short sling brigade. With that in place, any climber worth his salt and capable of getting there is immortal; he has the choice only of groping on, up and round the bulges, steep grooves and terrifying grasses above, or of falling clear and clean into the ample space below. There is exultation in that finality, despite aching arms, for beyond that thread Sirplum has only its excellence to give.

186

Tony Riley

High Tor, Derbyshire

Debauchery

by Nat Allen

High Tor is a limestone bastion. Massive in appearance, it stands above Matlock Dale, its lower scree slopes enswathed in thick woods. Many fine man-made walks interlace these tree-covered slopes and the summit plateau.

The Tor is situated on the east of the River Derwent and the A6 road between Matlock Bath in the south, and Matlock to the north. It is from Matlock, moving down the A6 road, that it is best seen, when its comparatively modest 150ft. walls of compact limestone belie its vast appearance.

The first climbing on High Tor was done in 1903, when J. W. Puttrell and his Kyndwr Club team ascended High Tor Gully. Like many of Puttrell's climbs, this was an outstanding achievement, for it was another fifty years before climbers, assisted by the use of artificial aids, began pegging and wedging the obvious lines. The early sixties saw the crag gaining in popularity, with the production of West's guide to limestone climbing, and Doug Scott's Derwent Valley book. For years, the main frontal face was the domain of artificial climbers; most of the weaknesses were climbed by such tactics, until this trend received a severe shock in 1961 when Steve Read led the Original Route entirely free, taking his protection from odd bits of ironmongery left by previous de-peggers – a tremendous effort by this dedicated limestoner.

In 1965, a young member of the Stoney Middleton-based Cioch Club put into practice the theory of free-climbing the expanse of unclimbed rock to the left of the Original Route and finishing, he hoped, above the conspicuous roofs of Fortress Wall, on the steep and apparently holdless Head Wall, crossing and climbing parts of four of Derbyshire's best peg routes.

Chris Jackson, accompanied by John ('Ackers') Atkinson, started his Cook's Tour of High Tor by moving first up the Original Route and tensioning across to a small ledge stance on Bastion Wall. Then a rising traverse was made, hopefully, to the left. 'At this point,' said Jackson, 'I protected myself with one of my ropes thrown over a handy peg in the Girdle Traverse.' This section moved on to Fortress Wall and the

problem was solved, the final section easing to the stance. So one of the finest expeditions on Peakland limestone, another daring free-climbing breakthrough, was made. Very much a feature of this period, the climbing was nowhere found to be excessively difficult, but the situations on the climb must have given good cause for apprehension. One piton runner was placed on the bulge below the Bastion Wall stance. Battered relics of ironmongery and nuts gave adequate protection.

Debauchery, like most of the dozen or so classics on High Tor, receives quite a lot of traffic, but the crag is rarely crowded, and one can spend a sunny afternoon, when most other crags in the area are less amenable after a wet spell, climbing on dry rock with the added luxury of having the place to oneself. The low-lying, sheltered valley, and the Tor's western aspect, contribute to the crag's quick-drying nature.

To start Debauchery, the climber. must locate the line of Original Route, which is the noticeable fault in the otherwise compact front wall. The first section is no more than a scramble up steep easy rock to a good stance and sapling belay at 40ft. From the stance, step left and move up a few feet to a foot-ledge. To the left again the wall is climbed on a sequence of excellent flake holds. At about 15ft., protection can be arranged to safeguard a move left into a shallow groove with a good peg *in situ*! Having clipped on to the piton, the climber must draw enough rope through to tension down, across to good holds on a more broken section. Hereabouts is an old peg, and a cramped stance can be taken. Most choose to continue up the next section to a good stance in a better position, to give protection for the second man. The rock is suspect as one moves cautiously to the bulge. Care must be taken here to fix a good nut runner in the crack, for the next section is a rather committing semi-layback, and the rock, while not being loose, demands steadiness on the part of the climber. The small ledge is reached, and a good angle piton is needed to safeguard this fine exposed position.

The second or last man must be competent to follow this pitch – and indeed the

Route Debauchery, Hard Very Severe, 220ft.
Cliff High Tor, Matlock, Derbyshire.
First Ascent C. Jackson and J. Atkinson, 1965.
Map Reference O.S. Peak District Tourist Map, 1–50,000 Sheet 119 (ref. 297590).
Guidebook C.C./B.M.C. *The Southern Limestone Area* by P. J. Nunn.
Nearest Road The A6 just south of High Tor. A footbridge leads across the river to the grounds that hold the Tor. A fee for entry should be paid if required, to maintain carefully established relations between climbers and the local authority.
Distance and time from cliff ¼ mile/300ft. Allow 10 minutes.
Good Conditions The route is more exposed to bad weather than others on the cliff but dries off quickly after rain.
Campsites and Bunkhouses Campsites at Black Rocks, Calver and Stoney Middleton. Huts at Froggatt and Grindleford. There are a number of Youth Hostels in the area.

Tony Riley

189

Above and right: Two photos showing the first big pitch of Debauchery. *Climbers: Chris Jackson and Jack Street*

whole climb – for a novice could find the pendule and the traversing nature of the second pitch a reversal of the lead.

Protection is arranged high in the corner to the left, and the slab is then traversed delicately leftwards to a piton on the bulge. With this welcome runner, a better resting position is achieved on the slab above. The climb now traverses left, across a delicate wall to a welcome horizontal fault. This section is very exposed, but reasonably well protected by two or three old pitons.

The fault has good hand-holds. After a step left into a shallow groove, the climbing eases. A slight bulge is ascended on to a grassy break, which is traversed leftwards to a tree belay on the top: a great pitch in a really exposed situation.

The descent is made by moving right to join a good track: after approximately 100 yards an obvious track descends a shallow depression through the trees, and a short scramble leads down to the track traversing the foot of the crag.

PENNINE AND PEAK
OUTCROPS **52**

Alcasan

by Paul Nunn

The Dale will never be free of the scars of industrialization. Narrow and confined, it has been rocked and shaken by high explosives, thoughtlessly wrecked by a succession of quarry companies. Dust coats the greenery with funereal drabness, blasting continues to devour the south side of the valley, wild life retreats and vegetation becomes sparse as the valley is picked to its geological bones.

Yet 'Stoney' retains some of its charm. The close village under Lover's Leap cliffs has a warm and intense atmosphere which is reflected in the character of the climbing.

A decade ago, few free climbs encroached upon Windy Ledge Buttress, 90ft. of natural limestone perched on a quarried base. Such a formidable looking wall was thought suitable for pegging, a view encouraged by looseness, a few existing artificial routes, and the sloth of long established patterns of thinking.

Among the most prominent of the cliff's features are the regular, horizontal, stripe-like strata, the bands which weave their way through the calcareous rock from end to end of the cliff, creating a natural suggestion of a traverse.

But these bands do not completely dominate the cliff's structure, for great blocks have fallen away to create overlaps, and occasional flaky fissures split the horizontals, while the cliff as a whole is warped into an S-shaped frontage. In traversing the bands these interruptions must be overcome, and it is this combination of natural line and complexity which makes Alcasan so appealing an expedition.

A great crack at the east end of the buttress was climbed by Frank Elliott in 1933, and it was from here that early probes were made. In June 1964, taking advantage of a previous semi-pegged ascent of the Flakes, Bob Dearman and Brian Moore traversed from Aurora into Scoop Wall. They used some pegs to reach Windhover and continued via the Flakes, before escaping up the crack of Kingdom Come. This notable effort was followed by freer ascents of the route, and an extension to the end of the buttress was made by Chris Jackson and Brian Moore.

The first two pitches of the ridge of

Aurora provide an ideal approach, via an arête of unprotected delicacy and a contrasting steep groove, to a pedestal stance a hundred and fifty feet from the ground. The first moves of the traverse are immediately exposed and difficult, following a slight easing in the angle of the rock and using small pockets in awkward combinations, sandwiched between a bulge below and a smooth white wall above. Fortunately, excellent protection is provided by a piton or two, before the shallow cave of Scoop Wall gives welcome respite.

Beyond is a black expanse of unsavoury rock blocking the way to Windhover arête. Loose at many levels, a shield hangs dauntingly amid the wall. A swing down on to the wall leads to the shield, which will doubtless peel away one day. The arête provides relief after a nerve-racking crossing. Above, there is a square stance and solid pitons. The second is scarcely better off than the leader, for he too must swing out

Route Alcasan, Hard Very Severe, 450ft.
Cliff Windy Ledge Buttress, Stoney Middleton, Derbyshire.
First Ascent R. Dearman and B. Moore, June 1964 (up to Kingdom Come); C. Jackson and B. Moore, December 1964 (added the two final pitches).
Map Reference O. S. Peak District Tourist Map, 1–50,000 Sheet 119 (ref. 224757).
Guidebook C.C./B.M.C. *The Northern Limestone Area* by P. J. Nunn.
Nearest Road A rough track leads off the A623 ¼ mile west of Stoney Middleton. There are parking places at the foot of the cliff.
Good Conditions A rapid-drying, south-facing cliff where climbing is possible in all seasons.
Campsites and Bunkhouses Camping by the car park below the cliff. Huts at Buxton, Froggatt and Grindleford.
Bibliography Mountain 9: *Stoney Middleton at the Change of Life* by Paul Nunn (an appraisal of the general history of the cliff and its place in Peak climbing).

Al Evans

Bob Keates

Bob Keates

on to the shield, facing the prospect of a fearful pendule should he fall through his own or the rock's failure. Through-leading ability is very desirable on this climb.

A short descent from the stance leads to the start of the black Flakes, which become easier after a first long reach to attain them. The rock here is more friendly and the protection very good, though the situation is still spectacular. A small stance in Kingdom Come is again secure, but the second needs to take care and should perhaps use a back rope to descend to the Flakes.

The last section of the climb is something of a 'crunch'. A swinging descent down a loose bulge on one or two droopy pegs leads to a tiptoeing move above a roof and a stance in slings. The smooth white wall beyond looks easier angled than is actually the case. It is perforated by small pockets for the hands, while fossilized sproutings must suffice for footholds. The peg runners are welcome as the standard of climbing escalates. Finally, a last long step, larger looser holds, a tree and grass bring to an end a route well calculated to wear down incompetent parties.

Alcasan is by no means the hardest climb at Stoney Middleton, but few others, for all their outfacing brutality, can really compare with its beautiful and persistent attrition.

Left: Moving up The Flakes pitch on Alcasan. *Climber: Chris Jackson*

Right: Traversing the final pock-marked white wall of Alcasan. *Climbers: Chris Jackson and Geoff Birtles*

Malbogies

by Mike Thompson

Way back in the fifties I was involved in the development of the then virgin Main Wall at Avon. Nowadays this is so criss-crossed with routes, part-routes, girdles, variations, direct starts and indirect finishes that it resembles those printed circuits which one suspects Ed Drummond slots into his cranium in the space where lesser mortals keep their brains. Things were different then. The wall was breached at the left by Maltravers and Malpractice and at the right by Mercavity, and that was all. The presiding genius was the young Chris Bonington; not the hirsute wheeler-dealer who now bestrides the climbing world like a commercial colossus, but a clean-faced Sandhurst cadet naïvely convinced that the rusty peg-hammer in his rucksack was really a Field-Marshal's baton. The same blind faith that took him time after time up the Main Wall led him to a commission in The Royal Tank Regiment where, though he could not drive a mini, let alone a Centurion, he believed himself to be embarked upon a career that would make Rommel look like Fred Karno. Only years later, after a series of embarrassing tank-collisions and a disastrous spell in margarine, did he Choose to Climb.

After Sandhurst the interests of national security took precedence over the development of limestone-climbing and our little group was dispersed around the globe, Chris to Germany, James Ward (who put up Maltravers) to Hong Kong and myself to Malaya. However, Bonington's commanding officer, in despair, sent him back to England on a driving and maintenance course and so, drawing on the low cunning which has stood him in such good stead ever since, he was able to sneak back to Bristol and, while I was holding back the Reds in Kuala Lumpur, pick the plum – the line we had all dreamed of, straight up the great expanse of vague grooves and emphatic overhangs in the very centre of the Main Wall.

I suppose it was pique at being out-manoeuvred (and the suspicion that it might be rather hard) that caused me to avoid the route; only the prospect of immortality in the pages of Ken Wilson's *Bumper Book of British Climbs* (and the £5 fee) induced me

to put aside my principles and transport myself (with the aforementioned Wilson) to the start.

Over the intervening years it has shed much of its ferocity and loose rock, the stance is lavishly upholstered with belay pitons and the whole climb grossly over-protected by peg runners. It has had to suffer the ignominy of being down-graded to VS but, even so, it is still the best route at Avon and, as they say, 'should be on the itinerary of any competent visiting party'. Fortunately, Nature has recently taken a hand to rectify things. The hold has fallen off the first move which in consequence is now much harder than anything else on the climb. One hopes that this will act as a deterrent to those who get up routes by dragging them down to their standards, and that the removal of, say, fifty per cent of the protection pegs will allow a little adventure to the climber and restore the dignity of HVS to the climb.

After fifteen abortive attempts at the first move, I teetered up the short wall on sweaty undercuts to the first little overhang which went remarkably easily to a slabby ramp ending in the Shattered Wall. It was difficult to decide whether I or the wall was more shattered by the time I reached the top, but the holds, like the sexual athlete's fantasy, kept on coming. Reaching the stance twenty feet higher is a little awkward (be sure to keep on the right). Looking down this 70ft. pitch I realized what a splendid, if tenuous, natural line it takes up the apparently featureless sweep of rock. Other harder routes may cross it, but there is no doubt that this is *the* line of the cliff. Looking upwards, square-cut overhangs extend in serried ranks as far as the eye can see.

Not content with having almost killed me on the first pitch by insisting that I should try to lead the crux without clipping into any of the protection pegs, Wilson added real insult to injury by preparing to lead through up the second pitch. 'How can I possibly be expected to do literary justice to this climb if I am denied the experience of leading it?' I demanded. The oracle was silenced and, taking advantage of this unprecedented, if short-lived, state of

Route Malbogies, Hard Very Severe, 190ft.
Cliff Main Wall, Avon Gorge, Bristol.
First Ascent C. J. S. Bonington and party, 1959.
Map Reference O.S. Sheet 156, Bristol and Stroud, 1–50,000 Sheet 172 (ref. 563743).
Guidebooks U.B.M.C. *Rock Climbs in the Avon Gorge* by B. Wyvill and R. Evans; *Avon Gorge* by Ed Drummond (published privately).
Nearest Road A car park below the cliff, just off the A4 (Portway) through the Gorge.
Good Conditions The cliff is a suntrap and the route is climbable in all seasons. It dries quickly. Avoid during hot summer afternoons.
Campsites and Bunkhouses There is a good camping spot behind the railings at the west end of the cliff.
Bibliography C.C. Journal 1957: *Three Climbs at Avon* by Chris Bonington (early explorations on the Main Wall); Mountain 20: *City Crag* by Brian Wyvill (general appraisal of the cliff).

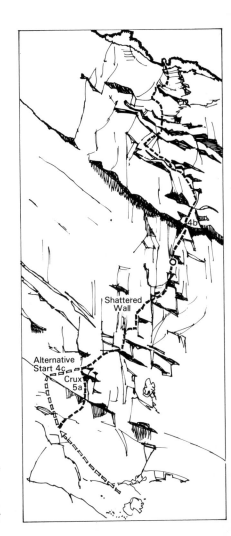

Ken Wilson

Ken Wilson

affairs, I quickly clipped him into every piton that came to hand and shot up the first overhang. Surprisingly, this is taken at its widest point and though spectacular is not particularly hard. Still, it is no place to hang around, especially with the oracle in full flow once again.

If the first pitch is the main meat of the meal, the second is the *Bombe Surprise* – a fantastic 120ft. romp through the overhangs. Technically little more than Hard Severe, it is wonderfully exposed and improbable. Time and again the way is blocked by jutting overhangs, and time and again enormous jugs materialize miraculously over the lips. Near the top a threaded honeysuckle (accompanied, of course, by an unnecessary peg) protects the final awkward move. A 150ft. rope should allow the leader to reach the ice-cream van and then, after belaying on the railings, he can return to the edge to watch the helmet of the second bobbing up and down as he navigates a sea of overhangs.

No 'spirit of the hills' nonsense pervades the Bristol scene. This is no place for the ecologically-inspired climber, macrobiotically nourished on compost-grown vegetables, fingering his way through his brown rice and boasting his impotent superiority in the wilderness by decrying the works of man. Avon itself is man-made and Nature plays only a supporting role. As you sit licking your space-rocket ice-lolly, the spectators gather at the railings with their inane questions. Look to your left and the red-brick bonded warehouses of the Wills Tobacco Company are framed by Brunel's Suspension Bridge. Look to your right and the Bristol Channel is obscured by clouds of poison emitted by the Rio Tinto Zinc smelter at Avonmouth. Look straight down and the bottom of the gorge is filled with lorries, buses, cars, trains, merchant shipping and untreated sewage. We have the slave-traders and merchant venturers of Bristol and the quarrymen who provided the limestone ballast for their ships, as well as the Wheeler-Dealer, to thank for Malbogies.

Right: The fourth pitch of Coronation Street (*see following chapter*). The route takes the crack above the stance then traverses round the Shield to gain a ledge above the leader's left hand. Sceptre Direct takes the crack in the background. *Climbers: Chris Bonington and Mike Thompson*

Cheddar Gorge, Somerset

54 Coronation Street

by Jim Perrin

It is fortunate indeed that perfection is no measure of greatness, for Coronation Street is far from a perfect climb; a flawed masterpiece, it towers above such elements as detract from its stature. There is no delicacy about it, nothing of the exquisiteness of formal perfection. One drives up from the cluttered distractions of Cheddar to park beneath its great raw wall. It is big, hugely so in contrast to one's environment: the busy gorge, the passing cars, the clustering, whispering people, and the great walls craning down over them. A magnificent natural environment, yet somehow familiarized, much of its atmosphere lost. Coronation Street starts by a rustic litter bin and soars; cars at the bottom give the scale. A system of grooves traces a staggered path up its seamed face: the effect is thrusting, powerful, sensational.

But defects it has: it is a very public climb; there is a certain nakedness about one's performance upon it. Scrutiny, vulnerability, the irritation of crass comments pricking into the vacuum of tense moments. And, as with other brands of sensation, one can say with perhaps a trace of prurience that it attracts a certain clientèle. To some there is an attraction in being on public view, and such as these seem to gather each weekend about its base, occasionally struggling up a few pitches, sometimes even breaking through into the upper reaches to put on a performance of *bravura* from the gallery. The element is strong, detracting from the pleasure of the climb.

But pleasurable it still is, even unique, hanging out as it does for 400ft. over a roadside car-park in oppressive verticality, every additional foot accentuating the exposure by the diminution of those doll-like and ever-present figures beneath. It owes its conception to Chris Bonington's choice of Cheddar as the venue for a television programme; in the absence of a suitable climb, he was forced to provide one, and thus Coronation Street. Created for sensation, it remains a sensational creation.

The first two pitches are common with Sceptre; grooves allowing of deeds darkly inelegant behind an arras of ivy, undistinguished, but useful in taking one clear of the lower vegetation and laying the basis of

a theme, with two hundred feet of air, which is to rise to a crescendo along with the climb. Above the second pitch a little bulge, after which Sceptre, frightened by the shape of things to come, scuttles off along primrose paths to the right. For Coronation Street the strait gate and narrow path of a clean, capped groove ahead. A brief prelude, this groove, leading into a major theme. The groove finishes at a stumbling-block-overhang, another groove out of sight to its left. Moving out left on slippery holds and jams appended to throbbing arms; lots of air, little elegance about the struggle to that groove above; a judicious knee, and pegs of twisted metal winking at the insecurity of your tenure. Thirty feet of easy climbing in the bed of a groove leads to a shattered overhang, the groove cleaving through it in bottle-neck formation to give the first really exciting moments of the climb. Beneath the overhang, rest and runners in abundance conspire to a willing delay from the way ahead: anxiety, and all spirit fled until the moment of action. The bottle-neck chimney is climbed tenuously on its right wall, feet high and the body leaning out unwillingly, fearful of air, while the shoulder eases itself round the bulge, the road absolutely beneath. Good holds, thankfully, a tiny shattered ledge, remote, a rusting bolt belay. Time and again the nature of this route seems to be in a sort of side-stepping, little angled walls and awkward bulges sidling round the boldness of some overhang into yet another breathless and bottomless situation.

Straight out of that small square stance a slender crack rises and runs alluringly to a great overhang, leftwards a boss of rock abutting against it, bulging, cut away, and held on by God knows what – the Shield, but no knight's comforting stance beneath, nothing but the long void. A gentle beginning, holds for hands and feet, albeit rickety, but ever-deteriorating and soon the feet sliding and that out-jutting boss to be circumvented. A commitment to the unknown in awesome position, a hand traverse on rounded holds with the feet heavy and free, a desperate breathless fight with ever-failing resources round to a stance in miniature, pegs and sit-slings. The position

Route Coronation Street, Hard Very Severe, 385ft.
Cliff High Rock, Cheddar Gorge, Somerset.
First Ascent C. J. S. Bonington and A. Greenbank, March 1965.
Map Reference O.S. Sheet 165, Weston-Super-Mare, 1–50,000 Sheet 182 (ref. 465540).
Guidebook *A Climber's Guide to Cheddar Gorge* by R. S. Dearman and D. W. Riley (published privately).
Nearest Road The B3371 Cheddar/Bath road at a layby immediately below the cliff. The climb actually overhangs this point and there is a serious danger of falling rocks. For this reason it is essential that climbers avoid the route whenever there is a risk of hitting bystanders or parked cars – particularly during weekends and virtually any time during the summer months.
Good Conditions The route dries quickly, particularly in its upper (harder) section.
Campsites and Bunkhouses It is possible to camp (discreetly) at various points in the Gorge in the winter months.
Bibliography *The Next Horizon* by Chris Bonington, Gollancz, London, 1973 (account of first ascent and subsequent TV extravaganza).

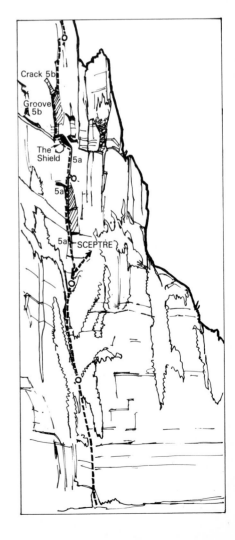

is such as to focus the mind on every discomfort, mistrusted pegs and an agony of air beneath.

The groove above: perhaps 90ft. long, two sections of roughly equal length but distinct character, separated by a small overhang and a certain displacement of line. It begins with some of the most technical climbing on the route; delicate, steep bridging to remind you of your feet, none too valuable a commodity thus far. Runnerless, more or less, the real thing; finger-and-toe free-climbing in a funnel of space. But a reverie cut short by that small overhang, that slight displacement of line, banishing balance, leading back into the themes of power and air. A hard overhang started over the void, a stretching, lurching, urgent overhang to drive another wedge of air into the back of your mind. Slimy finger-jams and fragile footholds, no trust in what little security around, until the groove opens to suppliant hands. The rhythm of a good crack, no footholds now but forceful jamming, momentum to carry you past awkward bulges, a crescendo of movement leading to the nerve-shattering finale of a final stance: a poor out-of-balance foothold of a stance, and belays whose duplication is the only proof against their duplicity; but a naked perch taken with pride, the route behind, spectators so infinitely far below. A short final pitch, a slabby wall to the right toying with you amusedly before leaving you free on the shrub-covered hillside. The consciousness of that great wall below, themes played out in aching muscle and a memory of air. Not a varied climb, not a private climb, but one built on a single theme to a grand scale, perhaps great.

Above: The fourth pitch can be split by taking a stance on the ledge just beyond the Shield. From here a steep groove is climbed by bridging and back and footing. This is perhaps the most technical section of the route. *Climber: Chris Bonington*

Left: Traversing the Shield during the first ascent. The footsling is not considered necessary these days. The climber is in virtually the same position as the leader in the photo on page 199. *Climber: Tony Greenbank*

203

Berry Head, South Devon

Moonraker

by Al Alvarez

Route Moonraker, Hard Very Severe, 250 ft.
Cliff The Old Redoubt, Berry Head, Brixton, Devon.
First Ascent P. R. Littlejohn and P. H. Biven, August 1967.
Map Reference O.S. Sheet 188, Torbay, 1–50,000 Sheet 202 (ref. 943562).
Guidebook West Col *South Devon* by P. R. Littlejohn.
Nearest Road An unmetalled road leads from the suburbs of Brixton to a car park near Berry Head and a short distance from the top of the cliff. A local council permit system is in existence for climbing in this area.
Distance and time from cliff 100 yds. Allow 1 minute.
Good Conditions The climb dries quickly but should only be attempted in calm conditions and at low tide.
Campsites and Bunkhouses Discreet camping in the Old Redoubt itself at the top of the cliff.
Bibliography Rocksport, January 1970: *My God have I got to do that?* by John Hammond (general appraisal of climbing on the cliff and description of an attempt on Dreadnought).

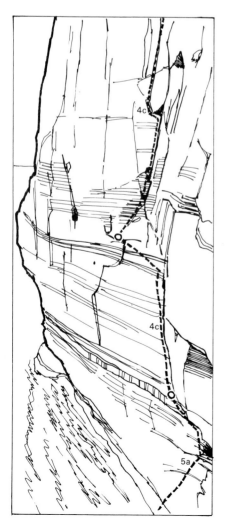

Even to the most hardened eye it is an imposing place: a big, impending wall with the sea battering along its base out to a ragged headland, and the vast mouth of a cave opening on its right. There are climbs that thread improbably through the overhangs on the cave's lip, with a hundred or more feet of space between the rock and the surging water; these look, quite simply, impossible. In comparison, the line of Moonraker is at least obvious: a series of cracks splitting the overhanging wall. It seems the most natural line on the cliff, but serious, straight up and down, not to be fooled with. Looked at from the opposite side of the cave, it seems to overhang from bottom to top. As it happens, this is not a trick of perspective; the rock leans out on you continuously, right up to the last few feet. Mercifully, the holds are generous, but you need strong arms and steady nerves.

You need them, in fact, even before you get to the foot of the climb proper. The top of Berry Head is a flat, pleasant, blowy place where couples and children and dogs wander among the ruins of what was once a Napoleonic fort, the Old Redoubt. But the grass on the side of the bay opposite the cliff steepens rapidly, then becomes bare rock overhanging the sea; another world, not for tourists. You step blind round a corner of sheer rock and move carefully down into the vast, dank mouth of the cave. It seems as big as a cathedral: a black, thundering dome, like a lunatic's skull, water boiling along its floor, birds flitting in the dark air. Rock pigeons, guillemots and kittiwakes all nest there.

The chances are that your feet will be wet before you even reach the climb, since the long traverse round the cave is just above the water-line – if you are lucky and the sea is docile. But the traverse, which starts easily enough, becomes progressively harder, so you may have more than your feet wet by the time you reach the piton stance a few feet above the water under the lowest of the inevitable overhangs.* You

*At low tide there is a ledge immediately above the water further left. At high tide the whole of the bottom pitch is out of reach; you must abseil directly from the top of the climb to the second stance.

dangle from the pegs, the sea banging and sucking at your feet. Above, what little you can see of the rock leans steadily out. The longer you hang there, the more deeply you ponder the climber's perennial question: how on earth did I allow myself to get into a situation like this?

There is no quick or obvious answer, since the first pitch is the hardest. You step up and right on to an outward leaning wall; it is undercut at its base, so the sea seems to surge dizzily below the tiny footholds. Small enough to begin with, the holds swiftly become even smaller and more widely spaced. By the time you reach the middle of the wall they thin to almost nothing at all. The sharp right edge looks like a haven of refuge. It isn't. When you pull gratefully off the wall you find yourself in a layback position at the bottom of a long, steeply overhanging crack. On the left is a ruin of a peg. You clip on a runner and then keep going with a vengeance. Mercifully, the edge is mostly perfect, like a layback in a textbook. It kinks to the left, still without a resting place, then continues even more unforgivingly. As a first lead into the unknown by Peter Biven, it seems disproportionately bold. Your arms strain like mooring ropes. The crack ends at a healthy chockstone under a roof in an overhanging corner. You are in balance at last. The move to the left again is harder than it looks, but it lands you on a good stance with another chockstone and a cluster of pitons which a picador would admire.

The wall to your right is the huge and hugely overhanging brow of the cave through which Dreadnought and Barbican pick their spectacular way. The wall facing you seems mild in comparison, at this point a mere dead vertical. But not for long. You move up deep cracks by a series of laybacks and hand-jams, straddling wide with your feet. The last fifteen feet overhang a little and are topped by another ruined peg. You go left horizontally and easily along the base of a triangular depression, roofed with the usual overhangs, to a stance at the top of a great, loose flake. For belay, there is a bong in a crack, a choice of threads and places for as many other pitons as make you feel happy.

The sense of security is precarious and brief. The right wall still leans out drunkenly, as though trying to peer into the dark yawn of the cave beneath; the facing wall now does the same. At the apex of the triangular recess, up and to the right, is a pouting lip of rock with a good crack behind it. You hand-jam up over it, straddling wide with your feet. It leads immediately to a second, even angrier lip: more jams, more straddling, as you move steadily up and out over free space. But the crack is deep and reassuring, and the foot-holds appear if you look hard enough. Then the crack straightens and thins; for ten or fifteen feet the only way up is by laybacking on the tips of your fingers. But the edge, thank God, is good.

Above, the rock is broken and it is possible to belay uncomfortably. If you decide to climb straight on, at least rest a little, for neither the crack nor the angle relents. Technically, it is the same mixture as before: hand-jams, occasional laybacks, big bridging movements with the legs – the style of climbing gritstone experts claim to love and the rest of us find simply fierce. Near the end, the angle moderates to the merely vertical but, as though to show who is boss, the crack goes blind. A finger-slot high on the right, a ballerina's toe-jam for the left foot and a final shuddering heave bring you to the last few, easy feet.

The grass on the top is flat, soft and probably strewn with disbelieving holiday-makers. There are wild rock roses to greet you and three pitons in the back wall. The beetling rock below seems another world. In release from all that tension, the blood pumps sweetly in your arms and fingers. As Confucius said about something else, relax and enjoy it.

Left: The first pitch of Moonraker.
Climber: unknown

Right: Bishop's Buttress on Chair Ladder (*see following chapter*). Bishop's Rib takes the centre of the buttress and Diocese climbs the impressive chimney on the left.

Ian Roper

Chair Ladder, Cornwall

56 # Bishop's Rib

by Pat Littlejohn

Route Bishop's Rib, Hard Very Severe, 190ft.
Cliff Bishop Buttress, Chair Ladder, Cornwall.
First Ascent J. H. Deacon and J. W. Oakes, 1956; M. B. McDermott, R. A. P. Mellor and D. W. Bateman (Direct Start), July 1963.
Map Reference O.S. Sheet 189, Lands End, 1–50,000 Sheet 203 (ref. 365216).
Guidebook C.C. *Cornwall*, Vol. 2, by V. N. Stevenson.
Nearest Road There is a car parking area in a field behind the village of Porthgwarra (ref. 369219). Continue up a road and track to a Coastguard Lookout above the cliff.
Distance and time from cliff ½ mile. Allow 10 minutes.
Good Conditions Dries fairly quickly but the bottom can remain greasy with sea rime and the top lichenous unless the weather is hot or windy. Avoid high spring tides.
Campsites and Bunkhouses Camping at Sennen. Huts in Sennen Cove and at Bosigran.

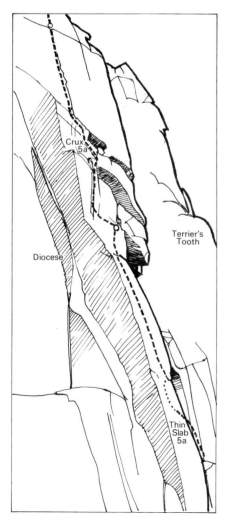

It is low tide. The waves, having launched their trillionth assault, now sigh and expire harmlessly well back from the cliff. The ramparts of Chair Ladder tower victorious above expanses of flat granite scarred with trenches and deep pockets, some filled with dead water left by the defeated ocean. Quite naked now, and in their other setting, the walls are vulnerable to a different sort of assault: man is permitted to approach.

Heralded by the sudden flight and angry cries of seabirds, two climbers descended the western end of the cliff. Fresh to the area, they eagerly assimilated their surroundings. A slab of ochre-coloured granite reared up above them for a hundred feet, losing itself in walls and buttresses higher still. It was tempting, but the first enticing profile of the main cliff drew them away. They passed beneath a handsome and complex crag, split by cracks, chimneys and gullies. Closer scrutiny revealed some fine walls tucked away, but always ledges intervened, stunting inspiration.

Further along the scenery improved. The narrow South Face rose steeply and without a serious break, but its central line was in the old style: it was not what they were looking for. A faint crack line in the stark lower wall of Wolf Buttress made them pause, but a glance at the buttress beyond committed this to the future. They were drawn to a compact and shapely mass of granite nearly two hundred feet high, and to the subtle line which climbed it full frontal – Bishop's Rib. Beginning in the gully on the right, the line rose across a slab into the thin central crack, which in turn led to a stance. Beyond, the route climbed the wall on the left, to reach an obvious line going leftwards through overhangs to a slight depression where the buttress leaned back a little. A deep crack in the slab above completed the serious climbing.

For these climbers the visual impact of the route at once set it above its peers, and the impression was not belied by the other determining factor of a climb's status – the quality of the actual climbing experience. After their ascent, the leader wrote an account.

Pitch 1: After a few moves in the dank interior, veer out on to the sea-smoothed slab, where a small nut runner helps soften the granite trench twenty feet below. Take a minute or so to learn the rock, then tiptoe leftwards – nicely precarious – to more comfortable holds in the thin crack line. It steepens above but the holds are positive, if spaced, and you soon reach easy ground and a neat, isolated stance. The only way onward is your way and it doesn't look easy, but take some time off to look around.

The sea has begun its steady advance and as you watch the stone landscape is gradually dissolved in foam. White gulls flash into view and disappear. Their cries echo and re-echo, seeming to magnify one's prevailing emotion. Often liberating and uplifting, they can become hostile and menacing at the slightest intrusion of anxiety over what lies above.

Pitch 2: Move left beneath an undulating wall of golden granite, then feel your way rightwards on near-jugs, heading for the rising traverse line. You can place a peg here, but it's better not to: it destroys the harmony. Just follow where the holds lead, and when they seem to let you down search out the little finger-slot at heart-height and rise through the stern bulges to gentler ground. You've cracked it now, so lean out and let the sensations bombard. On up into the crowning crackline, to savour the fulsome jugs and the roughest, toughest jams on the friendliest, sunniest, ruggedest rock anywhere. On the stance below the rambling summit towers, stretch out and let the sun penetrate. Or try, with a level gaze, to fathom the blue infinity.

Right: At the start of the rising traverse line on the second pitch of Bishop's Rib. *Climber: Frank Cannings*

Ken Wilson

Bosigran, Cornwall

Suicide Wall and Bow Wall

by Frank Cannings

Bosigran Face forms one of the retaining walls of Porthmoina Cove on the West Penwith peninsula, the south-western extremity of England; blunted, battered and cleansed by the fury of the Atlantic, it is a rock-climber's Utopia where the sun 'always' shines. The area is one of bleak moorland, with the skylines broken only by tall, derelict, tin-mine buildings. Throughout the peninsula a sense of wildness and isolation persists; the sea is moody; the moorlands mysteriously conceal a wealth of prehistoric relics and the place-names are those of an enchanted, make-believe world. The moors are covered by gorse, the headlands by thrift, honeysuckle and blackberry; over all hangs the aura of the ending of the land.

The rock is mostly granite, weathered and extremely rough. Flecked with feldspar, quartz and mica, it varies in hue from white to red, and is decorated with veins and sheets of black tourmaline. Bosigran Face towers over the beautiful Porthmoina Cove and its *aiguille* island. It is not a sea cliff in the modern sense. The sea does not forbid or inhibit direct access. It is a cliff beside the sea, with the climbs commencing from a platform well above sea level.

Nevertheless, the area represents the home of sea-cliff climbing in Britain. A. W. Andrews was climbing in the locality as early as 1902, and the first route on Bosigran Face, the Bosigran Ledge climb, was put up by Andrews in 1905. This route enjoyed the status of being the only climb on the main face for forty-three years.

There has never been a large climbing fraternity resident in the immediate area, and most of the climbing developments have occurred during holiday periods, with visitors leading the action. This persists today. The face is deserted on most weekends, but it is inundated with visitors at peak holiday periods.

In 1948, J. Cortland Simpson started the opening-up process with two extremely fine climbs, Doorway and Zig-Zag, but the cliff was still generally dismissed as impossible. This was partly due, no doubt, to the coating of long, hairy, green lichen which obscured the detail of the underlying rock.

The 200ft. high wall is fortified in its central region by a band of large overhangs, close to the top of the cliff. Beneath these there is a very large steep slab of black tourmaline, known as the Coal Face. Both Bow Wall and Suicide Wall neatly avoid direct confrontation with the overhang. This 'pleasure' is reserved for The Phantom and The Ghost. Bow Wall and Suicide Wall have a common start directly below the widest part of the roof, but they immediately diverge; Suicide Wall takes part of the Coal Face then twists round the left-hand side of the roof by way of steep walls and grooves, blackened by the seepage of stannic acid. Bow Wall skirts the roof on the right by a daring line up a wall which becomes progressively steeper. Finally it cuts back left across the lip of the great roof.

Peter and Barrie Biven, a pair of young gritstoners blessed with strong fingers, were introduced to Bosigran by Trevor Peck, who had partially dismissed it in favour of Chair Ladder. One can imagine the Bivens' joy on encountering such a vast quantity of unclimbed rock. They immediately added several new climbs, including Suicide Wall. Their first attempt saw Peter Biven clearing the Coal Face of ivy to gain the Pedestal, a precarious pinnacle stance on the left arête of the Coal Face. The crux traverses left across the steep black wall and was led by Peter Biven, in plimsoles and without any protection, in keeping with the methods of the day. On reaching the small ledge at the end of the traverse, Biven was unable to belay, as he was not carrying pitons. He reversed the traverse, a prospect that would scare many competent climbers today, and abseiled off from the Pedestal. The party returned the following day, armed with pitons, and completed the route. On the pitch following the traverse, Biven stood on Peck's head in order to place a peg which was then used for aid to gain a pair of cracks leading up to the next stance. Biven himself subsequently eliminated this aid, but the move was of a much higher standard than anything else on the route and the practice of balancing delicately on the unfortunate second's shoulder continued for many years.

The final pitch must have been a surprise for the pioneers. There is a very obvious

Routes Suicide Wall, Hard Very Severe, 210ft.; Bow Wall, Extremely Severe, 210ft.
Cliff Main Cliff, Bosigran, Cornwall.
First Ascents Suicide Wall – P. H. Biven, H. T. H. Peck and B. M. Biven, August 1955; Bow Wall – J. Brown (crux pitch), July 1957; B. M. Biven and H. T. H. Peck (finishing pitches), May 1958.
Map References O.S. Sheet 189, Lands End, 1–50,000 Sheet 203 (ref. 416368).
Guidebook C.C. *Cornwall*, Vol. 1, by P. H. Biven and M. B. McDermott.
Nearest Road The B3306 St Ives/St Just road at the Bosigran Count House (ref. 422365). A path leads across the moor to the cliff.
Distance and time from cliff ½ mile. Allow 10 minutes.
Good Conditions Both climbs dry fairly quickly and are reasonably sheltered.
Campsites and Bunkhouses C.C. Hut, The Count House; camping at Rosemergy Farm and Bosigran Farm.
Bibliography Mountain 15, *Cornwall* by Frank Cannings (general history).

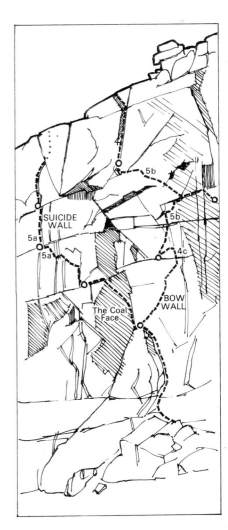

groove leering down above the top stance, and they must have rushed at this, expecting a plum pitch, only to be defeated by a smooth bulge 15ft. up it. A good jug on the right wall permitted a bold swing into a wide, enclosed crack. A layback out over the overhang above led to easy ground, and provided a spectacular finish to the climb. They graded the route Exceptionally Severe, and were obviously impressed enough to give it its intimidating title.

At that time (1955), there were numerous hard climbs of a similar standard in Wales and on gritstone. The ascent was therefore by no means a national innovation, but it did represent a sensational advance in local climbing standards. Overnight, the crag moved from the 1930s to the 1950s.

The climb did not have to wait long for a second ascent. Rawdon Goodier and 'Zeke' Deacon, a talented team of Royal Marine climbers, repeated it within a week. Nowadays it receives regular traffic and its grade has been reduced to HVS. The drop in standard is mainly a reflection of the improvement in protection techniques.

The first pitch of the climb is a pleasant scramble up an easy rake to the Coal Face. Usually it is avoided or soloed. The Coal Face pitch is delightful, once one realizes that the black, shiny rock is not slippery. The Pedestal stance is very exposed, being about 200ft. above the sea. It is now the cross-road of the face. The crux traverse pitch is only 25ft. in length, but it feels much longer. From the Pedestal it looks impressive and intimidating. A few steep moves, using small flat holds, and one is convinced that it is going to be desperate, until a reassuring position is gained at a series of flakes. There are two possibilities on this pitch. One is to use the flakes for handholds. There are adequate footholds until half-way across, where it is necessary to climb up a horizontal crack to get poor finger-jams. The alternative is to use the horizontal crack for the hands, and the flakes for the feet from the start. There is an ancient peg half-way across, on which too many people linger to rest. After this the footholds expire and eventually, when the stance is almost within reach, the handholds disappear too. Many people end up with one leg thrown up on the ledge, shuffling along on their bellies; others finish up on their knees or in other equally undignified positions. The secret is to move left as far as one can go with rounded handholds on the edge of the ledge. Then move left once more, whereupon it is possible to layback elegantly on to the stance. Another method, which nowadays might be considered unethical, was 'to place one's left foot behind one's left ear'. All in all this is not a pitch for a timid second; he is in for a substantial pendulum if he falls off any of the hard moves.

On the next pitch it is no longer necessary to crawl all over one's unfortunate companion. Years of pegging have enlarged the cracks, so that free-climbing the pitch is almost straightforward. Again, it is a short one. A popular alternative is the corresponding pitch of Beowulf, which takes the groove on the left.

The top groove is now taken by Paragon. Suicide Wall goes right into the overhung recess. Reaching this involves swinging from a large hand-hold with sufficient momentum to project oneself into the womb-like recess. Equipment snags and one is continually banging one's head against the rock, but eventually it is possible to escape by laybacking over the overhang.

After the ascent of Suicide Wall, Bosigran Face received its greatest onslaught, mainly from the Bivens and Trevor Peck, although Goodier and Deacon also participated. More hard climbs were done: Little Brown Jug and Paragon, which took impressive lines up steep walls; String of Pearls, the girdle traverse, which was completed early on during the development; and The Ghost and Phantom, both of which breached the great overhang. It became generally known that there were some good climbs in West Penwith. The Rock and Ice Club were early visitors and, although most of their stay was spent enjoying the seaside environment in a twenty-two man rubber dinghy, their most eminent member, Joe Brown, made a significant contribution by noticing a line up the sweep of wall to the right of the great overhang. Climbing with a young 'apprentice', he stormed the impressive wall

Ken Wilson

again using several points of aid. They subsequently discovered their *faux pas* and reclimbed the route 'cleanly', naming it Bow Wall. The route remained littered with relics of these early pegging exploits for some years. It received very few ascents during the next decade, and it acquired a reputation. When the flow of traffic later increased, the litter and the amount of aid was reduced. Today, it is free of aid and virtually free of pegs.

The first pitch sweeps up a reddish wall from the bottom of the Coal Face. It looks smooth and sensational, but is in fact well adorned with small flakes which make it quite simple. A short, exposed traverse (part of the girdle traverse) leads to a small, comfortable niche below the great over-hang. This is the sort of pitch to lead if you want to impress your uninformed friends. It's the second pitch that's the brute. A steep wall on good holds for 15ft. leads to a shallow groove. Strenuous finger-jamming takes you on to the Pancake, a peculiar dollop of rock which gives a good thread runner, vital for protection of the next moves. You are now aware of the diffi-culties. To the right is a smooth, steep slab, tucked away beneath a roof, with a blank wall beneath it. Using a poor fist-jam and a small hold on the slab it is possible to teeter up on to the slab itself. A precarious step right takes you out of the difficulties and enables you to rest your arms. The over-hang and the short slab lead to a small stance tucked beneath a little corner at the right-hand extremity of the roof. From here, a rightwards traverse across the lip of the great roof gives the next pitch. This was originally done with a couple of pegs, but is now climbed free with unbeatable exposure. As Peter Biven observed, 'there is precisely nothing between one's heels and the sea 300ft. below'. The climbing involves several very delicate balance moves on minute holds, followed by a swing up on to an arête and a small frightening stance. The final groove is straightforward, in pleasant contrast to all that has gone before.

Above: The first pitch of Bow Wall, something of a 'soft touch' in an impressive situation. The climbers are actually on String of Pearls but the routes coincide at the most difficult section of the pitch. *Climbers: Peter Biven and Mark Springett*

to the roof, climbed the series of over-hanging cracks, and then traversed right to belay on Doorway. His second followed up to the hard moves and fell off. The rope went slack, but remained motionless for some time. Brown, unable to communicate over the noise of the sea, soloed down Door-post to find the youth sitting it out on a small ledge. The route was left unfinished.

Shortly afterwards, the line was dis-covered independently by Trevor Peck and Barrie Biven who climbed it artificially and added the traverse above the great roof,

Right: The crux of Bow Wall, between the Pancake and the smooth slab. *Climbers: Dave Marshall and Ken Salter*

Adjectival and Numerical Grades

In order to rationalize the vagaries of the various grading systems at present operating in British guidebooks we are providing further details for the information of readers. Adjectival grading for climbs has doggedly persisted in Britain despite periodic attempts to replace it with more precise numerical systems. This doggedness has been nowhere more marked than in Scotland where a mixture of perverse mischief (to confuse Sassenachs) and native distaste for Southern innovations has preserved the Very Severe grade as the ultimate description of difficulty.

In order to give the puzzled climber some further clue, the Scottish guidebooks offer him a loosely graded list indicating the relative difficulties of the climbs. South of the border the hard climbs are now (by common consent) split into three grades – Very Severe (VS), Hard Very Severe (HVS) and Extremely Severe (XS). These terms encompass a combination of technicalities, sustained difficulty, loose rock, lack of protection and problems of retreat. Sometimes big, serious and frightening climbs were found to be none too difficult, whereas smaller, less serious problems might often be technically very hard. Thus in 1963 Pete Crew and Rodney Wilson instituted a numerical grading system designed to go hand in hand with the adjectival system and pinpoint the technical difficulties of each pitch rather than any attendant seriousness or looseness. This combination of adjectival and numerical grades was thus considered adequate to describe the problems of any climb.

Since that time, however, the original meaning of the three adjectival grades has become debased. Protection techniques have improved so dramatically that what were previously regarded as serious undertakings can now be embarked on without undue concern for factors other than technical difficulty.

Climbers of the seventies no longer equate the adjectival grade primarily with the overall seriousness of the climb and it is increasingly becoming simply an indication of technical difficulty, thus duplicating the numerals. With this trend have come demands for rationalizing the top end of the grading system either by shifting all climbs down one notch or by introducing a three-tiered Extreme grade – an idea already under trial in a number of areas.

To make the whole matter even more complicated the gradual change in the meaning of the adjectival grades has led to a confusing relationship between mountain routes and outcrop climbs. At one time the challenge of a hard outcrop route was comparable to that of a similarly graded mountain climb, but now with the whole concept of seriousness on big crags being debased by improvements in equipment such comparisons no longer hold true.

A climb like Cenotaph Corner for instance – traditionally graded Extremely Severe – is now a considerably easier proposition than say Carnage (HVS), a climb of similar length.

Thus at the time of writing the whole area of adjectival grading is under review but, mindful of the natural desire by many climbers (particularly visitors) to have some reasonable comparison of difficulty of the climbs in this book, a list of gradings is provided here. The climbs are given their commonly accepted adjectival grades together with numerical pitch grades to give a greater insight into the problems that will be encountered.

Those who see no point in such a detailed concern for grading are cordially invited to ignore the list altogether and refer to more traditional sources of information.

Dragon	HVS	4a, 5a, 3a, 5a, 4a
Gob	HVS	4c, 4c, 4c
Goliath	HVS	4c, 5a, 4b, 4a
King Rat	HVS	4c, 4c, 4a, 4b, 5a, 4a, 4a
The Needle	XS	4c, 5a, 4c, 5b, 4b, 5a, 4c, 5a, 4a
Centurion	HVS	4c, 5a, 4b, 4b, 3a, 3a, 5a, 4c
The Bat	XS	4c, 5a, 5a, 5b, 5b, 4b
Trapeze	HVS	5b, 4a, 5a, 4c, 4a
Yo-Yo	XS	5b, 5b, 5a
Carnivore	XS	5b/c, 4c, 5b, (5c), 5a, 4b
Raven's Gully	VS	4a, 4a, 4b, 5a, 4a, 4b, 3b, 4c(5b)
Shibboleth	XS	4b, 5c, 5a, 5b, 5a, 5b, 4c
Swastika	HVS	4c, 4a, 4b, 4c, 5a, 4b, A1/4c
The Old Man of Hoy	HVS	3a, 5a, 4b, 4b
The Great Prow	VS	4c, 4a, 4a, 3b
The Scoop	A4/XS	A3, A2, A3, A4, A1/5a
South Ridge Direct	VS	3a, 4c, 4c, 3a, 4b
Central Buttress	HVS	5a(4c), 3a, 5a, 4a, 4c, 4c(4c)
Ichabod	XS	5b, 5c
Central Pillar	XS	4a, 4b, 5b, 5b, 4b
Gormenghast	HVS	4c, 5a, 4b(4c), 4b
Engineers' Slabs	VS	4a, 4c, 4c, 4c
The Crack	VS	4b, 4b, 4b
Kipling Groove	HVS	4c, 5a
Deer Bield Buttress	XS	4b, 5a, 5b, 5a 5b,
Praying Mantis	HVS	5b, 4c, 4c, 5a
North Crag Eliminate	XS	5a, 5b
Extol	XS	5a, 5b
Gogarth	HVS	4a, 5a, 4b, 4a, 5b
Big Groove	XS	5a, 4b, 5c, 5a
A Dream of White Horses	HVS	4c, 4c, 4b, 4c
Mousetrap	HVS	4c, 4c, 4a, 5a
The Groove	XS	5b, 5a, 4c, 5a, 4c
Cenotaph Corner	XS	5a/b
Diagonal	HVS	4b, 5a, 5a, 4c
The Grooves	XS	5a, 5b, 5a
Great Slab/Bow-Shaped	VS	4b, 4a, 4c, 4b, 3b
Vember	XS	5a, 5b, 4a
Great Wall	XS	5c, 5b
White Slab	XS	5b, 4c, 5a, –, 5a, 5b, 4c
Slanting Slab	XS	5b, 5b, 4a
Dwm	HVS	5a, 5a, 4c
Vector	XS	4c, 5c, 5b
North-West Girdle	HVS	4c, 5a, 3a, 5a, 4c
Kilnsey Main Overhang	A3/S	A2, A3, 4a
Carnage	HVS	5b, 5b
Right Unconquerable	HVS	5a
Valkyrie	HVS	4c, 5a
Elder Crack	XS	5c
Suicide Wall (Cratcliffe)	HVS	5b, 5b
Chee Tor Girdle	VS	4b, 4a, 4b, 4c, 4c, 4a
Sirplum	HVS	4b, 5b
Debauchery	HVS	3a, 5b, 5a
Alcasan	HVS	4a, 4b, 5b, 5a, 5a, 5a, 5b
Malbogies	HVS	5a(4c), 4b
Coronation Street	XS	4b, 4a, 5a, 5a, 5b, 4b
Moonraker	HVS	5a, 4c, 4c
Bishop's Rib	HVS	5a, 5a
Suicide Wall (Bosigran)	HVS	4c, 5a, 5a, 4c
Bow Wall	XS	4c, 5b, 5b, 4c

Index